Counselling STER
Older People

A creative response to ageing

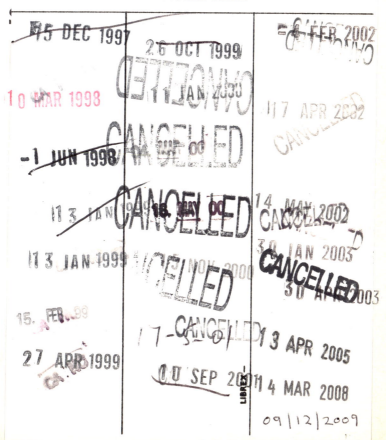

© 1989 Steve Scrutton

First published in Great Britain 1989
Third impression 1994

British Library Cataloguing in Publication Data

Scrutton, Steve
   Counselling older people : a creative response to ageing.—
   (Age Concern handbooks)
   1. Old persons. Counselling
   I. Title   II. Series
   362.6'6
   ISBN 0–340–42073–1

Whilst the advice and information in this book is believed to be true
and accurate at the date of going to press, neither the author nor the
publisher can accept any legal responsibility or liability for any errors or
omissions that may be made.

Typeset in 10/11 pt Cheltenham Light by Colset Pte Ltd, Singapore
Printed and bound in Great Britain for Edward Arnold,
a division of Hodder Headline Plc, 338 Euston Road, London NW1 3BH
by Athenæum Press Ltd, Newcastle upon Tyne.

Contents

Part 2   The employment of counselling skills in the problems of old age

Dedication

To Carole
for the moral support which enabled me to write

To Luke, Salim and Jude
for foregoing their dad during the long hours of composition

PART 1

The application of counselling skills to older people

CHAPTER 1

Introduction

The human race is unique amongst the animals in that we continue to live beyond the time when we have relinquished two roles which are vital to other species – the ability to work for a living, and the ability to procreate and nurture new offspring. Yet this very uniqueness brings with it problems which can be seen in the lives of many elderly people in our society. This book addresses itself to some of those problems, and to the potential value of counselling techniques in helping ageing people come to terms with the many losses old age involves.

The book is not intended to be a scholarly text out of reach of those who perceive their task as a straightforward tending of the needs of older people. The reader need not be alarmed by the thought that this is a difficult, complicated, intellectually demanding treatise on the arts and skills of counselling. This disclaimer is made because counselling is so often presented as a highly technical pursuit, to be practised only by professionally trained people who have a sound understanding of psychotherapy, or some other psychological discipline.

Instead, the book presents counselling as a simple but effective technique that is, in fact, unknowingly practised by many caring but academically unpretentious people every day, and which can and should be developed and used by many more.

It is directed towards the social worker, the staff of residential and nursing homes and day centres for elderly people, home helps, the nurse, the general practitioner, the priest or parson, and other professionals who come into contact with older people, but are perhaps uncertain about their attitude and approach to dealing with the issues and problems that face elderly people in our society. It also assumes that the relatives and friends caring for ageing people can find counselling a valuable and attainable technique.

At the same time, it takes a critical look at how elderly people are perceived within our society. Old age has, like death, become an issue which we do not like to discuss or delve into too deeply. The 'ageism' which surrounds our thinking and practice with older people is questioned and discussed at length, both in how it affects our attitudes to the ageing process, and the way it tends to structure the way elderly people function. Counselling can be a valuable technique for combating the power of ageist attitudes.

Talking with ageing people about their problems and difficulties, which is what counselling is about, is something we as a society have tended to under-value, even neglect. There is no known British text dealing specifically with counselling older people. The reasons for this will be discussed in Chapter 2. Yet the many thousands of people who care for older adults will know of their need for companionship, friendship, conversation and support in coping with the problems of ageing, indeed, of being 'old' within our society.

If readers, as carers of elderly people, feel after reading the book that they have more knowledge of elderly problems, and how these can respond to counselling; if they feel more confident discussing such issues with the elderly; and if they feel that such discussion can be helpful to them, then the book will have achieved its principal objective.

Before proceeding, just a word about the terminology used to describe 'elderly people' in this book. There is a growing awareness of 'ageism', which can be simply defined as those social tendencies which assume that 'old age' is a uniform category or condition, that the process of growing old is in some way a regular experience, and that elderly people constitute a homogeneous group.

At present we are still in what might be described as the 'apologetic' stage. Terms such as 'old biddy' and 'old codger' are obviously derogatory. Even terms such as 'old folk' or 'old timer' are rightly considered to be condescending. So we have entered a period of uncertainty. Terms like 'the elderly' and 'the old' appear to refer to groups rather than to recognize the individuality of elderly people. 'Elderly people' seems acceptable at present, but 'ageing people' or 'the older adult' may be taking over.

Without wishing to appear dismissive of the importance of a name, our present search for the 'correct' term appears to betray the uncertainty of younger people over what to call their elders. This is probably aided by the fact that elderly people have not yet asserted themselves as a group. Racial minorities have, to an extent, done so and they have thereby achieved a degree of confidence and self-identity which has enabled them to assert that they are 'black' – and proud of it. What many once thought to be a term of abuse has become the accepted terminology, by the insistence of black people themselves.

It is not unlikely that a similar transition will happen with our 'senior citizens'. They too will decide that the euphemisms we are inventing to describe being 'old' not only undermine them, but prevent them being proud of their age. Maybe old people will want to be called 'old'.

Counselling elderly people by its very nature emphasises the individuality of the counsellee. This book attempts to stress this vital point, but in addition tries to use the terms 'old', 'older', 'elderly' and 'ageing' in the appropriate places, according to the meaning of the words themselves. It makes no apology for doing so.

CHAPTER 2

Counselling . . . and the older adult

Counselling . . .

Counselling is essentially an approach to human communication. The subjects of counselling are troubled or unhappy people who, for whatever reason, are finding it difficult to live their lives in harmony with the world around them, or to lead their lives to their full potential. The problems they face, whatever their source, will be affecting their attitudes, their behaviour and their social relationships.

The primary objective of counselling is to involve individuals in a process whereby they can be helped to reflect on, and become more aware of, their current situation and the complexity of their own needs. It seeks to allow them to express their own feelings about their lives, without any attempt to impose our own ideas and views. Thereafter, it seeks to enable them to initiate and develop new and appropriate responses to their situation.

In doing this, the object of counselling is not to bring about change or manipulate personality, but through the development of self-knowledge and self-understanding to enable the individuals themselves to modify their own behaviour and outlook on life, and to do so in ways which are acceptable to them. Counselling is based on the idea that to talk about a problem is helpful – this is why counselling is sometimes referred to as a 'talking cure'. But it is more than this. Counselling is based on the belief that all behaviour, however odd or irrational it might appear, has meaning. The meaning might be difficult for the outsider to decipher, but will usually be found to have something to do with the inner emotional life of the individual. Counselling seeks to discover this meaning.

At its simplest, counselling is no more (and no less) than the development of warm, empathetic and understanding relationships with those who are experiencing emotional and social stress, giving them time, listening to their troubles, and responding to them with sympathy. At this fundamental level, counselling is no more than a 'theoretical construction' of a basic human skill, and as such the counselling of elderly people is probably practised spontaneously every day by many people throughout the world without necessarily being 'elevated' by the name. Sensitive and caring people who are good listeners, who like people enough to allow them to express their own feelings, and who are prepared to give depressed, confused, difficult and emotionally disturbed people time to express their feelings, are practising counselling.

The problem with this 'simple' definition of counselling is that the development of 'warm, empathetic and understanding relationships', whilst common, is not a universal human skill or attribute. So while it is important to present counselling as a method that can be practised by any caring person, it is also vital to stress that it is more than just 'being pleasant', more than just befriending, more than just 'talking to' people. Many people who do this might believe that they practise 'counselling', and have sound counselling relationships with older people, when in fact their role within the relationship is too dominant to be any such thing.

This is a common problem. Too often we do not listen to people who tell us about their problems, especially when they are no longer able to look after themselves. We do not spend time finding out what is on their minds. Often with dependent people we are too busy 'caring' for them to care. We assume that we know from the limited facts available to us how they feel, that we know best what they should do, and that our idea of what is 'right' or 'wrong' should determine what other people decide to do. The giving of advice, however good; the giving of directions, however correct; the use of exhortations, however well-intentioned, do not constitute counselling. Such techniques are practised within dominant/submissive relationships, and whereas such techniques are common with the 'professional' helpers of old people, they have no place in the counselling relationship.

Counselling is the art of helping other people come to terms with their own lives, and the problems and difficulties they are experiencing. It recognizes that it is not sufficient to care for others, but that others should be helped to care for themselves. Moreover, the counsellor seeks to achieve this through the efforts and the favoured 'solutions' of the counsellee. In this sense, counselling is more than mere communication, giving useful advice, friendship or influencing the attitudes and behaviours of others. It is a process of providing support and help aimed at making the troubled recipient feel 'better', but relying upon the internal strengths and resources of the counsellee in order to do so. The counsellor is also enquiring into the causes of problem behaviour and emotions, something even good friends will often shy away from, feeling perhaps that they do not want to pry or delve into difficult areas. This means that to counsel effectively, a special relationship, with very particular qualities, is essential.

The outcome of counselling is to assist the counsellee who is living through some kind of personal stress. The concept of social distress will be an important one throughout this book. We will be talking about elderly people who are facing many problems and difficulties which are causing them distress. Some will be major difficulties, others relatively minor. Some people will cope well with problems and difficulties which other people find intolerably stressful. This does not make one problem more or less significant than another. The feeling of distress is real to the individual, and it is towards these feelings that counselling is aimed. It takes the counsellee through a journey which starts with self-assessment, goes through self-awareness, and hopefully ends up with self-determination. The object is to help the counsellee to live life more happily, in less stress, and in greater harmony with others.

Counselling has various 'schools', all with differing procedures and styles of their own, and the argument between them can lead to the belief that counselling is a highly structured and complicated technique, with a 'right' and a 'wrong' way of going about the task. Too often, when counselling is mentioned it signifies formal meetings at standard intervals with professional people who, through their training, position or experience, perhaps as psychiatrists or psychoanalysts, assume that they are the only people qualified to use the technique. Some of the American literature (see, for example, Landreth and Berg, 1980) would certainly suggest this. Sargent (1980) also acknowledges this indirectly when he refers to his less technical contributors as 'non-traditional' in order to distinguish their approach from the more technical, medicalized models.

This professionalization of counselling denies that the techniques involved are a set of skills which are essentially a simple and very human means of helping people in trouble. It does so through the everyday and essentially commonplace techniques of close relationships, empathy, and good communication.

This book presents the counsellor as carer and friend, not as therapist and psychoanalyst. It presents counselling as a set of techniques which can be mastered by all those whose care is genuine, and who are prepared to give some thought to what they are doing.

It is the simplicity and the basic humanity of counselling that make it such an attractive, powerful and valuable technique for those who care for older people.

. . . and the older adult

This view of counselling will be developed in later chapters, but before doing so, it is important that we consider some of the reasons for the comparative neglect of elderly counselling as a technique.

The skills of counselling people in difficulty are well developed in schools, youth work, non-custodial work with young offenders, family therapy, marriage guidance, work with alcoholics and drug-abusers, potential suicides, and in many other spheres. As Halmos (1978) says 'The counsellor's influence on his society is in a process of rapid growth' and in most areas this is supported by a considerable amount of literature. In comparison, there is an almost total lack of literature concerned with counselling older people, and what does exist is American. The reasons for this neglect are interesting to ponder.

Is there an implicit assumption that old people do not require the development of 'theoretical constructs' such as counselling, that their needs are simple and can be accurately assessed and readily satisfied? Do we assume that age brings with it an easy ability to express personal feelings and needs? Or has the image of old age as a time of peace, tranquillity and serenity obscured the very real problems and insecurities felt by many elderly people?

These ideas have no substance. They are perhaps more a mechanism by which the young can shield themselves from the unhappier realities of being old, especially in our society, and even escape from the 'unpleasant' prospect of becoming old themselves.

There may also be an assumption that counselling older people is essentially similar to counselling any other age group, but even a cursory examination of this would suggest otherwise. Simple communication with the elderly is often not straightforward. Poor hearing may impair their ability to hold a serious conversation. Their eyesight may restrict opportunities afforded to the counsellor for body language and other means of non-verbal communication. Their health may be bad, their morale low through loneliness and grief, and their ability to look optimistically at the future seriously reduced.

Moreover, whilst the counsellor of other troubled age groups may have personally experienced the problems they encounter, it is unlikely that the counsellor will have had first-hand experience of old age.

So the neglect of counselling for ageing people would appear to lie in other, more significant areas. These are concerned with the social neglect of older people generally, something that can be witnessed in every area of service provision for older people. A BMA report stated that many doctors see 'geriatric medicine as a second-rate specialty, looking after third-rate patients in fourth-rate facilities' (BMA, 1986). The quantity and quality of social work provision for elderly clients, although taking up a high proportion of social services expenditure, has long been recognized as being inadequate, often carried out by unqualified social workers with limited resources (Barclay, 1982). Local authority building of sheltered accommodation is woefully inadequate. Public transport, on which many elderly people rely, has been severely cut back over recent years.

It is not possible to understand fully the reason for this neglect without reference to some of the ideas and concepts widely shared by people within our society about the nature of old age.

The justification of a social perspective to counselling

Counselling is essentially a person-to-person skill, in which the feelings and needs of the individual are centrally important, taking precedence over everything else including, most importantly, the counsellor's personal and institutional interests. However ideal this might seem, counselling should be ideologically neutral and should not be directed towards either political and social change, or political and social stability. The outcome of the counselling process should be neutral in everything except the personal dimension.

It is important to stress why the counsellor should strive towards this ideal even if, as we will see, it is an impossible one to attain. Often, when dealing with distressed and powerless people, there are two outcomes which can be achieved. One, which can be described as the conservative position, supportive of the status quo, is the tendency to be overbearing, to assume that we, the representatives of wider society, know best, that their dependence on our support allows us to over-ride their wishes. Their thoughts and feelings become of secondary importance. Their attitudes and behaviour do not give them a right to our respect. Counselling, in that it can influence the behaviour of an individual, can be seen in this way as a powerful technique which can be used to control behaviour for the benefit of personal, institutional, social or political agendas. It becomes a means of modifying behaviour in the interests of social control.

Equally, those with an interest in radical social change can see counselling as a means to politicizing the individual. They see troubled and problematic behaviour as the consequence of social inequity or injustice, and conclude from this that 'problem' individuals represent the just deserts of a corrupt and evil social system. They also see that disaffected individuals might prove to be natural recruits to the social and political objectives they support, and that counselling might be used as a means of raising the individual's level of social awareness, and radicalizing their stance on social issues. Counselling becomes a technique for the manipulation of individuals in the interests of social engineering.

The use of counselling for either social control or social engineering is morally suspect. It is also patronizing. The counselling that arises from either approach fails to attribute dignity, respect and esteem to the individual. It becomes tainted with hidden agendas, and is consequently dismissive of the rights of the individual. This is particularly easy when we deal with older people, especially the dependent elderly who are particularly vulnerable to the designs of their carers and susceptible to the hidden agendas of the counsellor.

It is not so much that either the conservative or the radical agenda should, or even could, be abandoned. Elements of both are present in any communication between two individuals. The counsellor requires some measure of control in order to counsel in the first place and most individuals need to be able to function successfully with other people in order to develop satisfactory relationships. Indeed, many older people might be happier and more content if they were able to conform more to the needs of the wider group or society, particularly when personal problems are initiated or exacerbated by an individual's inability or unwillingness to identify with the needs of the wider group.

Conversely, many of the problems of old age are closely linked to the injustice of social provision. The social dimension is an important facet in understanding the problems faced by ageing people. If it is entirely ignored in the counselling process it denies an important, indeed a vital, element in self-understanding. Knowledge of the social dimension is, as will be seen, an important conceptual tool with which ageing people can re-interpret, and then combat, many of the difficulties they face in their lives.

Too often, the difficulties and problems faced by individuals are seen to be the result of some form of personal failing and inadequacy. It is their fault that they are poor; it is their fault if they are depressed; it is their fault if they are lonely; it is their fault if they are in pain. They have made the wrong choices, or bad decisions in the lives they have led; or they are personally incapable of coping with the problems brought about by ageing. Explanations based on individual 'pathology' ignore the social dimension of problems faced by elderly people. It places blame on people rather than taking into consideration the context within which people live. It ignores the constraints placed upon them by social laws, social provision and social attitudes. What is worse, the ageing individual will themselves too readily accept pathological explanations of their own problems, and will often not be aware of the social structures which may cause some of their difficulties, and thus confine their ability to cope with them.

The existence of this social perspective within the counselling process may appear to run counter to the idea that the counsellee's problems must be central. Surely the counsellor should start from the counsellee's own position?

This is to misunderstand the idea of 'client-centred' counselling. It is not so much that all agendas must be abandoned in counselling. What is wrong is for the counsellor to deny that they exist. The counsellor will clearly have agendas, and they should not be hidden within the counselling relationship but discussed openly on the understanding that the counsellee can reject them without paying an unacceptable personal price for doing so. If, for example, the constraints of time or finance mean that some form of assistance is not available, the substitution of another and perhaps unwanted alternative may become the objective for the professional carer. This is an understandable objective which should not remain hidden but discussed openly with the counsellee.

So whilst counselling must place considerable emphasis upon personal feelings and perspectives, and give credence to people's interpretations of the origins of their difficulties, the counsellor also has to be able to see their situation in broader terms, and where necessary to help them re-interpret the other circumstances which have led to it.

Many older people are too accepting of their allotted social role, a role which for many is inadequate, unrewarding and unfulfilling. Their passive acceptance of the social structures bear heavily upon their lives, and does not usually represent a contented acceptance of their lot, as we are too often inclined to believe. Rather it is indicative of a sense of powerlessness about having an effect on the quality of their lives (Scrutton, 1986). Such resignation does little to remedy their feelings, but constitutes a self-fulfilling acceptance of the unhappiness of their circumstances. Moreover, old people often feel that acceptance of their situation is what is expected of them, and that to do otherwise risks losing the support of their younger carers.

Even those who refuse to accept their situation passively very often do not strike out against the forces which oppress them, but against those who appear to represent those forces, including professional carers. Often, those people who are merely closely available alternatives (such as relatives and friends) come in for the backlash. This can lead to anger and bewilderment, to the withdrawal of care and support, and indeed to the designation of a variety of labels connected with mental illness, confusion or senility. This is a common but self-defeating strategy which many older people adopt. It merely places already unhappy and discontented individuals in further difficulties, and leads to reactions which place even more obstacles in their way. This can confirm the 'mentally ill' and 'confused' labels on the individual.

Too often troubled elderly people do not possess a clear view of the social factors which make old age an unhappy and unsatisfactory experience for so many. Explanations which place the emphasis on personal responsibility and blame – individual inadequacy, poor health, unsuitable life habits and, above all, the 'natural' processes of ageing are easier to understand. Such factors are considered to be irreversible and universally applicable to all 'old people', and this fatalism is at the root of the powerlessness felt by many ageing people. Moreover, it is these beliefs which determine and restrict how they live their lives. The counsellor must seek to emphasize a wider interpretation of the counsellee's situation, and in doing so has to include explanations which are often far outside the thinking and experience of many elderly people.

Therefore, the counsellor clearly has the task of distinguishing between the factors of old age which are obviously irreversible by the very nature of the ageing process, and those which result from a personal acceptance of social factors which structure the ability of elderly people to lead fuller lives. The counsellor has to be aware of the existence of these social factors, and to be able to recognize them and their impact on the lives of particular individuals. Counsellors should have the ability to present alternative explanations, alternative ways of thinking about their problems which can liberate ageing people from the constraints imposed on them by a variety of social structures.

What are these structures? In going on to describe them it is important to point out that many of the dominant social attitudes and descriptions of old age have a basis in reality. No-one can or should want to deny the inexorable processes of ageing. The problem is usually that they are too readily applied prematurely or universally to cover everyone of a certain prescribed age. The task of the counsellor is to try to unravel the reality from the social construction.

CHAPTER 3

The social context of ageing

Dominant social values and ageism

Counselling should take an essentially optimistic view of the counsellees' ability to review and reconstruct their own lives. Is this possible? Is it possible, for example, that old age can be a time of hope? Is it possible that elderly people can enjoy their lives, rich in expectation and high in fulfillment? Can their last years be personally satisfying and socially valuable, a culmination of a lifetime's experience? All of us, no matter what our age, have to be able to hope, to have something to look forward to, and those who do not possess this will find it difficult to cope with the normal trials and tribulations of living.

That such questions have to be asked would seem strange indeed to traditional societies where the status of 'elder' is one of prestige and distinction, and where age is valued for its wisdom and experience. Philpot (1986) has compared the traditional and the modern attitudes towards older people in Japan.

> Japan is a country of contrasts. Caught between East and West, it almost defies the foreigner to analyse it. Has the traditional 'respect for elders', a cornerstone of Japanese life for centuries, diminished? Are elderly people (in a society that is ageing as rapidly as it is changing) as radically affected by industrialisation and the tentacle-like spread of cities as elsewhere?

He found that the roots of respect for elderly people were contained within Japanese culture and religion, and that despite the rapid development of industrialization and urbanization and the rush for growth, efficiency and change, respect for elderly people has ensured that they have not fallen behind, and old age still retains a certain authority and respect. It would be wrong to construct an idealistic stereotype of a 'golden age' for old people, but our own 'advanced' civilization has in many ways abandoned these perceptions of old age. The way in which aspects of the social status of older people have been lowered during the last two centuries has been outlined by Cowgill and Holmes (1972).

If other societies define and react to old age quite differently to our own, there is an obvious need to understand the dominant social contexts and attitudes in which old age is lived, and the structural and attitudinal impact this has on the lives of ageing people. Clearly, there are also different views and opinions held within a single society, such as our own. However, within each society there exists a body of ideas which can be described as dominant. This 'dominant ideology' consists of a complex set of social values which to a considerable extent determines how older people are seen, how they see themselves, and how they function or are allowed to function within the wider social context. It is these dominant ideas which establish the 'structures', the dominant constraints within which older people are forced to live their lives. As Estes (1986) states,

> This requires an examination of society's treatment of the aged in the context of the national and world economy, the role of the state, conditions of the labour market, and class, race, gender and age divisions in society. At base, this requires examination of the relationship of capitalism to ageing. It also begins with the proposition that the status and resources of the elderly, and even the experience of old age itself, are conditioned by one's location in the social structure and the local to global economic and social factors that shape that location.

Dominant ideology reflects the interests of the most powerful groups in any society. Laws are passed which not only work in the interests of these groups, but often work against the interests of weaker, or minority groups. These can involve racial minorities, the 'working' class, handicapped people, women, and, of course, elderly people. Sets of values and assumptions exist which act against the best interests of the people who belong to these groups, and arising from this comes racism, classism, sexism and ageism. Each comprises a set of negative attitudes, practices and values which form a stereotype of the group, and affects the way the group is treated and the way it is able to function within the wider society.

Ageism in our society is being increasingly recognized as a powerful influence, developing a stereotype of 'old people' which diminishes and undermines their social status. It consists of several different myths, outlined by Dixon and Gregory (1987).

1. *Myth of chronology* – the idea that elderly people are a homogeneous group by virtue of their age alone, i.e. once your age reaches a 'magic number' you automatically become old and part of the group 'the elderly'.
2. *Myth of ill health* – that old age automatically involves physical

deterioration and that illness in old age is part of normal ageing, not disease processes, and therefore is irreversible and untreatable.

3. *Myth of mental deterioration* – that elderly people automatically lose their mental faculties, slow down and become 'senile' (i.e. mad).

4. *Myth of inflexible personality* – that personality changes with age to become more intolerant, inflexible and conservative.

5. *Myth of misery* – that elderly people are unhappy because they are old.

6. *Myth of rejection and isolation* – that society rejects its elderly people and is uncaring towards them, and the elderly people prefer to 'disengage' from life, i.e. withdraw into themselves.

7. *Myth of unproductivity/dependence* – that elderly people are not productive members of our society, because they are not engaged in paid employment and therefore are inevitably dependent upon others.

Ageism is endemic in society and resides within all of us. Indeed, it resides within the minds of those who have themselves become 'old'. They will have learnt that to be old is to conform to these stereotypes, and accept the ascribed elderly role within the social order. They will take the attitudes they held as young people and internalize them when they reach old age. Perhaps they expected little of elderly people, and now they will hope for little more of themselves than they once expected of others. And, generation by generation, we perpetuate and intensify such attitudes.

This is the nature of ageism. It prevades the thinking, attitudes and expectations of young and old alike. The result is that both the old and their carers accept the socially constructed view of old age, not because that is 'the reality', but because our social beliefs are so powerful they become self-fulfilling. Dominant ideology reflects the way things 'are' rather than how they either 'might be' or 'should be'. They are not natural perceptions, true and incontrovertible, but beliefs which have been developed by dominant social forces over the years.

> Society creates the framework of institutions and rules within which the general problems of the elderly emerge, and, indeed, are manufactured. Decisions are being taken every day, in the management and development of social institutions, which govern the position which the old occupy in national life, and these also contribute powerfully to the public consciousness of different meanings of ageing and old age. (Townsend, 1981)

The paradigm of old age today is perhaps the individual, living alone, socially isolated, managing on inadequate income, suffering from poor health, poorly housed, dependent upon younger carers for support, and seen generally as a burden. There is another popular image, more concerned with leisure, pleasure and contentment. It used to be associated with living on the south coast, but is now more concerned with wintering in hotels in Spain. But this applies to only a few older people. We seem to use this alternative image to deflect some of the more awful realities of life for most older people, but the biggest fear we all have is of the unhappier reality. Yet it is not necessary to see old age as unproductive and futile. If large sections of society do so, then we might legitimately ask how it is that we have arrived at such a judgement.

The origins of ageism

The value placed on age

Youth is more highly valued by dominant social attitudes. It is associated with beauty, energy, enthusiasm, vigour, new ideas, innovation, change and progress – all highly valued attributes. The old can offer only experience, competence, loyalty, continuity, security, and reliability to a society that seems to have outgrown such values. The immaturity, rashness and naivity of youth seem so often to be forgotten, along with the role that the experience of age can play in guiding it. Dominant ideology sees the future, and the people of the future, as crucially important, and older people have little role there. In much the same way that we have learnt to consider commodities as 'disposable', people have become commodities with a 'value' to be bought and sold, and once they have outlived their value, they too become disposable.

Productivity

The basis of dominant social attitudes to old age surrounds the concept of productivity. The value we place on individuals, and therefore the financial and status rewards that are available to them, is largely assessed on the basis of what the individual produces. Old people are generally considered to be 'unproductive'. Their productive years lie behind them, and whilst they are considered to have 'earned' their pensions, this does not cancel out their current 'non-productive' status. Hence, old people are frequently seen as a burden on the rest of society. The projected rise in the number and proportion of old people within society in coming decades, which is a frequent topic of discussion at present, serves as a constant reminder to ageing people of their dependent social status, and the 'drain' that they have become on future public finances.

To the extent that elderly people are unproductive, they have become so because of developments in social policy concerning retirement. Many people have retired because they were expected to do so, even compelled to do so. On the one hand we do not expect elderly people to work, presumably as a consequence of modern social philanthropy, but on the other we 'blame' and penalize them for their unproductive years of retirement.

The concept of productivity, so important within capitalist societies, is one that is central to the value we place on elderly people. It explains and justifies some of the circumstances and conditions in which elderly people are expected to live. Thus, state pensions can be fixed at minimal levels. The most significant effect of retirement on many pensioners is the drastic reduction in living standards. The consequence of this can frequently be seen in the misery of cold and hypothermia, and the stark choices of 'food or heating' which many retired people face, and which periodically surface in our national and local media.

The problem with linking the concept of old age with the capitalist ethic of productivity is that it does not appear to permit the philanthropy which is supposed to characterize our modern 'welfare state'. The capitalist ethic (that is, to those who deserve, most; to those who do not, least) might explain why elderly people are treated in the way they are, but such an explanation would clearly not be suitable for those apologists of dominant ideology who wish to support and perpetuate the wide disparities of income and wealth that exist within our society. They would clearly wish to perpetuate the myths of 'conventional' social wisdom that society does everything it can to value and revere its older citizens. They would deny the link between productivity and elderly poverty. Therefore, other explanations have to be found which coincide more appropriately with the explanations of dominant ideology. The submission here, however, is that these other explanations are secondary, although they form the basis of our ageist attitudes.

Religious belief

Ageism can be found firmly embedded in some of our pervasively influential Christian values and beliefs. The 'other-worldliness' of our Christian heritage teaches us that the problems of this world are not as important as our place in the next; that suffering is part of our preparation for the next life, and that the imminence of death, and therefore the closeness to a 'better' world, is something to be welcomed rather than feared. It is not the intention here to enter a theological debate, and more sophisticated and recent trends in religious thinking might argue that this is not the real message contained within Christian belief. Yet whatever the pure religious message might or might not be, the social message for many people who are now considered old is often clear. Their beliefs are less sophisticated, simpler and more traditional. These tell them to forget their troubles in this life, for they are only temporary. Happiness, contentment, fulfillment and all that is 'good' will be available in abundance in the next life. It is quite pointless for them to worry about their present condition.

The 'this-worldliness' of counselling is therefore pitted against the 'other-worldliness' of religious belief. Such attitudes not only allow old people to justify their social status and situation, they stop the development of dissatisfaction which would otherwise be embarrassing to dominant social ideology. In turn, this means that too often it is the more superficial interpretations of the Christian message that are presented to us.

Psychology and the ageing personality

The absence of a full and coherent developmental psychology of old age has not helped in dispelling some of the myths contained within ageism about the elderly personality. Indeed, some important elements within the massive growth of psychological theory this century have tended to indicate an ageist message. Nowhere can this be more clearly seen than in the work of the father of modern psychology, Sigmund Freud, who himself wrote that,

> ... psychotherapy is not possible near or above the age of 50, the elasticity of the mental processes on which the treatment depends is as a rule lacking – old people are not educable. (Freud, 1905)

This view has had an on-going effect on the attitude towards elderly people within psychology.

> ... orthodox Freudian doctrine has long held the notion that basic personality characteristics are developed and set at a very early stage of development, well within the first decade of life. These basic characteristics, so this view goes, are little, if at all, amenable to modification. Consistent with this, then, is the conclusion that with advanced age the point of no return (with respect to behaviour or personality change) has long since passed. (Schwartz, in Sargent, 1980)

The idea of the elderly personality as a fixed and unchanging entity is fundamental to understanding the lack of counselling approaches. To the extent that counselling is generally associated with personal change and growth, this widely held psychological assumption (perhaps more obvious in the public mind than in more modern psychological ideas) discounts the potential value of counselling for older people.

It also provides a 'scientific' theory which 'explains' why older people tend to get into difficulties in the first place, and then are unable to solve their own problems.

Social relationships and disengagement

The theory of 'disengagement', first postulated by Cummings and Henry (1961), suggests that old people will tend voluntarily to relinquish their social roles and responsibilities, and indeed withdraw from many aspects of social life and participation generally. This theory still enjoys widespread popular credibility although it has been heavily criticized, and largely discredited in academic circles. The theory suggests that it is quite natural for elderly people to withdraw willingly from the social pressures and responsibilities of everyday life, and in doing so, it tends to validate the social processes which make older people redundant and obsolete, and replace them with younger people with more up-to-date skills. Withdrawal thus becomes academically acceptable. Ageing people do not withdraw because they feel undervalued, bereft of a social role and unable to meet the financial costs of full social engagement, but rather because it is considered to be part of the 'natural' processes of ageing.

This, in turn, affects the way that we believe older people should be treated. What they require is time for reflection, rest and sleep, and the removal of all unnecessary pressures and responsibilities. They do not need nor do they want an active, energetic and interestingly full life. Therefore it is best that we do not disturb them too much, lest we upset them by doing so.

This quiescent and peaceful image of old age helps to make the loneliness of old age more acceptable. Elderly people do not make new friends so readily, and given that they are likely to lose their long-standing friends through death, it is reasonable to expect that older people should be increasingly on their own. Loneliness becomes an understandable, acceptable and natural hazard of old age.

Allied to this is the belief that relationships are less fulfilling in old age, that much of the fun and enjoyment associated with being with other people has to be left in the past. Sexual relations are a typical example, it being widely believed that it should not be practised by people beyond a certain age, and that if it is, it is unusual, even a source of amusement.

The medicalization of old age

Ageism associates old age very closely with pain. It is tacitly accepted that elderly people become increasingly prone to sickness and ill-health. To an extent this is based on truth. However, ageism takes what is a normal tendency and transforms it into an extreme and depressing inevitability. Thus, arthritis will progressively wrack their bodies with pain. Their heart and other vital organs will decline in vigour and vitality in an inevitable process of wasting, leading to a series of ailments for which there is little defence. As bodily functions decrease, constipation, incontinence and other conditions will increase. They will lose control of their limbs, muscles will weaken and their sense of balance will diminish. Sight and hearing will fail. The process is pre-ordained, and little can be done to halt the inevitability of personal decline and ill-health.

The medicalization of ageing is consistent with an image of old age as a process of inevitable physiological and biological decline. It suggests that the process can be temporarily halted only by skilled intervention by professional medical staff. These claims and the fatalism of dominant attitudes towards elderly health need to be seriously examined. Certainly, evidence from the more fit and active elderly, those who have not given into dominant social concepts of disengagement and physical decline, would suggest that a sensible attitude towards the care and maintenance of the body, for example through good diet and sensible life-style, keeps mind and body in good shape far longer than conventional wisdom would have us believe. Dominant ideology suggests that it is the fit elderly, and not the sick elderly, who are the exceptions to an otherwise general and unavoidable rule of nature. This is not necessarily so. Baltes and Schaie (1974), reviewing available evidence, declared that research which had indicated a general intellectual decline over a normal life span was 'largely an artefact of methodology', and that 'people of average health can expect to maintain or even increase their level of performance into old age'. Two contributors to Birren and Schaie (1977) confirm this. Botwinnick outlined studies which had shown no decline in verbal and reasoning ability, and others showing some small improvement. Rabbitt suggested that older people were able to compensate for their limitations, by being able to 'conserve and exploit their intellectual resources more fully than do the young'. These findings need to be made more generally known, and should certainly be known by the counsellor of older people.

One consequence of this has been that the care of ageing people has become increasingly medicalized. If decline is inevitable, if there is nothing that we can do to prevent old people becoming frail, sick and dependent, we have to place our trust in the medical experts. The medical profession have in turn led us to believe that they alone can maintain the body. The fact that people now live longer has been attributed, in no small measure, to medical science by the medical profession, and this has been largely accepted. There is, however, little or no evidence to support such a claim. Indeed, Illich (1977), Doyle (1983), Thunhurst (1982) and others have argued persuasively that improved nutrition, public sanitation and better conditions of work have had more to do with this trend than the medical profession. Indeed, there is some evidence to suggest that when infant mortality is removed from the statistics, life expectancy is not significantly greater now than it was prior to the Industrial Revolution.

The medicalization of old age is a major factor in modern society. Certainly, the medical view of ageing holds considerable sway in the care of older people. When they become ill, or indeed face other problems more concerned with their social lives, it is often both easier and quicker to respond to them by the use of drugs. Palliatives rather than cures are usually offered. Pain can be controlled, but the source of pain is rarely diagnosed. Depression can be treated with anti-depressants but these do not reach the cause. Fears and worries can be tranquillized, but they are rarely discussed. In this way, medication can be used to hide the underlying problems. And in doing so, it can help us to avoid the time-consuming process of looking deeper into the causation of many elderly conditions.

Another common form of medical ageism occurs when provision which would be available to younger people is withheld from older people, presumably because they have less life expectancy, and therefore less to gain from such treatments. They are also less productive and therefore the rewards of saving life, or improving the quality of life, are not so significant. This classic and all too common form of ageism again teaches us something about the value dominant social attitudes place upon old age. The argument seems to be that, as the elderly are in a natural and unavoidable decline, there is nothing that can usefully be done. The medical profession, whilst it is quick to claim that it prolongs life, also readily accepts the inevitability of decline and illness in old age. This is especially so when it discovers that it has no answers to a particular situation or ailment.

Indeed, the situation is worse than this. Medicine has too frequently offered treatments and drugs which have been found to be positively harmful. Polypharmacy is common with elderly patients, and professionally sanctioned drug abuse often leads to results far worse that the condition the drugs were originally intended for. There have been a series of mini-scandals in which a succession of drugs prescribed for elderly people, often for many years, have been found to be dangerous and withdrawn from the market. Fortunately, we have not yet had one of Thalidomide proportions.

The result is that ageing people increasingly receive the worst of all possible deals. On the one hand, their health problems have been progressively medicalized, to the virtual exclusion of, for example, personal responsibility or alternative medical viewpoints. But on the other, medical science actually has little to offer elderly people except palliatives and so, in fact, does little to help. It would appear that we have for too long placed reliance upon those who have had little of real value to offer.

The medicalization of many problems of old age, together with our often misplaced confidence in the efficacy of medical responses, tends to hide what is becoming increasingly obvious to many, including many younger medical practitioners – that medicine has neither the time for, nor the real answers to, many of these problems.

Counselling is a process which needs to be increasingly adopted, not least by those working within the medical profession. Yet it is a time-consuming activity, especially when compared to the rapidity with which a prescription can be written. If society gave doctors, social workers and others the time to counsel older people this would have enormous professional and cost implications. It is clearly easier to allow old people to remain content with the belief that they are ill because they are old, and that as illness is a medical problem, they should be satisfied with, and indeed grateful for, their drugs.

The mental processes of ageing

Old age is believed to lead to a natural diminution of mental abilities. Increasing numbers of older people are becoming confused and suffer from some form of senile dementia. Again, the reasons for this trend are not clear, but the general observation has been adapted and widely interpreted to be a 'natural' and irreversible process of brain deterioration with age. Yet there are examples of senility with much younger people, and obviously many examples of extremely old people who are entirely sensible, which suggests that the direct causal relationship between senility and age is not entirely straightforward.

Here, perhaps more than with physical ill-health, counselling should question dominant attitudes and opinion. Studies comparing the brains of 'confused' and 'cogent' elderly people have not revealed any significant differences (see Chapter 18). But many modern drugs used for other illnesses and conditions have been found to be instrumental in creating confusion in elderly people. Again, medicine can be seen as potentially harmful as well as a beneficent force in elderly health.

The experiences of many people who have lived to advanced years would seem to indicate that the human brain can function adequately for a natural life-span of anything up to hundred years and more, given the right circumstances. And the 'right circumstances' have perhaps as much to do with social, emotional and financial circumstances as with anything else.

Dependence

Dependence is also closely associated with old age. Again, it is widely assumed that old people will inevitably become a burden upon those who have to care for them. The fear of becoming dependent is common with ageing people, and one which leads to many difficulties and misunderstandings. Like other aspects of ageism, dependency and old age are clearly associated. Indeed, many young lives, mainly female, have been spent caring for aged relatives, and for carers in such situations, concepts of duty and obligation will often conflict with desires to fulfill personal needs.

Consequently, ageing people who do not want to be a burden fight against becoming dependent. When they are troubled, or lonely, they will often endure their circumstances rather than burden others with their problems. The link between old age and dependence can therefore actually reduce the opportunities elderly people feel they have to discuss their situation with younger people, especially with those they know care deeply for them. This is often reinforced by younger carers if they are for any reason reluctant to take on the responsibilities of their care. Where older people sense this obvious discomfort or denial, they may decide that others do not want to discuss their problems. Consequently the problems remain suppressed.

For many elderly people, the worst aspects of dependence are a loss of human rights, a loss of individual freedom and choice and with these, a loss of human dignity. At a point where the dependence of ageing people becomes self-evident, they are often given practical help rather than emotional support. The result is that the nature of their problem remains undiagnosed. What many want is not just practical support, but an opportunity to discuss their feelings about having to ask for such support. This is usually ignored.

The provision of physical services can be no more than a sop to the feelings of carers, and is often seen as such by the dependent elderly. The provision of routine and practical services can serve to reinforce and highlight their incapacity. People enter their homes to do their housework, to cook their meals, and to provide other services about which they are likely to have strong feelings. Many feel deeply the loss of personal respect and dignity. This consequence of care is usually not intended, but it is present largely because we do not have the time to discuss their dependency with them.

Death and decline – the purpose and meaning of old age

The expressed wish of many elderly people for a quick and early death becomes more understandable as the nature and impact of ageism are studied. They are made to feel a burden, the future is expected to bring only further inevitable decline, and their death therefore seems to constitute a 'happy release' from the expectation or reality of suffering in old age.

If this is so then the value of providing protracted and complicated forms of care, such as counselling, can be seriously questioned. Care becomes a matter of making ageing people as comfortable as possible for as long as they remain alive – and little more. Too often, caring for older people is seen as a task devoid of hope. As long as old age is considered to be a period devoid of personal growth and development, then the resources required for counselling will not be forthcoming. It is the absence of hope, together with the impact of social ageism, which permits us to allow older people to live in poverty, to become confused or senile through loneliness or distress, and to die of neglect or hypothermia.

Dominant social attitudes towards death are mixed, and often apparently contradictory. On the one hand, any discussion about death is avoided – perhaps because we feel that it is an unpleasant subject which reminds us too much of our mortality. Ageing people often find that they have no-one with whom to discuss their fears and anxieties about what may be the next major stage or event in their lives.

Yet at the same time, death is clearly an issue. The 'happy release' attitude exists in both young and old alike, although as such its existence is only tacitly admitted. Conversely, euthanasia does not find widespread popular approval. Does this mean that people do not have the right to take their own lives, even when they decide that they no longer have any reason to continue living? Or does the desire for euthanasia arise from dominant social attitudes which are internalized by elderly people? Clearly, the attitudes we have about death constitute a dilemma, and the whole issue will be dealt with more fully in a later chapter.

Yet the personal experience of many elderly people would indicate that life in advanced age, even when accompanied by declining powers, can be full and meaningful. Death should not be a subject that is avoided, least of all with those who are closest to it.

The importance of understanding ageism in counselling older people

Dominant ideology, in all its aspects, often mistakes the description of old age within existing social settings with a prescription for what old age has to be. In most of what has been described there is an implicit assumption that ageing people are set in their ways and not capable of significant change. They are represented as rigid in their thinking, and immutably set in their life-styles. They are not open to new ideas. They have become anachronisms, people who have lived beyond their time, and therefore are of no further value. Moreover, they have become so by virtue of their age, and the process of ageing is natural, pre-determined and inevitable.

Here we have to return to the earlier submission; that the purpose of ageism in our society is to explain why older people are not entitled to a larger share of social resources. Ageism serves to devalue elderly people in all the ways outlined in order to make it appear that what is happening to them is the result of natural rather than structural processes.

Dominant ideology represents a powerful determinant of the attitudes we hold about, and the attitudes held by, older people. In order to be effective the counsellor has to be aware of these attitudes, and recognize that they will colour the views, attitudes and self-image of the elderly counsellee. The counsellor has to tackle them by raising them within the counselling process, and seek to apply them appropriately to the individual concerned.

Yet it is important to stress the limitations of counselling in this respect. Whilst it can help individuals overcome some of the impact of ageism in their lives, by itself it will do little to change the social structures which produce it. Many will say that our time would be better spent on 'political' solutions which would have an impact on the lives of all elderly people. Such critics might question the wisdom and even the morality of helping ageing people adjust to living in a society which is so inherently ageist. Such criticism is valid. Counselling is not a solution to the social forces and attitudes which can make old age such a depressing experience for many. But, as Halmos (1978) says,

> . . . there are two kinds of betterers, two kinds of righters of wrongs: those who would rectify the anomalies of society before giving a personal helping hand to the individual, and those who would consider the personal assistance of the individual as more urgent and potent than the bettering of society.

So it remains important that the counsellor is aware of, and capable of drawing attention to, the injustices of social life. Amongst all the other effects of ageism, it has led to caring practices which can be extremely conservative and debilitating. Phillipson (1982) came to this conclusion after examining a number of features of professional practice towards older people.

> Apart from some limited areas of innovation, the overall impression is one of stagnation and conservatism in day-to-day work. Older people appear trapped within models of ageing which emphasise the deterioration and loss of function accompanying old age. Such models are, however, at last being challenged, not least by older people themselves in their own political organisations.

The counselling process can play an important part in combating the impact of ageism on individuals, and in relying on older people to decide on their own solutions, to challenge it as a group. The counsellor has to have a view on the ageist creation of old age in order both to understand and interpret the social context in which the individual lives, and to help that individual cope with it. How else can troubled individuals begin to assess their lives? By questioning dominant social attitudes about the nature of old age, the counsellor can transform elderly attitudes from hopelessness to hope. If it is insufficient to change both practice and provision for elderly people within the confines of ageism, it is also expecting too much of the ageing individual to change and grow unless they are aware of the social factors which structure their own lives.

CHAPTER 4

The counselling agendas of old age

The experience of growing older in our society brings with it many emotional and social traumas. How the elderly react to these depends on many factors, but principally on the way that they have learnt to deal with problems in their younger years. All elderly people will have spent a life-time dealing with a variety of problems and difficulties, and the way they face old age will depend crucially on what they have learnt from those experiences. This means that each ageing person will bring a characteristic response to the process of ageing; some will bring wisdom, openness, flexibility, gentleness and kindness; others will bring prejudice, dissatisfaction, rigidity, frustration and aggression.

Whilst the elderly personality is already well established, it is not as 'rigid' as many would have us believe. One objective of counselling elderly people is to assist them to adjust realistically to the problems and consequences of normal change in the ageing process, and to prevent them becoming tyrannized by it. Even those who have dealt successfully with the problems they faced in their younger years are likely to experience some difficulties in coping with increasing age, but they will at least bring with them the skills and confidence gained over a lifetime.

Other people will not be so fortunate, bringing instead an inadequate social base and many emotional scars that will have developed over the years. Some will have failed to make close and lasting relationships, or to master the art of communicating their feelings. It is these people who are likely to be the most vulnerable to the problems of old age as they will have fewer resources with which to cope.

So in dealing with the problems of ageing people, the counsellor is not working with fresh material, but with individuals who have experienced a considerable amount of life and been shaped, and sometimes mis-shaped, by it. Therefore, it is important for the counsellor at an early stage to determine whether they are dealing with counsellees whose difficulties are a recent experience directly related to ageing, or those who have longer-standing problems with their roots in earlier years. It is also important to distinguish between individuals whose difficulties permeate their entire personality, and those who are finding adjustment to a new stage of life temporarily hard.

This chapter looks at the problems which are specific to growing old within our society. It deals with the problems that all ageing people will face, notwithstanding their personal ability to cope. In doing so we have to recognize that every elderly person is a unique individual, despite passing through the common experience of ageing. In particular, it sets out to examine the extent to which the social performance of older individuals is socially constructed for reasons outlined in the last chapter, and the extent to which they are the 'natural' problems of old age. The following chapter will then look at the task of working with those whose problems date back to earlier stages in their lives, and in particular to how a person's life history will affect their ability to cope with the processes of ageing.

Counselling for young and old alike is usually geared to the 'problem' emotions – depression, despair, anxiety, frustration, stress, low self-esteem and so on. If the myth that old age is a peaceful and tranquil time were correct there would be no reason for counselling, but the reality for many individuals is often far removed from such an idyllic picture. There are many factors in the ageing process which can create troubled emotions, and which are therefore the legitimate object of counselling support.

Indeed, the problems of living into old age should not be underestimated. Old age brings with it problems few of us have faced up to, often because it is more comfortable for us to deny them; they might, after all, happen to us one day.

The last 100 years have probably witnessed the most rapid peaceful process of change experienced in any century of human history. It is a useful exercise for any younger counsellor to consider life as it was during the early years of an older person's life. These are the years in which we all learn to comprehend and cope with life, and which most of us treasure as 'the good old days'. It would be strange indeed if the rapidity of change during this century had not made it difficult, even impossible, for some older people to cope. Many of the old 'certainties' will have been lost, and new and puzzling realities will have taken their place.

The problems of old age usually surround the issue of loss. Throughout our childhood, youth and middle age, we all develop roles and functions which give us our social status, our personal identity, and a meaning to our lives. At the same time we form relationships with important people who then become central figures in our social and emotional lives. Together these provide the very reason and purpose of life for us. As the years pass many of these roles are shed, and many good friends are lost or pass on. Research has consistently found that loss is the most significant contributory factor in elderly distress, and it is the difficulties that such loss brings that serve as the basis for counselling older people.

The loss of significant people

Most people face the loss of significant friends and relatives throughout life. Even in childhood, grandparents and older relatives die, perhaps parents too. Older brothers and sisters move away from the childhood home. For many, parents separate and leave home. Friends move to other places, or we leave school and lose contact with them. There is no way that we can anticipate the loss of significant people in our lives; it happens regularly to everyone at all stages of life, and it is invariably painful. Perhaps by the time we reach our later years we should have become used to the process of grieving and loss, but this is rarely the case.

Indeed, as we grow older the loss of friends becomes more rather than less painful. The young usually form part of groups which have regular and dynamic processes of forming, losing and re-forming relationships, so if loss is not exactly painless, it is at least considered redeemable. There are other people to meet, other situations to enter, other challenges to face. The young want to socialize and, in most cases, need to in order to work for their living. Life goes on, and grief must of necessity take its place. Yet even the young, with all these apparent advantages, do suffer socially and emotionally, and such loss can at times become intolerable. If so, some form of formal or informal counselling is often available to them.

The problems of loss in old age are often more bitter and intense. The avenues available to the elderly for finding 'replacement' relationships are more restricted, limited both by the duration and importance of the lost relationship, and their more restricted social contacts. These factors are often exacerbated by a variety of others, such as ill-health, the decline of their physical abilities, their mental approach to life, and their financial ability to participate in social life. Older people will no longer have access to 'work' relationships, which for so many have been the main source of friendship and companionship. So each successive loss often has the effect of increasing loneliness and isolation. Indeed, loneliness is the most common consequence of losing close friends and, in turn, elderly morale and happiness is more deeply affected by loneliness than any other single factor. In extreme situations, the loss of significant people can lead to losing the will to live.

The impact of personal loss, and the increasing inability of older people to find replacements, is often the result of the social expectations of old age. The theory that elderly people 'disengage' from social life is probably only marginally a 'natural' process. In the main, disengagement occurs because of the dominant social expectations that old age brings with it, increasing debility, incompetence and loneliness, and for many these then become self-fulfilling. It is for these reasons that counselling can help in both ameliorating grief, and in encouraging older people to maintain their engagement in social life.

The loss of the parental role

Elderly people have usually lost two crucial roles which will have often formed a significant part of their earlier lives. The parental role is one that fills a significant part of people's lives, especially women, and particularly those women who have not worked. The total dependence of the young child on parents diminishes gradually over a period of years, but the relationships that parents form with their children mean that parenting provides for many a deep and lasting meaning in their lives. As children reach adolescence they begin to establish their own social life, and increasingly in modern society these lives are quite separate and distinct from the lives of their parents. When, as young adults, they eventually leave home to begin their own inde-pendent life-styles, parental investment in both time and energy is suddenly unnecessary, even positively unwanted. This is particularly difficult for some when the youngest or last child leaves the parental home. The rational response to this is that the process is quite natural, and should be expected. Yet, whilst there should be joy in seeing children making their way independ-ently in society, there remains for many a 'gap' in their life which many 'ex-parents' find difficult, even impossible, to fill. How can 'redundant' parents fill the now empty hours? This is particularly difficult when there has been too much time and energy invested in children, and not enough in developing their own lives separate from their children.

As more years pass, the former caring/dependent roles are gradually but often completely reversed. The declining powers of parents make them increasingly dependent upon the care of others, and it is the children who mostly take on this role. The cycle of dependency is complete when former parents begin to feel not only unnecessary, but a burden to their children. Many ageing people feel this reversal of the caring role very deeply, and often with an intense sense of shame.

Retirement

The loss of productive, paid employment constitutes another significant loss of role for ageing people. Retirement involves many losses. The daily routine of passing time in productive work is replaced by the passing of time with apparently little or nothing to do. The companionship available at the place of work is lost. And the financial loss which retirement brings involves for many a significant reduction in their life-style, in the opportunities realistically available to them, and thus in their expectations of life generally. For many retired people it becomes financially impossible to fill their increased leisure time with worthwhile and satisfying pursuits, and this is particularly so for those who have either not used their leisure time constructively in earlier life, or those who have invested their entire energies in their employment. The social class issues in this respect cannot be underestimated.

> For many working-class groups . . . there is a greater degree of discontinuity between life in work and life in retirement. The factory environment itself enourages the development of a very limited range of skills, few of which have relevance beyond the factory gate. If work does have an influence on the non-work area of life, it may only be in a negative sense. People working different shifts from week to week may find it difficult to participate actively within the community; people doing assembly work may often be too tired to go out. The result of such practices may appear at their most acute in retirement, when individuals will require a far broader range of activities and relationships than their work environment may have allowed. (Phillipson, 1982)

For many people brought up in the generation that is now 'elderly', 'leisure' and 'spare time' were terms which had little practical meaning in their lives. Life was always more concerned with struggle and work. Consequently many people entering old age, and faced with many hours in which they feel they have little to do, are at a loss to know how best to fill them constructively. Many will have spent what spare time they had in passive rather than active leisure pursuits (watching television, or drinking at the local pub) and where this has been the case, they are likely to experience more difficulty in coping with an enforced increase in leisure time. Only those who have been able to afford the time (and the money) for more active pursuits and hobbies will necessarily find retirement a release. Retirement counselling is therefore an important aspect of the counselling of older people, and this will be considered in more detail in a later chapter.

The loss of financial status

The income of retired people falls dramatically. Again, this is particularly relevant to the working class retired, and particularly those who have to rely on the basic state pension. Many are unable to maintain their former standard of living. Tight budgeting is required, and any 'life-savings' remain untouched in case of a 'rainy day'. Too often, the daily concerns of older people are worries about the basic necessities of life – keeping warm, clothing themselves adequately, and having enough food in the house for the next meal. These fundamental financial problems can often lead to despair and anxiety which generate emotional difficulties and neurosis. It has been calculated that over two million people live close to or below the 'official' poverty line, which many regard as unacceptably low in any case.

Social status also declines with the loss of financial status. We have seen how retired people are considered 'unproductive' in a society which ascribes status, as well as income, on notions of a person's productive worth. The 'growing proportion of elderly people' within the population is frequently cited by the media as a 'burden' upon tax payers. Old people have become a problem. How are we to fund this growing number of retired and dependent elderly people? These attitudes undoubtedly affect ageing people themselves, and their view of their own status and value in society. It makes many feel like scroungers, dependent upon social security which many still see as charity. They develop a self-image of being a burden, centred around concepts which to their generation have connotations which are not always apparent to younger people.

Declining physical abilities and poor health

The process of physical decline is generally seen as a medical problem, and a physical condition which the doctors, armed with modern drugs, have to ameliorate. The idea that physical decline may have an emotional side is less readily recognized. Yet an individual who has been physically fit, able to cope for themselves, dependent on no-one and proud of their independence will often find it difficult to cope emotionally with the increasing incapacities of old age. People who have never asked for help will need to do so, and for many this will be a deeply humbling experience, quite contrary to the self-image they have previously established for themselves. Moreover, their hopes and expectations for the future, many socially prescribed, will suggest that their ability to fend for themselves is only likely to decline. They realize they might eventually need to have assistance to accomplish even the most basic and most personal daily tasks, such as bathing and toileting. Both the contemplation and reality of this can cause considerable emotional turmoil, and can be deeply distressing to individual pride. Dependence, imminent or actual, should therefore constitute an important agenda in the counselling of older people.

Again, it is necessary to point to social class differences in life expectancy, health and physical incapacity of people generally, and of older people in particular. The relevance of this was pointed out in an Age Concern survey which found that 35% of people in more affluent 'AB' social groupings, but only 19% of those doing unskilled or semi-skilled manual work, were considered 'very fit'. Correspondingly, of those in the highest group for incapacity,

9% were from professional or managerial backgrounds and 22% from semi-skilled or unskilled jobs. (Quoted in Bosanquet, 1978; Doyle, 1983 argues this case more fully.) Again, the implication for counselling is that we are dealing with issues which arise as much from social organization as from the nature of old age, and that the social, emotional and economic realities of life need to be a normal part of the counselling agenda.

The loss of independence

The ability to lead our lives in the way we see fit, albeit subject to the laws and mores of social life, is an important cultural element in our society. When an individual is no longer able to be independent, many psychological consequences can occur. Anxiety and depression often follow as a reaction to the loss of former skills or abilities. When this happens through illness or accident to younger people, we are aware of the likely feelings that must accompany it. However, when disability and handicap arise through old age, particularly when this has been a slow and gradual process, we often fail to recognize that the loss may be equally significant to the individual. There is no legitimate reason to believe that the onset of handicap is any easier to accept merely because of increasing age.

When ageing people can no longer cope with living on their own, the spectre of residential or hospital care arises. This prospect is often made worse by notions which we should have consigned to the past, namely, the social stigma associated with the old Poor Law workhouses, and the regimentation of the early (and many existing) elderly person's residential establishments. But the effects of institutionalization in hospitals or homes, however caring they may try to be, are always likely to be detrimental in a society which values freedom and independence so highly. The process of preparing, allocating and receiving ageing people into institutional care is therefore a crucial stage in the final years of many people's lives. Counselling should be an integral element of this preparation. It is an essential method for determining the personal desires, wishes and needs of elderly people. If institutional provision could more accurately reflect these individual needs, they would then provide a more acceptable and relevant service to the more dependent elderly.

The effect of attitudes on the experience of old age

Ageism, and the stereotyping of old age, forms the basis of individuals' acceptance of their own lives as ageing people. We have seen how 'decline' into the dependence of old age is not entirely the result of 'natural' life processes, but to a considerable extent is socially constructed. The 'disengagement' of older people from social life is what they themselves expect, and what in turn is expected of them. The social construction of attitudes to ageing does not by itself create the ageing process, but it enhances and accelerates it. To what extent ageism becomes self-fulfilling in successive generations of old people will clearly depend upon the individual's personality, life-style, health and circumstances.

Given this, the task of counselling is not to reverse the ageing process itself but to assist the individual to reduce the rate of physical decline by rejecting the stereotypes. This can be achieved through increasing personal knowledge of the process of growing old, and enhancing the confidence of the individual to live life to the fullest possible extent for the longest possible time. Counselling should seek eventually to overcome the fatalistic and pessimistic models of old age. Such models purport to be 'descriptions' of old age, but in fact they become prescriptive in limiting and confining the hopes and expectations we allow elderly people to maintain. Many ageing people are trapped into these prescriptive patterns, and counselling should help them to understand better what old age is in their own experience rather than what elderly stereotypes tell us old age should be.

These are some of the issues which might or might not be relevant to any ageing individual, in whatever combination or degree they might arise. They are clearly problems of sufficient importance to contribute to emotional and social distress at some level in most older people. At the very least they can cause the individual worry, and if this worry is not adequately dealt with this in turn can lead to stress and then to physical and mental illness, to social disengagement, and ultimately perhaps to stress-induced confusional states.

Yet counselling should not be solely, or even principally, concerned with these 'pathological' aspects of ageing. Ideally counselling should be available long before the problems and difficulties of ageing reach such extremes. Indeed, perhaps the absence or the inadequacy of counselling provision for ageing people has contributed in part to the high and increasing levels of such pathology in the lives of elderly people today. All counselling is concerned with helping people come to terms with the paradoxes of life. Halmos (1978) states that 'psychological evidence is accumulating in support of the notion that sanity and an acceptance of dissonance may correlate with each other.' This is an important concept in counselling older people for its very nature creates the most paradoxical of all paradoxes – the belief in a happy and contented old age at a time when decline and death are quite naturally important concerns. The juxtaposition of the hopes and expectations of life amidst the grief, pain and illness of old age, and the imminence of death, presents a counselling task of immense proportions.

Generally, ageing people want to talk about their health, their incapacity and their death. It frightens them. It worries them. They are not in control of what is going to happen to them, or when it is going to happen. Their very existence is uncertain. In a sense it always has been, but the young can and often do discount such thoughts. The old can no longer do so because of the very imminence of death.

Too often, younger people refuse to discuss such matters with them, denying them the opportunity of coming to terms with their mortality, and their very humanity. We deny them the chance to look at their final years with a degree of appropriate optimism, for it is largely by discussing worries and concerns that we are eventually able to put them to one side, and look to more hopeful horizons.

When death is so close, there is often a need to make sense of life. What has their life been about? Have they wasted it? Has it had any real meaning or significance? Bland reassurance, which is too often the response elderly people receive, is of no value, nor indeed does it constitute a counselling approach. Counselling should seek to enable individuals to find meaning in life for themselves.

And then there is the question of what follows death? Are the religious precepts that we have been taught (whether accepted or rejected during our lives) relevant or meaningful to this final part of our lives? Is death just a return to ashes, or is there a better life hereafter? Whether we believe that the soul is resurrected after death or not, old age certainly resurrects such questions even for those who have spent little of their lives concerned with religious matters. Counselling does not have an opinion on these, or any other questions, but should be seeking to help ageing people come to terms with their own beliefs.

And what will become of those who are left behind? Will they be able to cope in their permanent absence? The answer to this question, positive or negative, can produce concerns for the individual. We might not like to think that our death will leave others unable to cope, but at the same time the prospect of our dying and others' lives continuing as normal seems to many to be a judgement on their value. All such concerns should be considered and discussed where appropriate in the counselling process.

All these agendas make the counselling of ageing people a vital technique for all those relatives, friends, doctors, social workers and others who work, or have significant contact, with elderly people. It is surely no longer acceptable to ignore them as we so often do in our dealing with them.

CHAPTER 5

Life history

It would be quite wrong to assume that ageing people only have problems associated with their age. They are individuals with a unique set of experiences. Their life history has made them what they are, to a large degree determining the nature of their social participation. Understanding this is vital. It is difficult for the counsellor to understand anyone, and certainly not older people, without being fully aware of the past which has created them.

This highlights the importance to the counsellor of piecing together a full and accurate life history, almost as the first act of counselling. Many questions need to be asked.

When were they born, and where? This gives the counsellor some general insight into the times and circumstances in which they were born, and during which they spent their most formative early years.

What was the composition of the family, and where did the individual fit into it? Much of their individual character was formed from the experiences, circumstances and quality of these early family relationships.

What were the dominant factors in family life – the occupations and life-styles of their parents, their social class allegiances, their religious and other beliefs? Such factors are often crucial in the understanding of individual social and emotional expectations of life.

What importance was attached by the family to education, and to social advancement? What were their early hopes and desires for the future? How has the individual fared in life in comparison with these early expectations?

What were their main periods of employment? Was work a satisfying and fulfilling experience?

What was the nature of their life-style during successive stages of their life? How fulfilling and satisfying were these experiences?

How did marriage and family life affect them? Or what were the reasons for an individual not marrying, or not having children? How formative was this stage of their lives, and to what extent have they been able to happily relinquish these former roles?

How satisfactory are their current relationships with life-long friends and relatives, and in particular, their relationships with their children?

All these factors will have been crucial in the formation of personality, and the kind of personal qualities ageing people bring with them to cope with their final years. The information the counsellor is able to gather about the counsellee's life history is therefore vital.

The form on page 38 was developed in order to outline the kind of areas in which information may be useful. As such it provides a useful guideline for all prospective counsellors. Within these boundaries lies a wealth of information that might well give clues to important factors in the life of the individual. A multitude of relationships, satisfactory and unsatisfactory, terminated and continuing; a variety of social attachments and commitments; limitless hopes, desires, wishes and impulses; an infinite number of insights and beliefs on the nature of life and society; innumerable conflicts, despairs, disappointments, and an equal number of methods of dealing with them. And all these, plus much more over a considerable number of years, have contributed to the elderly person who now requires counselling. To obtain this information may require many hours of careful and sympathetic conversation. The effort is, however, both necessary and worthwhile for it can help not only in eliciting vital information and insight, but can also assist in the formation of a good counselling relationship. The time taken over this by the counsellor can indicate that we are genuinely interested in the counsellee as a person rather than just as a 'problem'.

Moreover, the counsellor's task is made easier by the fact that reviewing one's life is a common and often a pleasurable experience for ageing people. But what, specifically, is the counsellor looking for?

All people are the product of their past life. Experiences shape us as people, and make us what we are. They help to form our personality and character. As individuals, we do not respond to situations randomly, but through a complex system of learned responses and attitudes. These make our responses more regular. Patterns become discernible and therefore, to some extent, more predictable. Therefore, when we are faced with problems and difficulties we will respond in our own particular way.

Some people seem dogged by ill-fortune; some by tragedy; others regularly pass over opportunity. Some people appear always to be surrounded by friends who support them; some seem to be regularly let down by other people; others seem to have few friends. Some people respond passively; other aggressively; others sink into depression. Some people appear always to look optimisitically to the future; others remain forever pessimistic.

LIFE HISTORY

Name _____

Date of birth _____ Place of birth _____

Mother _____ died 19 ___   Father _____ died 19 __

Religion of parents _____

Brothers and sisters

	Name	Born	Address if alive	Died
1.				
2.				
3.				
4.				
5.				
6.				

Main addresses whilst with parents

1. _____
2. _____
3. _____

Marriage

	Date	Place	Spouse	Date ended	Reason
1.					
2.					

Marital addresses

_____ from _____ to _____
_____ from _____ to _____
_____ from _____ to _____
_____ from _____ to _____

Children

	Name	DOB	Left home	Present address
1.				
2.				
3.				
4.				
5.				

Other significant people

Name	Relationship	Address

Main employment

Subject	Spouse

Hobbies and interests

_____
_____
_____

Date of admission to full-time care _____ 19 ___

Whatever the pattern that can be found, it often gives the counsellor some useful insights into the problems of the counsellee. It helps to explain how individuals look upon life, how they take up challenges, how they respond to difficult situations. It also offers some idea of how people are likely to respond to situations in the future. It is in many ways, the key to understanding an individual's social performance.

The unconscious world of meaning

In looking for patterns the counsellor has to make a distinction between the internal and external worlds, the conscious and subconscious experiences that individuals bring to their current problems. Many believe that human motivation is simple and straightforward, that we understand what we are doing, why we are doing it, and are fully aware of the likely outcome. This rational view of human behaviour, that we act according to known motivations and drives which are (or should be) under our personal control, is difficult to square with human experience. The belief that we know at all times how we think, feel and behave, and what motivates us to do so, is false. Even if we have sufficient knowledge of psychological theory and have taken into account significant or traumatic events in our lives, and believe these explain the problems and difficulties we have experienced in life, it is seldom as straightforward as this. Experience is continuous and cumulative, involving, as has been outlined, an enormous volume of daily interchange with people and things, often trivial and inconsequential. But often the repetitive and persistent minutia of life have more lasting efforts on how people subconsciously choose to lead their lives than the obvious but occasional traumas. The habits, beliefs and emotions that determine our responses to people and situations are more strongly associated with the everyday events taking place over many years and accepted by us without conscious thought than with isolated incidents, however traumatic.

So elderly individuals, like all of us, are a product of their own history at both a conscious and subconscious level. Decisions taken at one stage of life inevitably affect what happens at subsequent stages. Counselling is usually of greatest help when it is able to throw light upon crucial life events and decisions, and help the counsellee to a new understanding and view of them. This is why the counsellor of ageing people has to start at their birth rather than at the commencement of 'old age'. Many aspects of understanding ourselves are denied to us because we consign some of the unwanted and uncomfortable aspects of our lives to the subconscious. Freud called this a 'seething cauldron' of all the wishes, impulses and desires which we are told are socially unacceptable, or which we feel would be dangerous or anxiety-provoking if we admitted them to our consciousness. The unconscious, then, consists of those aspects of ourselves and our experience which have either been disallowed to us, or which have been made unacceptable to us by some external moral force.

The problem is often that what is repressed are quite natural human desires and feelings which have nevertheless become social taboos. Often they have been inhibited by some dominant social, religious or moral imperative; sometimes the source of inhibition has been parents, or some other significant individual during childhood. Many individuals have never fully evaluated or come to terms with their inhibitions, which leads to serious conflicts arising between conscious desires and the unconscious restraints. This can often develop into a level of internal confusion and disharmony that can have an extremely negative effect on an individual's ability to lead his or her life.

When counselling older people it is important to remember that the moral imperatives which have been applied to the individual may have been far stronger than, or of a different nature to those which now apply. This can often make them more difficult for the younger counsellor to comprehend.

Despite the influence of psycho-analysis, many people still feel that the unconscious is a suitable place for disposing of their unwanted or disqualified feelings and desires. Indeed, consigning unwanted emotions to the unconscious can be, and often may seem to be, an appropriate means of emotional survival. We do this when we decide not to discuss critical issues with people who are clearly disturbed by them, often because we prefer to avoid the issues involved.

Indeed, much traditional religious teaching, which may be an extremely powerful force in the lives of many elderly people, suggests that we should be able to deny or repress some of the more basic human motivations, particularly those which surround sexual matters. But as Freudian analysis has indicated forcefully, such defence mechanisms entail sacrificing part of reality, part of ourselves, and the energy used to sustain subconscious denial could be better employed in other directions. At more extreme levels, the loading of our subconscious can lead to irrational, illogical and apparently senseless behaviour which can only be understood when we understand the contents of this part of our mind.

A developmental psychology of ageing

The consequence of such internal psychological disharmony is often tragic for the individual, when powerful and pressing forces operating from within the subconscious begin to dominate our conscious world. The origin of such disharmony is not usually attributable to advancing old age, but is rooted in earlier times. For a more concise and analytical understanding of how it occurs, it is useful to read the work of Erikson (1965).

Erikson developed a 'developmental psychology' of ageing, which maintained that unresolved issues from earlier stages of life to a large extent influenced the way the individual dealt with problems and difficulties in later life-stages. Erikson described eight life-stages in which the individual has to resolve a particular psycho-social issue or crisis.

1. Early infancy (0 to 18 months), and the development of basic trust or a sense of mistrust.
Infants whose early experiences do not allow them to feel that their emotional and physical needs will be satisfied will, according to Erikson, fail to develop a basic trust in people and in life generally. This can lead to psychological problems, connected with an inability to form trusting relationships with other people, and which will consequently reduce their ability to tackle the issues faced at subsequent stages of development.

2. Early childhood (18 months to 3 years), in which the child develops either a sense of autonomy or a sense of shame or doubt, and

3. Childhood (3 to 6 years), in which the child develops either a sense of initiative or a sense of guilt.
Children want, or need to feel, a developing sense of their own personal identity, separate from that of others, even the people closest to them, so that they are able to have and express a will of their own, and to initiate their own actions. Erikson describes these stages as being 'decisive for the ratio of love and hate, co-operation and wilfulness, freedom of self-expression, and its expression'. Failure to do so leads to a concern about personal weakness, incompetence, powerlessness and badness, leading to an inhibited ability to act according to their own initiative or desire.

4. Middle childhood (6 to 12 years), in which is developed a sense of industry or alternatively, a sense of inferiority.
The 'inner self', consisting of the confidence and belief we have developed in ourselves, has now been formed, and the child is now able to move out into the world in a competitive state with others. This stage is concerned with getting things done and completing them from our own personal efforts. Most children enter the wider world with some degree of inquisitiveness and optimism, but many will fail to live up to their own expectations, or the expectations of others, and this will lead to feelings of isolation, inferiority, despair and a possible drift into mediocrity or inadequacy.

5. Adolescence (12 to 20 years), in which the individual develops either a sense of ego identity or identity diffusion.
Adolescence, with its transition to full adult life and responsibilities alongside major hormonal, body, social, sexual and emotional changes, is a time when all the issues of earlier stages, even when successfully resolved, undergo a major reconsideration and reassessment. Do our own inner desires and wishes coincide or conflict with the wishes and desires of others? Where there is a feeling that inner desires and social realities conflict, this gives rise to

major doubts about our personal identity, sexuality, social ability and general purpose in life.

6. Early adulthood (20 to 35 years), and the development of intimacy or a sense of ego isolation.

Erikson associates this stage with the crucial ability to feel ready and able to commit ourselves to other individuals in new, mutually satisfying, fulfilling and long-lasting partnerships. This indicates an ability to share and therefore to give to our relationships a degree of personal commitment, and to relinquish a degree of personal independence. Where this struggle is resolved in favour of isolation, the individual develops a sense of being alone, and is in danger of becoming self-absorbed. Such individuals will tend to shy away from intimate relationships with others.

7. Middle adulthood (35 to 60 years) sees either the development of generativity or a sense of stagnation.

Generativity is seen as a personal interest and involvement in establishing and guiding future generations, mainly (but not totally) expressed through productive employment and child-rearing. Stagnation implies a general feeling of lack of personal involvement and fulfillment in life.

8. Late adulthood/old age (60 years onwards), in which the elderly individual either develops a sense of ego identity or drifts into feelings of despair commonly associated with old age.

This stage refers to the kind of issues and outcomes considered in the last chapter.

Erikson's stages are meant to indicate only an approximation of the main struggles encountered at each period of life. The 'end' of one period does not indicate that particular crises have been resolved one way or the other, but the degree to which they have been resolved, positively or negatively, will be important in later stages. Those whose life journey has been relatively successful will be able to place their life in context, and view the last stages of their lives more philosophically. They will feel that their losses are unfortunate, but will tend to be more successful in finding ways around them which enables them to remain essentially optimistic. Those who are unsuccessful will tend to view the ageing process as catastrophic, unfair and debilitating, and their pessimism will restrict their ability to cope adequately with the realities of old age.

Clearly, the success or lack of success experienced at each stage will have implications for how the individual is able to progress in their life. Hence, the counsellor will need to be aware of the degree of unresolved business from each stage of life. The non-trusting adult may well have had difficulties in their infancy. Those who show an inability to act for themselves may well still retain unresolved insecurities from their childhood. Those who are uncertain about their identity and role may well have been carrying those doubts since their adolescence. Those who are failing in their personal relationships may have been doing so since their early adult years. Those who feel isolated and detached from life around them may have had similar feelings since their middle years. So within all these explanations of an individual's successful and unsuccessful adaptations through life stages can be seen many aspects of how different people adapt to the problems of old age.

These are just some of the regular patterns displayed by elderly individuals which are rooted in their past history of experience.

The emotions

Failure at any stage of this developmental journey through life results in the individual experiencing troubled emotions which are, as we have seen, the main focus of counselling. What are these emotions?

The main emotions which cause problems in our lives are:

(a) depression and despair,
(b) anger,
(c) frustration,
(d) anxiety.

To some degree these emotions are experienced by everyone at each stage of their lives, and mostly we are able to cope with them. Counselling becomes useful only when the feelings involved become either unbearably intense, or indefinitely prolonged. Each emotional state can lead to attitudes and behaviour which restrict the individual's ability to lead life to its full potential. They affect our outlook on life. They cloud our judgement. They cause us to act in ways which would otherwise be considered quite untypical of us.

At times when troubled emotions appear to be taking over our lives, there is a tendency to 'send for the expert' – the doctor who takes control through the provision of drugs, the psychologist who offers some form of therapy, or the social worker who assesses what practical support might be required. All these professionals have, in turn, become used to 'taking control' or taking over the responsibility. Yet this tendency is both unwise, and ultimately, self-defeating. Other people can, at best; only provide palliatives for they do not and cannot know the origins of the emotions. Only the individual feels them; and only the individual can overcome them.

Counselling is based on the premise that every person, even if they appear to have given up hope, or become totally prone to anxiety, or irrational in their anger, have within them the only source of control available. Even the most damaged emotions are, in the last resort, controlled only by the individual who owns them. It is their ability to re-assert control, to overcome their feelings, which needs to be re-established.

Self-image

The counsellor's route to helping the individual regain personal control is through the concept of self-image. We all have a picture of ourselves as people who possess or lack certain skills, abilities, aptitudes and qualities. We all function within a social setting in which we see ourselves fulfilling or failing to fulfill particular roles. We construct this picture or image of ourselves throughout our lives, and it is a powerful motivating force. Self-image is what leads us to great achievements and success, and enables us to progress through life's stages with a feeling of satisfaction and achievement. Alternatively it holds us back from achieving anything. For some, it is the cause of ongoing failure, impotence and incompetence, constantly dragging us down to deepening levels of depression and despair.

Self-image consists of two factors. First, there is the 'ideal' self, which comprises a set of images individuals harbour about the kind of person they should be, or would want to be, what level of performance or achievement they should be attaining, and by what standards they should judge themselves. Set against this is the 'actual' self; the individuals' own assessment of their actual social performance.

When there is a serious imbalance between these two factors, self-image is likely to be low, and this can have a major impact on the way that individuals decide to live their lives. Where the ideal self is unattainably perfect, or where assessment of social performance is unfairly harsh, the imbalance between the ideal and actual self will lead to low self-esteem. With ageing people, this is particularly important where individuals refuse to recognize declining powers and ability. Inability to attain the level of social performance they feel is necessary leads to depression and despair, anger, frustration, and to an unnecessary anxiety about the future.

If the imbalance is in the opposite direction, where the ideal self is easily attained, self-esteem may be satisfied at a much lower level of social performance, but in this situation people fail to live fully or reach their potential as individuals. Again this is an important concept with older people, particularly when faced with dominant ageist attitudes which persistently underestimate the abilities and contributions possible in old age. So whatever the combination of ideal and actual selves, imbalance will have a profound effect on self-image, and the way individuals determine to lead their lives.

Every individual needs to feel a sense of personal worth. Everyone needs to have an identified social role. Everyone needs to have a realistic optimism regarding the future. For older people, each of these elements of self-image can be particularly difficult concepts to maintain and develop, for they are essentially optimistic factors which have to be applied to a stage in life popularly believed to possess little about which to be optimistic.

The problem is that whilst the counsellor has to take an optimistic stance, this optimism cannot be passed directly to the counsellee. It has to be gained, and then internalized by the counsellee. Hence the counsellor of the troubled ageing individual has to be able to pursue new ways of looking at the present, the past and the future, and to discuss these with the counsellee. Counselling has to 'de-condition' the way that older people look at themselves; they have to be encouraged to look again at their supposed limitations and failings, and look more optimistically at what it is possible to achieve in old age. The value of counselling in facilitating this process of personal change has now to be considered.

CHAPTER 6

The counselling relationship

The following three chapters are concerned with the process of counselling. Through the medium of this book, it is possible to distinguish three aspects of the counselling process – the relationship, the skills, and the process of personal development. In practice it is quite impossible to do so, so inextricably linked are these three factors.

Two people are primarily concerned in the counselling process, the counsellor and the counsellee. It is the interaction between them that constitutes counselling. The quality of counselling depends essentially on the quality of the relationship established between them. In this sense the 'skills' of counselling are secondary. As Rogers (1951a) has said,

> In our experience, the counsellor who tries to use a 'method' is doomed to be unsuccessful unless this method is genuinely in line with his own attitudes.

This is an important point for any would-be counsellor to remember. Counselling is not a complex body of skills that takes precedence over the more ethereal interactions that take place between people. Technique, in other words, is subservient to the people involved.

In 'behaviourist' approaches there is quite a different set of priorities. The behaviour rather than the person is the central point of concern. Change through a process of conditioning, rather than growth through a process of self-understanding, is the objective. A body of scientifically established responses is applied to observed behaviour which seek to reinforce the required behaviour. The 'human' factor, unquantifiable and therefore 'unscientific', is removed as far as possible.

Counselling is a perceptual 'art' rather than a scientific technique. It relies heavily upon the unquantifiable impact of human relationships, first to determine the problems which trouble the counsellee, then to develop self-awareness of these problems, and finally to enable the counsellee to determine and carry through their favoured response. But to successfully facilitate this process of personal growth requires certain vital attitudes and approaches by the counsellor.

The work of Carl Rogers has been particularly important in developing an understanding of counselling relationships, and will be central to the general approach to counselling adopted throughout the book. The approach to relationships has a number of important facets, particularly for the professional person involved in working with elderly clients. These, and their inter-relationships, are represented in the diagram below.

Client-centred counselling

The counsellee is always centrally important within the counselling relationship. Counselling is a 'client-centred' approach within which should exist a concern and interest in the well-being of the counsellee. If this concern is genuine, there should be no problems. Difficulties will arise when the counsellor finds the counsellee to be particularly awkward, or their behaviour particularly hard to accept. Ageing people like anyone else, can be difficult to relate to; not all old people are lovable, contrary to certain public perceptions. Many can be positively cantankerous, others seemingly 'content' with their depression, others quite rigid in their thinking and their life-style. The counsellor may feel that it is difficult in such circumstances to develop the warmth that allows them to relate closely with the counsellee.

A non-directive approach		Non-judgemental attitudes
Genuineness	THE COUNSELLEE	Trust and confidentiality
Unconditional positive regard		Emphathetic understanding

A non-directive approach

Counsellors cannot enter into a relationship with the sole intention of directing counsellees to alter their attitudes, to change their behaviour, or to take control of their emotions. It may be that we believe that this would be in their best interests, but it is often like telling a drowning man to swim when he does not know how. It is likely that all counsellors will have their own agendas – certain objectives to fulfil, perhaps based on their view of the best outcome for the individual concerned, or professional tasks to achieve – but where these can be harnessed and made secondary to the needs of the individual, the counselling process is undoubtedly enhanced. The reasons can perhaps be best understood by stating the case negatively.

A directive relationship has many implicit assumptions. One is that the director knows best. The other is that the directed are not capable of coming to their own solutions for their own problems. Such relationships are unequal, comprising a dominant and a submissive party. They work only if the submissive party can do what they are told, wants to do what they are told, and if there are no internal or external restraints preventing them consistently carrying through what they are told. They work only if the submissive party remains submissive; when directives are ignored or refused the basis of the relationship crumbles. Besides, if the solution to a personal problem depends upon submissiveness this does not augur well for its continued effectiveness when the director is no longer around.

Non-directiveness and respect for the worth of other people are closely linked. Directiveness suggests that we know what is in the best interests of other people, and this demeans the individuality and dignity of those people. We remove personal responsibility from them because we believe that they are incapable of taking responsibility for themselves. We assume that their lives will be best guided by ourselves, thereby assuming a wisdom and importance which is justified only in the most extreme circumstances. We deny the individuals their right to self-determination, their ability to make sound decisions for themselves. We deny their potential for personal development and growth. We fail to treat them as people of worth, and by our own behaviour, we subtly devalue them.

Non-judgemental attitudes

Another problem arises when the counsellor is faced with individuals whose behaviour is, or has been, personally or morally unacceptable to the counsellor. Perhaps an elderly lady has been caught shoplifting, or an elderly man found to be interfering with little girls. Perhaps an elderly person has taken to regular masturbation, often in the presence of other people. Perhaps it is merely that they are rude, or offensive in the way they treat other people, including the counsellor. There are any number of reasons why counsellors of older people should find themselves in difficulty in this respect.

Whilst it may appear to be an idealistic position, the counsellor has to try to be 'morally neutral' about what the counsellee has either done, or is currently doing. The objective of the counsellor is to understand the feelings and attitudes which underlie behaviour. In doing this, any hint of disapproval or condemnation on the part of the counsellor can result in the erection of barriers which entirely prevent the formation of an adequate counselling relationship. Counselling is practised in order to discover the causes of difficult or unacceptable behaviour, bitterness, bad temper, frustration, sorrow or grief, not to make personal judgements about these things.

Clearly there are limits to anyone's 'moral neutrality' but it is important that the elderly counsellee is accepted as they are, rather than as we might want them to be. Where a counsellor's limits are reached considerable care has to be exercised. The troubled counsellee, particularly if their attitudes and behaviour have caused problems and difficulties to others in the past, will be used to disapproval. The additional disapproval of the counsellor is likely to be equally ineffective in obtaining change, confirming only that we are no different from anyone else who has tried to help in the past. Unfortunately, this does not deal with the feelings of the counsellor. Many techniques exist to overcome this. Our feelings can be presented as the view of society generally. Or we can express concern about the effect such attitudes and behaviour can have on other people and how they, in turn, will respond to them. Or we can present our views within the counselling relationship simply as our feelings and opinions, which should have no particular significance within the relationship apart from the need to be frank and honest with each other. To counsel is not to dismiss all personal views and values, but it does involve the need to express them in a way which is not going to alienate the counsellee.

Unconditional positive regard

If the work of counsellors is to be helpful to the individual, they must seek to look positively at the counsellee. Rogers (1951b) talks of the need for 'unconditional positive regard'.

> When the therapist is experiencing a positive, accepting attitude toward whatever the client is at that moment, therapeutic movement or change is more likely to occur. The therapist is willing for the client to be whatever immediate feeling is going on – confusions, resentment, fear, anger, courage, love or pride . . . The therapist prizes the client in a total rather than a conditional way.

Counsellors should not look upon elderly counsellees as inferior or abnormal in any way, despite all the difficulties their emotional condition or their social behaviour might present. Rather, counsellees have to be seen as individuals in difficulty who have the capability, through their own inner resources, of overcoming their own problems and redirecting their own lives through their own efforts.

What does this mean for counsellors? They have to believe that ageing individuals have a worth and dignity of their own. They have to respect their right to self-determination. They have to rely upon the counsellees' inherent capacity to choose their own values and attitudes, and that they are capable of doing this in their own self-interest. Moreover, counsellees have to do this even if they select ways which counsellors feel are wrong or inappropriate.

Empathetic understanding

The counsellor should try to view the world as the counsellee sees it. This involves trying to place ourselves in the mind, and the situation of the counsellee.

> . . . to assume, in so far as he is able, the internal frame of reference of the client, to perceive the world as the client sees it, to perceive the client himself as he is seen by himself, to lay aside all perceptions from the external frame of reference while doing so, and to communicate something of this empathetic understanding to the client. (Rogers, 1951a)

In this way it becomes more likely that we will be able to understand some of the apparently illogical or self-damaging aspects of the social performance of the counsellee. It is vital that the counsellor avoids denying the problems of the counsellee, as perceived by the counsellee. Nothing is usefully served by denying the problems and difficulties others feel. It is sufficient that they feel them for us to take them seriously. To deny them is to fail to respond, and leads to the belief that we do not really care how they feel. Our own feelings and interpretations about how another person feels are of little value in this respect. Therefore the ability of the counsellor to enter into the mind of the counsellee does not just involve 'having sympathy' with them. Sympathy is often patronizing, and is by its nature unhelpful. The counselling relationship also requires empathy.

> This means that the therapist senses accurately the feelings and personal meanings that the client is experiencing and communicates this understanding to the client. When functioning best, the therapist is so much inside the private world of the other that he or she can clarify not only the meanings of which the client is aware but even those just below the level of awareness. (Rogers, 1951b)

Empathy enables the counsellor to form some tentative explanation or interpretation of what is happening to counsellees; what they are thinking, why, and linking this with their social performance. This is clearly an essential stage in the process of counselling. The counsellor will have some idea of the problems the counsellee faces, but until some ideas are formed about why such problems have arisen it is difficult to focus on the direction that counselling should take.

Yet there are also obvious dangers in the concept of empathy. It is never really possible to be certain that we know what is going on in the mind of another person, particularly if they are facing difficulties or problems that we have not experienced. Nor can the counsellor assume that any particular insight holds good for any length of time. Consequently, there is a continual need to test and retest the assumptions that we make, checking that what we believe to be the attitudes and feelings of another person are, in fact, accurate. Therefore the counsellor can never be dogmatic. Certainty in counselling relationships is a dangerous illusion, doubt a spur to the further clarification and updating of our understanding which is so necessary to the counselling process.

Genuineness

Counselling should be a two-way process. This means that the counsellor should be able to relate honestly to the counsellee, being capable where necessary of revealing the counsellor's own feelings.

> The more the therapist is himself or herself in the relationship, putting up no professional front or personal facade, the greater is the likelihood that the client will change and grow in a constructive manner. (Rogers, 1951b)

Counsellors often have to share parts of themselves too. This means that we have to be prepared to talk about ourselves openly and honestly, sharing with the counsellee the feelings and experiences we have in common. We should not believe that counselling relationships with older people can be a one-way process, and that they can be expected to tell us about their most guarded thoughts and feelings if we are not prepared to talk about our own. People are more likely to share with others who are prepared to admit to their own feelings and weaknesses.

There is no room for false professional fronts, for the maintenance of social distance, for assumptions of superiority, and similar considerations often associated with 'professional' relationships with clients. It is important that counsellors present themselves as people rather than as 'a doctor', or 'a social worker' or 'a priest'. The counsellor should not assume a special status or authority within the counselling process, or within the life of the counsellee. The counsellor has to be prepared both to talk and be talked to honestly and critically. For people in difficulty or under stress, there is no more depressing person than the paragon, the person with no personal difficulties, the person with all the answers. Such people highlight assumed inadequacies rather than ameliorate troubled emotions. The counsellor has to be a 'real' person to be helpful.

Trust and confidentiality

In any relationship requiring openness and honesty, particularly when dealing with issues surrounding personal emotions, trust is essential. No-one openly reveals their feelings to people they do not trust. If we believe that someone is likely to be unsympathetic, or use information in ways we would not want, we remain cautious and guarded about what we reveal. So the counsellor has to have, or has to develop, a sense of trust through every action and comment made. The counsellee has to be able to have firm grounds for believing that the people who offer help are trustworthy.

Confidentiality is an essential basis for a trusting relationship. The sharing of intimate details of their lives, details which if generally known might lead to either embarrassment, guilt or anxiety, is not likely to be risked if counsellees have any suspicion that they might be passed on to others, or even that they might be used to determine plans for their future which might run counter to their wishes. In general, information obtained by the counsellor is strictly confidential, and whilst the transmission of information to others can take place, this should be done only with the expressed permission of the counsellee.

The counselling relationship described is obviously an ideal towards which to strive rather than an attainable reality, but it is no less important for that. It is likely that the closer we come to attaining the ideal relationship, the more effective we will become as counsellors. The further we are from it the more aware we should be of our limitations as counsellors.

No-one can be entirely non-directive, or non-judgemental. But within the counselling relationship it is important that we try to recognize the existence of our own agendas, be open about them, and attempt to ensure that the focus of our concern remains the expressed needs of the counsellee. So we should ask ourselves about our agendas. Are we looking for change? Do we have a time limit? What do we expect for ourselves from our efforts? What is important is that our agendas do not over-ride the concern we have for the counsellee, and lead to feelings which will prevent the counsellee's problems being central. 'Why can't they be more reasonable? Why do they go on making these demands on me? Why can't they just conform to my wishes? Do they not realize that they are making my life difficult? And especially when I am being so reasonable and nice to them – it is so ungrateful!' If these are our over-riding concerns, the seeds of counselling failure are present.

Personal and professional agendas are nearly always unhelpful, particularly when there is a juxtaposition of control issues with counselling. For example, it has been known for the responsibility for educational counselling in a school to be linked with responsibilities for discipline. Police officers have also been given the task of counselling young offenders. This places people in an impossible position. Less extreme examples of the same situation would be the doctor with a busy waiting room, the social worker under pressure to place (or not to place) ageing people in care, and residential care staff whose work is so much easier with quiet, uncomplaining and compliant residents. In these situations, the need to clear the waiting room, the constraints of departmental policy, and not upsetting compliance, can all become more important than the needs of the individual.

What should be clear is that the relationship discussed here is one which is not achieved by authority or status. It is not achieved on the psychiatrist's couch, or over the doctor's consulting desk, or by fleeting visits by a social worker. It is achieved only by those who are prepared to give their time to a troubled individual. It is achieved by those who are genuinely concerned, and who recognize the essential integrity and dignity of personality of individuals in difficulty.

This is particularly important when working with older people. Perhaps more than any other generation, our elders do not respond well to being manipulated or compelled into situations which are not of their choosing, no matter how well-intentioned such actions might have been on our part. Yet when ageing people become frail or incapacitated it is too easy for those who care for them to assume rights and responsibilities in their lives which are unjustified, and often deeply resented. This is particularly true of physical frailty. The declining ability to look after themselves is often mistaken for an inability to think and make decisions for themselves. We might have to feed them, to dress and undress them, to toilet them, yet if we as carers ignore their dignity and feelings we are in danger of making our caring an imposition, much resented by the individual concerned.

This presents many problems for the professional worker. Not least of these is the power that many have in providing or withholding services, or their ability to assess the needs of counsellees in ways which can have a major impact on their life. Equally, the power of doctors, or even the young relative upon whom the ageing person feels dependent, is equally significant. All such power tends to 'skew' the relationship away from the genuineness Rogers describes. Counsellors of older people, more than most, have to develop the ability to present themselves as safe, non-threatening people, who, whilst they might possess certain powers, are not likely to use them except with their willing and informed consent. The requirement of honesty within the relationship should ensure that there is no denial about the power the counsellor possesses. Such a denial would be neither genuine nor honest.

Professional carers have to be aware of their power, and not use it knowingly or unwittingly within the relationship. This is easily done. We can gain compliance with an explicit or implicit threat to remove our caring. Even the possibility that we might do this, even if we have no intention of doing so, can be a threat to elderly individuals. They are careful not to say or do anything that might upset us, or which is contrary to what they believe we want them to say or do. Ageing people, as we have seen, will speak frankly and honestly about their innermost thoughts only if the relationship is one of mutual trust and confidence, and the one-sidedness of many professional–client relationships has therefore to be seriously addressed.

The task of forming mutual relationships with ageing people is also affected by certain dominant attitudes towards old age. Our society does not expect elderly people to make demands – it is increasingly they rather than children who are expected to be 'seen but not heard'. Even those who do make demands are not necessarily heard, or they do not have their demands met. Most older people have internalized a more deferential attitude to professional carers than exists with younger people. This has arisen from two separate social phenomena. The first is generational. Older people were brought up during a period when, generally speaking, there was more deference expected by, and shown to, professional people. The second relates to class. A high proportion of 'dependent' elderly people have their origins in working background where, again speaking generally, more deference was shown to their 'betters' than is the case today. What results from this social background is a tendency amongst many older people to hide their feelings simply because they are used to accepting their lives without complaint, and being grateful for even the smallest act of kindness or care. To complain, for many elderly people, is to appear ungrateful. Moreover, as pain, grief and unhappiness are increasingly accepted by dominant social attitudes as normal concomitants of old age, ageing people feel that there is no point or purpose in complaining.

All such attitudes can prevent genuineness within counselling relationships. Indeed, they are features of counselling older people which perhaps distinguish it from the counselling of other groups. It is too easy to accept the non-complaining, fatalistic facade of older people, easier to walk away believing that there is no emotional turmoil, no upset, no pain, than it is to search further to discover their real feelings.

The problems of the carer–counsellor, the 'informal carer', the close friend or relative who is caring for an ageing individual, have also to be considered. Whilst having the benefit of knowing the ageing person more intimately than the professional carer, problems can arise from being too intimately involved. Our own emotions, our own feelings are then involved and this can mean that we are not sufficiently dispassionate to interpret all the factors which are contributing to the problems. It may also be that we are ourselves part of the problem, but are unable to see it, or our elder is unable to admit it to us.

This does not make the task of carer–counsellor impossible, as many would suggest. It just makes it more difficult. It is important that carer–counsellors are aware of the problems, that they challenge and re-investigate long-held assumptions, that they carefully analyse their feelings and are open about them. If this is done then the carer–counsellor is potentially the most important counsellor of all.

Sometimes it becomes obvious that certain people are unable to counsel a particular individual, for reasons that are not immediately apparent. Some will prefer a counsellor of the same sex, others of the opposite sex. Some will trust younger rather than older people, and vice versa. Some will confide more readily in people of high status, others the reverse. Sometimes a past incident might adversely colour an elderly person's judgement of a prospective counsellor, and this might be quite unknown to those concerned.

However, such prejudices and preferences are not common. What is more important is that potential counsellors' present themselves as warm, caring and understanding people with a genuine concern and interest in the counsellees as individuals. Indeed, elderly people who experience warmth and positive regard can seem to benefit even if they are, for some reason, unable to participate in communication. This is seen in people recovering from illness, or just in becoming more happy and contented in their lives. Such benefits leave little doubt that these factors are an essential pre-requisite to successful counselling.

Yet the counselling relationship is not on its own sufficient. Certain skills need to be developed and understood to obtain the full benefit of counselling for the ageing person. It is to these skills that we must now turn our attention.

CHAPTER 7

The skills of counselling

Counselling is the art of communication, but a very special kind of communication. We have seen that it is communication with another person who is experiencing some kind of emotional trouble, or acting under stress in some way. It seeks to allow individuals the freedom to explore, express and to 'feel' their feelings in safety. It seeks to assist individuals in the process of defining their own problems and difficulties, in increasing their personal knowledge of self. It seeks to help individuals to measure their problems against the social realities, and to find their own resolution to their particular dilemmas. The skills of counselling are concerned with enabling this communication process, whilst at the same time dealing perceptively with the problems that the counsellee faces.

The counselling relationship, non-threatening, non-disapproving, empathetic, genuine.

Listening, and establishing a relaxed, non-threatening atmosphere.

Assisting *self-expression*.

Interpreting what we hear.

Building a *working hypothesis*.

Focusing on difficult areas. *Challenging*.

Facilitating *decision-making*.

Avoiding *giving advice*.

Establishing a relaxed and non-threatening atmosphere

The first meeting with a counsellee should be as relaxed as possible. The counsellor should seek to be as warm, supportive and caring as possible. The early conversation should be light and inconsequential. A cup of tea, or similar, is always a good relaxing agent, always to be offered or accepted depending on the venue. Sitting comfortably is also important, and preferably as close as possible, facing each other.

The counsellor should be as relaxed as possible. Signs of tension are easily transmitted and can quickly put the counsellee on edge, wondering what is to come. This is particularly important when the counsellor is known to have authority and power to make important decisions affecting the life of the counsellee, or even where the counsellee is reliant upon the support or care provided by the counsellor.

It is always wise for the counsellor to be aware of any possible worries that the counsellee might have about the meeting, and have ready some words of reassurance about the purpose of their meeting. Where such worries exist the inconsequential chatter must not be allowed to continue too long. It becomes important for the counsellor to move on to the main reasons for the meeting, and to begin the process as openly and honestly as possible. This is where the counsellor can briefly outline the agendas, leaving the counsellee in little doubt as to his or her intentions.

It is the responsibility of the counsellor to move into the difficult area of feelings, and to do so as gently as possible. Again, the counsellor should have prepared the ground thoroughly before the meeting starts, outlining the main areas of concern, and how they are to be introduced. Moving carefully into the main reason for the meeting is a crucial skill. It is important that the counsellor is able quickly to focus the meeting upon the concerns, interests and feelings of the counsellee. Assurance that you are primarily interested in how they feel, what they want, and what they want to do is important in this respect. This is an invaluable early strategy for outlining the purpose of the meeting, and perhaps the possibility of a series of meetings.

Listening

Perhaps the most fundamental skill which helps counselling to transcend other forms of communication is listening. Unfortunately, the ability to listen to the problems of another person is not a universal human trait. Most of us have tendencies to pass information outwards rather than to allow it inwards. Politicians manipulate, entrepreneurs exploit, teachers disseminate information, priests sermonize, bosses of all kinds give orders, even friends give advice. It is perhaps strange that, whilst we pride ourselves on our commitment to individual freedom and self-expression, listening to the problems of other people, and responding appropriately to their needs as expressed, is less common. All of us, to some degree and in our own way, are ready to lecture and opinionize, but too few to listen.

Sad to say, professional groups are little better, and possibly slightly worse, than average. Mayer and Timms (1970), in a noteworthy social work text, found that there existed a massive level of misunderstanding between client and social worker concerning individual need. Clients would arrive with specific problems, often of a financial nature, but what they received was questioning directed at matters that seemed entirely irrelevant to the needs they were presenting. Clients who needed money would become upset at what they considered inappropriate questioning, but this would suggest to the workers that they had touched a sensitive point, confirming some personal theory that it was not really money that the clients required. My more recent experience would suggest that matters have not improved significantly from this early social work text, especially concerning social work with elderly people.

Listening is the real starting point of the counselling process. To arrive there the counsellor has to stop talking, and in order to stop talking, answerable and leading questions are required.

Assisting the listening process

To listen without saying anything does not encourage anyone to talk, or to continue talking. The counsellor needs to give continual reassurance of interest and concern. This can be achieved in a variety of ways – non-verbal communications such as gestures of understanding and approval or facial expressions which mirror the expressed emotions of the counsellee, and reassuring touches of support and encouragement. To this can be added simple verbal interjections such as, 'Yes, I see', 'I understand'. 'That must have been awful'.

Reflecting back is also a useful technique. Instead of asking a question, the counsellor picks on a sentence or phrase used by the counsellee with the purpose of bringing further responses or clarification. There are also times when we need to ensure that we understand what is being said, and this can be done by asking simple questions or making comments which help elucidate or develop what the counsellee is saying, such as, 'So you think that . . .', or 'You mean that . . .', or even 'I'm not sure that I follow what you mean . . .'. At the same time, this confirms to the counsellees that you are interested in the way they are thinking and feeling, and that you are making every effort to see their point of view.

Certain questions can also help counsellees to describe their feelings in more depth. 'Tell me more about how this made you feel', and 'What did you do when you felt like that', give counsellees permission, and perhaps a feeling of safety, to talk further about themselves. This kind of encouragement becomes increasingly necessary as more difficult 'problem' areas are discussed. It gives counsellees 'permission' to talk about difficult areas, and indicates that we are willing to listen to all the emotion that they may harbour, but which they felt no-one else wished to know about.

The choice of words

The counsellor must also be aware of the words that are being used, and the possible impact that they may have, or the possibility for misunderstanding that may arise from them. Tyler (1969) outlines some of the problems.

'Still another difficulty has to do with the specific words the counsellor uses. The one thing he wishes not to do is to arouse defensive attitudes. Certain ways of putting things are more likely than others to affect people adversely. Words like coward, stupid or effeminate should probably never be used unless the client has used that very word himself. It is as feasible to say, 'You can't bring yourself to attempt it' as 'You haven't the courage to try'. Either is an expression of a painful emotional attitude, but the second is much more likely than the first to arouse defensiveness. Much the same rules apply here as in ordinary tactful conversation. This does not mean that reality should be watered down or glossed over. Counselling differs from most conversation in that problem areas and unpleasant facts are faced, not ignored or side-tracked. They need not, however, be presented brutally.'

Yet on the other hand, for the counsellor to be too conscious of saying the right thing at the right time in every situation represents a state of mind that can only hamper the counselling process. It can end in silence, this being considered preferable to choosing an incorrect word or phrase, and this is clearly nonsense. What needs to be remembered is that even when the 'wrong' word or phrase is used, in error, it can be rectified. 'Why have you reacted so strongly to a word which I intended so innocently?' 'Who has said this, or called you this before?' The existence of a good counselling relationship will overcome such mishaps, as long as they are not too frequent or too insensitive.

Interpreting what we hear

The ability to listen whilst another person talks does not merely entail being aware of the words spoken to us. The counsellor has to be able to extract from the words being used the feelings and meanings which often lie just beneath the surface. The words people use are too often interpreted literally to signify little more than their immediate and most rational translation. Thus, when we are told that everything is 'OK' we prefer to believe that this is so, although what people say can often contain far deeper and more subtle feelings and personal emotions.

Older people, perhaps more than most others, will often express certain feelings, such as contentment or resignation, when they do not represent their real emotions. Indeed, words can be used which will often hide the very feelings which are at the root of the individual's problems, and which represent the reality of their emotional lives.

Such human behaviour may be confusing, and it would be easier if people would say what they meant. The fact is, however, that we do not always do so. Even the rules of social politeness, which suggest that we should not burden others with our problems, will lead us all to respond to enquiries after our health with an automatic 'Very well, thank you' when often we may be feeling poorly or even downright miserable. These daily lies of politeness are compounded when we face major difficulties and problems. Our disingenuous responses have many functions. In part they avoid the need to talk of difficult subjects. They say to others what we believe they want to hear, or refrain from saying what we believe they do not want to hear. They hide from others the pain we are feeling.

It is these functions that the counsellor has to overcome. We have to encourage counsellees that talking about the issues which worry them might be helpful. We have to assure counsellees that we are prepared to listen to their difficulties. We have to demonstrate that we are aware of their feeling of pain, and that we are interested in talking to them about it. In this sense, the counsellor has to be a mind-reader, but the problem of 'reading' the true feelings of the individual can be made easier by two factors. The first is the relationship; as we have seen, people are only prepared to talk openly to those who they feel are genuinely concerned, and who have both the time and the interest to understand.

This can be augmented through the skill of matching what is being said to the known personal circumstances of the counsellee. In other words, the counsellor must seek the real feelings of the counsellee through careful listening to what is being said, how it is being said, and how this appears to relate to the real situation. Therefore, the art of good listening is perceptive, involving a degree of interpretation of what is being said, the reasons it is being said, and how what is being said relates to the realities of the situation.

Building a hypothesis

Counsellors will by this stage start to form their own views about what they are hearing. Indeed, the beginning of the counselling task is the process of gaining understanding and insight into the life situation of the counsellees. This should take into account a wide variety of factors, their interests and aptitudes, their feelings, their relationships with others, their strengths and weaknesses, their medical condition, their past life, the effect of significant life events, and the way they view their future prospects. Links and connections will begin to be made between the way counsellees think or feel and the way they behave. Patterns of behaviour will emerge which will indicate that the individual reacts to similar situations in similar ways. Soon, a comprehensive and coherent picture of the counsellee will start to build up.

Such a hypothesis attempts to describe a whole person, and not to separate certain aspects of an individual's life for special attention. It should recognize, and try to make sense of, the inter-connectedness of our lives. Yet, having done this, it should pay particular attention to the emotions rather than to the 'facts', or the rationalizations and justifications we all tend to use in order to shroud our feelings, especially in times of stress.

> 'What the counsellor does is to concentrate on how the client feels about the incidents or facts he is reporting rather than on the facts themselves, and then to respond to what appears to be the most significant part of each complex sequence . . . Counselling is concerned with strain rather than with the facts. (Tyler, 1969)

This means that the 'fact' that an individual has become an 'old person', or suffers from regular illness or pain, or has become dependent upon others, whilst an important part of our understanding, is less important than how these facts make the individual feel. It is largely how an individual 'feels', their self-image, which determines the quality and nature of their social performance.

Recognizing the internalized self-image of the counsellee is an important perceptual skill in arriving at a working hypothesis. Self-image, its origins, its present restrictive function and its future debilitative consequences are important elements in an individual's life, and gaining an understanding of them is vital. If counsellees are able to reach a better understanding of their own self-image, they can often overcome the social role into which they have been fixed, and develop newer, healthier ones.

In building a hypothesis, the counsellor may be assisted by the 'personal construct' theory of Kelly (1955). It is not possible here to go into great detail about this complex theory. But in short, Kelly suggests that an individual's social performance is determined not so much by external events, but by self-erected mental structures through which the individual sees life, interprets it, and decides how to respond. According to their particular view of life, individuals always act in an orderly and predictable way. Understanding an individual's particular viewpoint is therefore vital, and explains why the early stages of counselling are concerned primarily with listening. It is clearly important that we understand the basic outlook of an individual, not because it is necessarily right, but because it determines the way that individual behaves. We have, therefore, to understand the world as seen by the individual, shaped by a complex system of expectations which have been developed throughout a lifetime.

The individual's 'personal construct' ensures that reactions to particular situations occur in predictable patterns. If we are to understand why older people do not respond to situations in more logical, less self-damaging ways, we must try to understand the system of prediction which the individual is using. If elderly individuals see life through helpless, defeated eyes, where they become resigned to pain and disappointment, loneliness and despair, their reaction to new situations will not be positive. Negative outcomes will in turn serve to confirm the correctness of the 'negative' view of life. The counsellor must not only understand that this is the way the counsellee's life is predicted and determined, but has eventually to help the individual develop a more positive set of expectations. These will, in turn, allow individuals to respond more positively to the problems they face.

Confirmation and clarification

Counselling requires a continuous process of confirmation, clarification and re-clarification to ensure that our hypothesis is a reasonable one. Counselling empathy requires constant testing because we can never be certain that what we believe to be the feelings and attitudes of the counsellees are accurate. Only the counsellees can be certain of this, and unfortunately they may often be quite unaware. The difficulty that arises from this concerns the attempt to confirm and clarify a hypothesis about which the counsellee has little or no conscious knowledge.

The process of confirmation and clarification attempts to solve both problems. By asking certain questions, the counsellor can ask the counsellee to consider certain propositions, and then together they can examine their validity. Such questions might be, 'Does the fact that you feel this way make you respond like this?', 'Can you see the similarity between the way you reacted to this situation, and the way you reacted to that?', 'Does the way you respond help the situation, or make it worse?', 'Can you think of another time when you have done this, or felt like this?' In this way, both counsellor and counsellee can clarify, test out and refine the hypothesis, so that it more accurately reflects the actual feelings, situation, and state of mind of the counsellee.

Focusing on difficult areas

It is now clear that the counsellor is doing more than listening. New concepts, new ideas, new connections are being introduced into the discussion which are presenting the counsellee with alternative pictures of reality. Many of these are challenging and difficult for the counsellee to accept.

The counsellor is also to some extent directing the course of the discussions when making a selection from the many possible areas of interest. This choice becomes progressively more difficult when the counsellor feels that 'problem' areas need to be opened up. This is a difficult skill to develop, as evidenced by the rules of 'social politeness' which often run counter to what the counsellor wants to do. We are taught not to focus on the more difficult aspects of what we know about other people. To dwell upon the problem emotions of others is frowned upon as 'morbid curiosity', likely to lead only to highlighting and prolonging them, thereby causing unnecessary pain. Yet often the only pain which is saved by social politeness is our own. It is difficult to understand how personal problems can be resolved by refusing to talk about them. Problems 'forgotten' are rarely actually put out of mind. And strategies designed to bring out these problems do not cause distress themselves but merely bring out distress which is already present within the individual.

Focusing upon problem emotions means that the counsellor has to be able to pass back information to the counsellee. Hopefully by this stage the counsellee will be sure of the counsellor's genuineness. Yet the counsellor has to have the ability to focus on difficult and distressing areas in a way which is not threatening to the counsellee. It should arise from concern and interest in the counsellee, not from a prurient self-interest or inquisitiveness on the part of the counsellor. This can be achieved by regularly outlining why we feel that it is an important area to discuss.

To whatever extent counsellors choose the focus of the discussion, they should continue to see their task as one aimed at helping counsellees develop their own exposition of their situation, and their feelings about it. All the skills of presenting as a 'non-threatening' person, and the techniques of assisting counsellees to talk are necessary here. They can be essential if counsellees are to be encouraged to continue talking about the painful feelings they have about themselves and their lives, happy that they are being treated with dignity and respect.

Challenging

As counselling proceeds it does not always continue to be the sympathetic process of listening, support and approval. Whilst the process of talking about feelings will often by itself lead counsellees to new insights into their own lives, at other times this will not happen. When such a situation arises, the counsellor may need to challenge the counsellee if any further progress is to be made. Often, counsellees can use the counselling process as a social prop, and not one which leads to re-examination, change and growth. This can be particularly true with ageing counsellees, who enjoy the company offered to them through counselling,and who perhaps are not committed to the idea of change 'at their age'.

Challenging also refers to the need that sometimes arises to confront the counsellees with alternative understandings of the problems they face. This will often happen when counsellees have placed blame on other people and not looked at their own contribution to their problems. It may have become apparent to the counsellor that counsellees are 'locked' into feelings which are affecting the way they are leading their lives, but are apparently more content to hold on to the feelings than to resolve the difficulties which arise from them. Many people, including elderly people, are quite content with their apparent misery.

The counsellor might be convinced of the existence of certain repeating cycles within the current relationships of the counsellee, which the counsellee appears either unwilling or unable to break. Where it is necessary, and when it is appropriate, the counsellor sometimes has to embark upon a measured 'confrontation' with the counsellee over such matters.

> Without this, it can be all too easy for the client to gain comfort and reassurance from a warm, accepting counsellor without making any progress in resolving his difficulties. The client may recognize and identify his problems but come no nearer to finding solutions or resolution.
> The counsellor who is in touch with her own feelings will soon become aware of the client who is 'stuck'. The counsellor may feel bored or irritated. She will recognize that the client is repeating himself or demanding a particular reaction from her. (Brearley and Birchley, 1986)

Confrontation with this sort of information is often an essential and necessary step in the counselling process. People will often play games with their emotions, perhaps in the hope of gaining sympathy, or confirming their particular view of other people or of life generally. The variety and extent of 'the games people play' with their emotional lives have been outlined by Berne (1968). Such games can be played with the actor entirely unaware that they are doing so.

The way confrontation is handled should not be destructive to the counsellee. Repetition of the same or similar ground can be stopped by a gentle reminder, followed by asking why it is that a particular story or incident is so important. This itself helps to focus counselling upon potentially useful areas, whilst at the same time asking the counsellees to examine the particular 'game' they are playing. Questions such as, 'Do you feel that you might be doing this in order to produce this kind of feeling or situation?', can lead counsellees to a re-examination of their motives.

The roles attributed to, and accepted by, the counsellee also have to be challenged. Those who have accepted ideas about their worthlessness, their impotence or their badness will not usually be able to help themselves unless and until they are able to modify their self-image.

When a major confrontation is anticipated, counsellors should ensure that they have sufficient time available to pursue the matter fully, and at the end r :urn to some reasonable level of mutual understanding.

Making decisions

Helping the counsellee to make decisions is the ultimate goal of the counselling process. The skills of facilitating decision-making are discussed by Tyler (1969).

> There are times when in order to proceed with his life, a person must make a decision. It may be one that is large and far-reaching or it may appear relatively small and trivial but . . . (of) special significance for the person who makes it is that his choice will help to determine the pattern of his unique development over time. Each life decision is to some extent irrevocable, since even if one goes back to the fork in the road and takes the other turning, he cannot eradicate the effects of the experience the first choice has brought him.

The ability of older people to develop and grow through making decisions is restricted by many of the attitudes of our ageist society. In order to make decisions ageing people have to view the future in a way which allows them an active and influential part in their own lives. There must exist the idea that new attitudes, new determinations, new approaches, new behaviours, fresh outlooks and new challenges are quite possible even in old age.

The counsellor has many problems to deal with in this respect. Have elderly people any right to choose? What influence can they expect to have over their own lives? What value are they to anyone? These and other questions have to be treated sensitively and honestly. The skills of counsellors are ultimately judged by the extent to which they are successful in facilitating personal action by the counsellees in dealing with life problems. The particular problem with many ageing people is that they do not recognize that they are capable, and have the energy to deal with their own problems and feelings. They feel lacking in worth and value. They feel that they have no future towards which to strive. They feel unwanted. All this leads to less activity rather than more, and the counsellor has to try to convince older people of the need for self-action.

The dangers of advice

The counsellor should never resort to the giving of advice. It is often tempting to do so, especially when problem attitudes and behaviour begin to frustrate our attempts to obtain mutually beneficial change. Counselling ends when advice is given. To advise is to give an opinion about what another person should do, and should be avoided.

The counsellor will sometimes discover that the counsellee has certain ideas about the nature of the counselling role, and the counselling process generally. This problem has to be addressed, especially when there is an assumption that our task is to solve the counsellee's problems. This clearly has to be remedied by repeated reminders that change can only be brought about by the counsellee's efforts and that consequently, the only part that the counsellor can play is to help decide what is to be done, how, and when. It is often in such situations, especially when the counselling relationship is good, that the counsellor's opinion is likely to be sought. 'What would you do if you were in my position?', 'Why don't you tell me what to do?', and similar questions, should always be passed back to the counsellee. 'I am not you, so it's best that you decide; but we could talk over the options you have.' Referring the problem back does not allow the counsellor to fall into a trap, for most people will normally do what they want to do, regardless of the best-intentioned advice. Often, troubled individuals will take action based, however loosely, upon your advice and return in triumph to tell you that it was completely unsuccessful. This is in turn used to confirm that their situation really is hopeless, and that even our support and help does not work. It proves to them that it is their *situation* which defeats them, not themselves, and there is nothing that anyone can do about it.

Advice can also stop a different kind of counsellee from telling us what he or she wants to do, because this might mean disagreeing with us. It can also lead to the efficacy of our advice becoming the burning issue of discussion. So an essential skill of counselling is to avoid completely the giving of advice, and to allow counsellees to take what eventually must be their responsibility to arrive at their own decision, in their own time and in their own way. Ultimately this also adds to the dignity and confidence of the counsellees, for when decisions are made and they work, individuals can themselves take the credit for their success rather than the counsellor.

CHAPTER 8

The process of counselling

Counselling, as we have seen, seeks to involve troubled individuals in an experience of transformation or healing. But how is such a process achieved? What is the nature of the journey through which the counsellee has to pass?

Social distress – a restricted, inadequate or disturbed individual whose *social performance* is in some way leading to personal difficulties.

Self-expression allows individuals to explain their attitudes, outlook and feelings about their total situation.

The counsellor constructs a *working hypothesis* which attempts to see meaning and connections in the counsellee's social performance.

The working hypothesis is *tested and refined* through the process of discussion and questioning.

The development of *self-awareness* in which the counsellor transfers to the counsellees the meanings and connections in their social performance.

Decision-making, by considering alternative responses to their social, distress, leading to new forms of social performance.

The emergence of individuals who are more aware of their situation, and the problems they face, but are able to cope with the pressures, strains and disappointments that life entails.

Social distress

The counselling process starts with the troubled emotional lives of individuals, whose feelings of worthlessness, inadequacy, fear or vulnerability have affected their lives in serious and possibly damaging ways, and whose relationships with other important people have become difficult, unbearable or have broken down. Their self-image, for a variety of reasons, will be extremely low. It is not that such people are necessarily 'inadequate', but that they feel themselves to be inadequate. These feelings are reinforced by dominant social ideas of individual pathology, that is, if something is going wrong in their lives it must be their own fault. This is because they are inadequate, corrupt or lazy. From such a viewpoint, everyone obtains from life what they work for, and in the end most people eventually obtain what they deserve.

This view of social distress has to be challenged, and a theory which emphasizes the social origins and nature of personal distress developed to replace it. Sherman (1981) has developed a useful alternative theory which he called the 'Social Breakdown Syndrome', which involves a more comprehensive explanation than those which focus entirely upon individual pathology. This has the advantage of combining many of the different factors that can interact to cause social and emotional demoralization in older people.

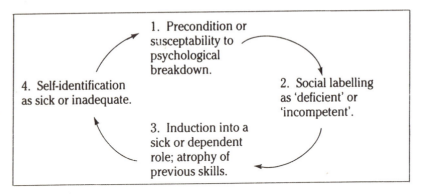

1. Precondition or susceptability to psychological breakdown.

2. Social labelling as 'deficient' or 'incompetent'.

3. Induction into a sick or dependent role; atrophy of previous skills.

4. Self-identification as sick or inadequate.

Sherman describes this as the 'vicious circle of increasing incompetence'. The circle demonstrates that it is a combination of many factors acting upon each other which contributes towards a troubled personality. What Sherman's circle perhaps does not emphasize sufficiently is the impact that dominant social ideology about the nature of old age has upon personal problems of older people at all levels of experience, emotional, social and financial. If society generally under-values old age, is it any wonder that old people do not experience a sense of personal worth? If society has no use for old people, is it any wonder that older people feel that their lives are without meaning? So to a considerable extent the individual, and the problems that ageing people experience generally, are structured by dominant social attitudes and values, and this element needs to be added to the circle.

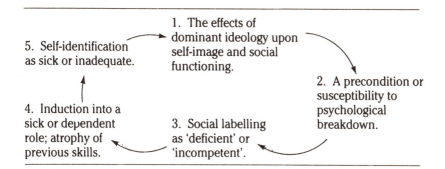

5. Self-identification as sick or inadequate.

1. The effects of dominant ideology upon self-image and social functioning.

2. A precondition or susceptibility to psychological breakdown.

4. Induction into a sick or dependent role; atrophy of previous skills.

3. Social labelling as 'deficient' or 'incompetent'.

It is into this cycle of social distress that the counselling process seeks to break. The causes of social distress are not uniform. Feelings and situations which some people cope with adequately can become quite unbearable for others. Social distress arises directly from self-image. Who do we believe ourselves to be? What is our role, our value, our usefulness? What is the meaning and purpose of our lives? These enormous questions beset us all at various stages of life, but as we have seen they can be particularly problematical for older people. The self-image of older people is closely linked with morale, which for many has sunk so low that they often do not wish to continue living. They have had to accept the loss of many of their former social roles, the loss of status, a declining ability to lead entirely independent lives. How is the individual to adjust? It is when morale is very low that we find it difficult to cope with the problems and difficulties of life, and when counselling can become vitally important.

The counselling process focuses upon self-image, and ultimately aims at modifying it in a constructive way. The task of the counsellor is to try to help ageing individuals modify their self-image so that it is more in line with reality. It is important to stress that our self-image has the power to determine our attitudes and social behaviour.

The actualizing or formative tendency

All behaviour, no matter how apparently irrational or senseless it may seem, is logical and purposeful according to some particular viewpoint. The counsellor may not be able to find the reason readily, or we may not like or agree with what we find, but nevertheless the reason will exist. The counsellor's task is to find these reasons within the emotional life of the individual.

From within these emotional origins, counselling maintains that all human behaviour is modifiable, and that this modification can come principally through an increased level of self-awareness. This confidence reflects the essentially optimistic nature of the counselling process, perhaps best expressed through Rogers' (1951b) concept of the 'actualizing' or 'formative' tendency, which he described as:

> an underlying flow of movement towards constructive fulfillment of its inherent possibility, which resides in every organism.

The actualizing tendency rejects the explanations of individual pathology, of inherent badness, laziness or inadequacy. In their place is the belief that human problems arise from the interaction of individual experience with unfavourable social and environmental conditions. The 'healthy' personality, towards which the counselling process is aimed, is one which is able to react appropriately and continuously to circumstances. It has to be able to cope with fluctuating events and changing personalities, and to do this involves a variety of social skills. When successful the individual is able to maintain an equilibrium. The failing individual is one who has become fixed, unable to react appropriately to the people and circumstances around him.

The actualizing tendency suggests that even these failing individuals are at all times capable of growth and development, so it is an essentially optimistic view of the human condition, and this is particularly important when working with older people. Rogers (1951b) himself reflected on his own advancing years and, applying the actualizing tendency to the problems of ageing in a chapter which asked the question 'Growing old: or older and growing?', he concluded that 'I sense myself as older and growing'.

Such optimism about the human condition is very different from the dominant social stereotype of old age. The most important element of this optimism is that the counselling approach implies that growth is a continuous process during which our potential capacities can be drawn upon and developed at any period of life, including old age. This view is necessary for two reasons. First, because the lives and experiences of many elderly people prove it is true; and second, because it would be important, even necessary, for the counsellor and the counsellee to believe it even if it were not true.

Self-expression

Counselling is often called a 'talking cure'. This is misleading because counselling is more than this, but it does provide one valuable element of the process. Many people will have experienced the relief of being able to talk to another person about their feelings and difficulties. It is at the heart of the old saying 'A trouble shared is a trouble halved'. Often the counsellor of ageing people will experience this when, after talking with them for a short period, many of the pressures and worries appear to be visibly lifted from their shoulders. They immediately brighten, become more animated and are often quite grateful that someone has taken the time to listen to them. Such gratitude underlines the importance of merely giving older people our time, and listening to them.

The emotional release that is offered by self-expression has to be enabled by the creation of the right atmosphere. We talk more openly and freely when we feel easy and relaxed. Older people will not discuss their feelings unless they feel safe in doing so. It is only the relationship that exists between the counsellee and the counsellor that will help in this respect. The fact that we are doctors, priests, social workers will not necessarily be of any advantage to us, nor does it give us any right to expect intimate revelations. Our status and position stand for nothing when compared with patience, tolerance and a willing ear. Giving our time and devoting our attention to what they say is therefore crucially important in the process of counselling.

Yet in another way, enabling self-expression is often relatively easy. Ageing people usually relish any opportunity they have to express their feelings. Many feel that they have so few opportunities to do so.

Listening and self-expression are closely linked. We should at this stage be as non-judgemental as possible about the things being expressed, however wrong, misguided or unjust they might appear to. We should restrict ourselves to trying to understand, and then try to help them expand and develop what they want to say. Wherever possible, the counsellor should try to elicit their feelings beyond the more superficial emotions of anger, hate and hostility to the deeper emotions which involve the sadnesses, disappointments, inadequacies and griefs they are experiencing. The 'superficial' emotions are those often presented initially. They can be real and strong, affecting the way we lead our lives. Yet normally, the 'angry' emotions have their origin in deeper and often more significant upsets and disappointments.

Blocks

The process of counselling is not always smooth or straightforward. We cannot assume, for example, that counsellees are going to be willing or able to immediately divulge the full nature of their feelings and difficulties. Time is required, often to summon the courage necessary to talk about their real problems and difficulties.

Even when people appear willing to talk to us about their difficulties, it is not always the real problems that they will initially present. The counsellor should not therefore take up the first issue raised by the counsellees which seems satisfactorily to explain their situation. To jump too quickly on the problems raised early in the counselling process may even prevent the real reasons coming to the surface. They must naturally be pursued, but always giving counsellees the opportunity to move on to other, more crucial issues. How quickly 'the' issues will be raised obviously depends on a number of factors – the difficulty of the issue, the ability of the counsellees to express their ideas, and the quality of the counselling relationship.

Other resistances or blocks to communication can be more than an initial reluctance to talk about the main issues. Individuals often utilize these deeper blocks, consciously or unconsciously, in order to hide the 'unpleasant' truth from other people, and perhaps from themselves too. Such blocks in older people might take the form of stubbornness, violence, confusion or depression. Many ageing people hide behind the facade of 'being all right', and this is often one which is most difficult for the counsellor to penetrate (Scrutton, 1986).

Essentially, all these blocks to communication and self-expression are to do with feelings of inadequacy, and poor self-image. It is important to understand the nature and origin of blocks and resistances. In the very earliest stages of life, individuals react quite spontaneously to the stimuli which confront them. Young babies have no knowledge of the social niceties which will thenceforward determine their social response. Thereafter, children will be taught by parents, relations, friends and teachers what is expected of them, and what is considered to be appropriate and inappropriate behaviour. Within this process of socialization, individuals will learn that some emotions and feelings are not acceptable; this may cover such areas as masturbation and sexual activity, crying (especially in boys), and the expression of the more 'difficult' emotions of anger and grief.

Often the result is that the child, and subsequently the adult, in order to avoid punishment, will suppress feelings which might in fact be quite normal and natural, and indeed necessary to the human condition. Where this is so, people feel unable to express their pain and grief, their anger or fear; they will learn to be ashamed of the various 'taboo' feelings they have. They have to be suppressed or displaced because they are associated with 'wrong' or evil', and perhaps also with pain and punishment. Painful events in later life can also lead to the formation of blocks.

The work of Freud, and subsequent psychoanalysts, has indicated that when the pain of unexpressed feelings is not recognized or acknowledged, the subconscious mind ensures that such recognition never re-emerges at a conscious level, but it can nevertheless be a major subconscious influence on the social performance of the individual. Clearly the identification of blocks represents an important area of work within the counselling process, and when successfully tackled can reveal a wealth of information, and the reason and meaning behind much previously misunderstood behaviour.

Yet the counsellor of older people has to realize that the blocks may not necessarily be those current in modern attitudes and beliefs. They are likely to be more closely related to past sexual and religious taboos which, because they are not as powerful in modern society, are not so immediately apparent to the younger counsellor. The recognition of blocks within ageing counsellees is therefore an important skill, but like so many others in counselling it is a perceptual rather than a concrete skill. The way in which particular individuals have reacted to a particular restraint, and how this in turn has affected their general social behaviour and attitudes, has no firm rules which can be laid down.

The threat posed by the counselling process

Self-expression can be a threatening process, bringing to the surface many deep-rooted fears and anxieties and uncovering hitherto denied emotions. The skill of achieving it is closely connected with the counselling relationship, developing the mutual confidence and trust that is essential for real sharing. Through the relationship, the counsellor is able to explore with the counsellee all the feelings, especially the negative feelings of inadequacy, guilt and worthlessness, which they harbour about themselves. Within the safety of the relationship, the counsellee can be helped to examine the emotional origins, meanings and purposes of their behaviour. They can examine the reasons why they have had to deny the existence of those feelings.

This is the part of the counselling process which many dislike because it necessarily creates stress and anxiety in the counsellee. It seems to open up all the disturbing conflicts and inconsistencies which have been at the heart of their problems. It seems to stir up emotions and rake over apparently quiescent turmoil. As Rogers (1951a) says:

> In the case of a radical re-organisation, the client may go through the most racking torment of pain, and a complete and chaotic confusion. This suffering may be associated with rapidly changing configurations of personality, being a new person one day, and sinking back into the old self on the next, only to find that some minor episode puts the new organisation of self again in a position of regnancy.

This leads to accusations that counselling can actually create more problems than it resolves, indeed, that it can actually contribute to increasing people's problems. As Rogers indicates, the accusation is based upon a measure of truth. Where counselling is effective, it will produce a degree of pain. Most processes of change are painful. So why not leave the troubled individual alone? Such accusations lie not with counselling, but with a kind of primitive logic which associates pain with whatever is most closely at hand. Thus, when pain is seen to arise within the counselling process, counselling is thought to be the cause. Such reasoning is faulty for two reasons.

First, it is unlikely that counselling actually creates distress not previously present somewhere within the individual. Counselling may reveal turmoil and bring it to the surface, but if it does, that turmoil will have existed long before the commencement of the counselling process. Moreover, feelings lying dormant will have already produced an individual who is troubled, unhappy and anxious, and the individuals behaviour will already be moving him or her inexorably deeper into emotional and social despair.

Second, the process of increasing self-awareness is itself an essential prerequisite for emotional health. Emotionally troubled people cannot be expected to deal with their emotions until they are able to understand what those emotions are, how they have arisen, and what can be done to overcome them. Contradictions and dilemmas exist in the lives of every individual, but they become a problem only when we deny their existence, or fail to recognize and come to terms with them in our daily lives. The journey through painful feelings is part of coming to terms with troubled emotions, and then devising a realistic strategy for emotional and social survival and the re-commencement of personal growth.

We should not avoid the chance of helping others because of some misguided sense of 'doing harm', but we do have to recognize that the counselling process might cause some temporary uncertainty and pain. If the quality of the counselling relationship is good it should prove more than enough to handle the outcome, and if it then assists the individual towards a resolution of emotional troubles, the short-term distress has been worthwhile.

Increasing self-awareness

Whereas the primary objective of the counselling relationship is the development of the counsellor's understanding of the counsellee, the primary objective of the counselling process is the development of self-understanding, or self-awareness. It is always surprising how little we, as individuals, understand of the emotional basis of our own social relationships and behaviour – about the way we present ourselves to other people, about aspects of our personality which others find attractive, and those which are not so attractive. If we could all step back and watch ourselves in our daily lives, we might all learn a great deal – and with some effort, we could all no doubt be nicer, more attractive people. Counselling seeks to present troubled individuals with a 'mirror' through which they can assess their social performance, and the reasons which lie behind its success or failure, its quality or lack of quality. The counsellor, in a variety of ways, has to feed back to counsellees the impressions they give to others, and the way they 'come across' to other people.

Enabling self-expression allows counsellees to explain to us where they stand at the present time. The picture they draw will use various materials gathered from the past, and how this has affected the way they currently feel.

Self-expression therefore represents a static picture. It is not helpful in telling us why individuals are where they are, and it is unlikely to give us real clues about possible future developments. Self-expression is essentially reflective rather than contemplative.

If there is to be change and development in a person's life, it can only come from within the individual. It cannot be imposed from without. Change which is imposed by some form of 'authority' or 'expert' is rarely effective in the long run. We have seen that giving advice is bad counselling, but it is also insufficient. What the counsellor has to do is to provide counsellees with the necessary knowledge and information to enable them to bring about change in their own lives. The counsellor has to be the enabler rather than the enforcer of change.

The working hypothesis reached by the counsellor has to be transferred to the counsellees, not through direct transmission, but by helping them achieve their own insights. Helping counsellees achieve greater self-awareness involves many different areas and levels of understanding:

1. It means helping counsellees to recognize the situations, the events or the people that provoke stress, and how they react to the stress in their lives.
2. It means helping counsellees to understand how they have coped with such stress in the past, and the positive or negative results of such coping behaviour.
3. It means helping counsellees to look closely at their own emotions in order to decide whether they are necessary, or an on-going indulgence (on the basis that certain people enjoy the 'benefits' of sympathy and concern, so actually make use of their social distress) over which they could exercise more control if they wanted to do so.
4. It means helping counsellees to recognize their personal needs, and how these can best be fulfilled in their later years.
5. It means helping counsellees to make connections between their unfulfilled needs, their emotions, and their social performance.
6. It means helping counsellees to become aware of repeating patterns of relationships which have led to unhappy situations throughout their lives and recognizing the part they themselves play in bringing about these recurring patterns.
7. It means helping counsellees to look closely at their attitudes and beliefs, about themselves, about other people, and about life generally as an ageing person, in order to determine the effect these have on their lives, and upon the people close to them.
8. It means helping counsellees to make connections between what has occurred in the past, and how this affects what they are achieving or failing to achieve in the present.
9. It means helping individuals to understand the social factors which affect their ability to lead their lives, and in particular, the impact of dominant social values and ideas concerning old age.

10. It means helping counsellees to make connections between personal expectations and the dominant social expectations about old age, and in particular how these have restrained their ability to enjoy their old age.
11. It ultimately means helping counsellees to look at their current self-image, and deciding how this can be improved or modified, and what has to be done in order to do so.

Decision-making – modifying social performance

In the last resort, self-awareness requires the personal acceptance that responsibility for doing something about feelings or circumstances is a personal one, which cannot be effectively decided by other people. Changing the patterns of our social performance can only take place from within our own selves, and through our own volition. So whilst self-understanding is the vital ingredient of the counselling process, and whereas individuals might have developed significant insights into their own social performance, what individuals decide to do with these newly discovered insights is also of vital importance.

The most important factor that militates against changing our social performance is personal doubt. Any decision in favour of change has to be allied with the ability and the confidence to change. This is a bigger task than a momentary resolution, based upon the desire for change. Many older people have accepted their depressed and unhappy status. They have become defeatist. They lack confidence in their ability to effect change or improve the quality of their lives. There must first be the desire for personal change, and thereafter the confidence that change can take place. Ageist attitudes often contribute to despondency. Old people, we are led to assume, are too set in their ways, they are now too old to change. When these feelings are internalized, ageing people too readily believe that they are what they are, and they are likely to remain that way. Their feelings of hopelessness are confirmed by any assessment of prospects.

The question 'Is change possible?' is therefore an important one. Is it possible to move out of grief or bereavement? Is it possible to make more of our later lives? If the answer is 'no' then it may be that counselling has not yet reached a sufficiently advanced stage in the process, and we may have to return to earlier stages. Yet this is not necessarily the case. Asking for change can be likened to persuading someone to climb a mountain. Refusal does not necessarily indicate that the individual is incapable of doing so. It might be that the individual does not see the value of climbing a mountain; or perhaps does not have the confidence to set about the task. And many older people may be quite right in refusing the prospect of change – it may be in their best interests. The counsellor has to be realistic in balancing the potential value of change against the personal costs that change might incur. It might be that they genuinely do not feel that they have the energy or even the interest to effect change in their lives.

If the answer is 'yes, change is possible', then certain choices have to be made about how individuals are going to tackle the problems which face them, and the counsellor will have a role in enabling counsellees to make those decisions. The object of the decision is to arrive at responses which enable individuals to cope more adequately with their situation. There are several stages through which coping behaviour can be developed.

1. Deciding upon the nature of the personal task that needs to be accomplished.
2. Discussing the available options open to the counsellee, with all the possible consequences and outcomes of each option.
3. The process of making a firm decision.
4. Deciding what is to be done, and who is to carry out the tasks involved. There may be some limited involvement by the counsellor to prepare the way for the counsellee.
5. Supporting the counsellee through the process of change.

The goal – improving social and interpersonal relationships

So what do we want for the counsellees, or rather, what should they want for themselves? The ultimate aim of the counselling process is to achieve significant improvement in the social and interpersonal relationships of the counsellee. We are looking for individuals who are adaptable and flexible, who live in the real world of the present and can cope adequately with whatever problems and difficulties it presents. We are looking for people who know their needs and wants, their likes and dislikes – but who are realistic about when they are likely and not likely to be fulfilled. We are looking for individuals who are able to strive for satisfaction, but who are also able to defend and protect themselves from disappointments and setbacks. Certainly, we are looking for individuals who can accept responsibility both for themselves and others, who can use their initiative to control events rather than drift aimlessly through life. We are looking for individuals who feel reasonably content with their present lives, although perhaps with lots of unfinished business to complete. We are looking for people who can accept that the past has passed and, whilst remembering it with fondness, can also look to the future and view what it might bring with a degree of optimism and hope. The counselling process will never achieve such an ideal, but it is nonetheless a good objective for the counsellor to aim at.

CHAPTER 9

Group counselling and older people

Counselling on a one-to-one basis can sometimes be a difficult process, not least because there is no more depressing aspect of old age than to be asked to contemplate personal problems in isolation. For the more depressed and lonely people who have few if any outside contacts, counselling can appear to deepen the very feelings that it is seeking to alleviate, especially in the early stages. Moreover, it is the social situation rather than the individual that is the source of counselling problems. Attempts to help people in distress are less successful when treated in isolation from the social context in which they live. Any work undertaken on an individual basis should always focus attention on the broader social context in which the individual lives. The next two chapters concentrate on work which can include and involve individuals with groups of people within a social context.

Whilst individual counselling recognizes the uniqueness of human problems, group-based counselling recognizes shared problems. The group process often opens areas that many individuals would normally not discuss. Within the process of group interaction, attitudes become apparent, opinions are expressed, and behaviour is displayed, all quite spontaneously within normal social conversation and discussion. Groups can provide the 'social lubricant' that one-to-one situations often lack. The group is a microcosm of life, embracing the exchange of ideas and information, compromise, decision-making, making friends; and conversely the frustrations and antagonisms which build up between people. Groups can help members express their needs and feelings more safely; but equally important is the learning and insight that can be gained by the counsellor into the feelings and behaviour of the individual.

Older people have many topics of conversation to share. The 'good old days' and childhood memories of their early years; money and the cost of living; illness and other physical ailments; their hopes and expectations for the future; loneliness; bereavement, loss and grief. All these and much more are likely to be discussed, and in some respects are more profitably discussed in groups than on an individual basis. Older people are often keen to form groups especially if they are lonely or isolated.

Groups for social activity

There are several levels of group operation, all of which can be useful in work with older people. They can be valuable purely as a means of providing social companionship, activities of all descriptions, and intellectual stimulation. There are many informal groups of older people whose purpose is to meet these very needs, groups organized by residential and day-care units, luncheon clubs, church-based groups, social clubs and many others. They can help their members maintain a sense of belonging and personal worth, and also perhaps something to look forward to during the hours when they are alone. All this provides an important service for the social and mental health of many older people.

Yet such groups are extremely limited in their scope. Often they are organized by younger people who merely expect ageing members to be passive recipients of organized events. Older people are expected to play little part in the running of the group, beyond perhaps a simple process of consultation. Moreover, the aim of such groups often tacitly implies that there are no issues in old age beyond meeting simple basic needs such as companionship and leisure. Both their establishment and function suggest an element of ageism – that older people themselves are not capable of organizing and deciding appropriate agendas. They tend to deny that older people may have issues and agendas that they may wish to discuss, and they ignore the fact that many older people have the ability and interest to organize matters for themselves. Certainly, insufficient attention is often paid to concepts of choice, self-expression and self-help. Clearly, whilst such groups may fulfil a valuable and useful social purpose, they could offer much more.

Groups and social engagement

Person-to-person counselling can lead older people to question socially constructed ideas about old age, and encourage them to take a more direct and active part in a society of which they are still full members. In this respect, the formation of groups of older people for counselling, and a host of related purposes, can be useful. The opportunity provided by groups for individuals to share their problems with other ageing people can help to recontextualize individual feelings of helplessness, and assist in refocusing their minds more positively on the prospects of the future. It can help older people realize that they are not the only ones with problems, a belief which the isolated and depressive nature of personal circumstances can sometimes encourage. It also helps them realize that there are other people who have similar problems and difficulties, and that they are not alone in their plight. Often, such a realization arising from contact with other ageing people can alone be worth several face-to-face counselling sessions.

The counsellor is often able to observe the spark of insight and realization which can arise from contact with another troubled individual. Such contact can often help individuals to move out of their own, often closed world of despair. They can begin again to focus on another person outside themselves, and relate what others have to say to their own situation. Often, they will begin to respond sympathetically, and with a concern that was once reserved for their own situation. They may even come up with possible solutions to the problems faced that will be equally attributable to their own situation, although they may be quite unaware of this until their attention is drawn to it.

For groups to function at this level, opportunity has to be given for full social contact between members, and the emphasis has to be placed not on activity, but on group interaction.

Active or informal counselling through the use of groups

In addition to providing companionship and activity, groups can be used for informal counselling. The inclusion of a counselling element into such groups is based on the understanding of their potential value in facilitating and enabling personal change, by helping group members understand their own thoughts and feelings, and in changing their coping behaviour to the situations in which they find themselves within the group. Involving an individual in a group process can be a powerful method of helping older people. The group can provide an opportunity for socialization, and for sharing problems and feelings with others who might be experiencing similar difficulties. Groups can help members to discuss their feelings and needs more safely, and the mutual support given can help them develop new coping strategies for dealing with them. Indeed, involvement in a group can sometimes be the only way to encourage more withdrawn people into a counselling situation, especially those people who feel too awkward or vulnerable in a one-to-one situation. Ideas about not 'burdening others' with personal problems, that discussing them denotes some kind of 'personal weakness', are common within the older generations, especially when the prospective counsellee has a strong sense of personal dignity and pride. Sometimes, such defences can be almost impossible to break down on a person-to-person level. Sherman (1981) outlines the value of group techniques of counselling:

> . . . just hearing the problems of other group members is often very helpful. The member finds that his or her own problems are not unique. Also, by acting as auxilliary counsellors for others, members of the group learn how to combat their own self-defeating attitudes and behaviour. The fact that there are several persons in addition to the group leader who can reflect and provide feedback about such negative attitudes and behaviours makes it more likely that the individual member will take such information seriously and do something about it. The force of group approval can be an important incentive in this regard.

Informal counselling implies that group members are not seated and asked to discuss a particular topic or situation. The group is seen as a vehicle which creates social situations involving interactions between two or more people. There are many situations of happiness and joy, tension and frustration that this can produce. As these interactions occur, the issues and situations which arise can form the basis of small group discussions. This is particularly useful when such situations relate to some of the more general problems faced by individual group members.

Informal groups should be organized on the basis of free self-expression if they are to be most helpful. Their value is reduced if 'difficult' subjects are not discussed, or if difficult situations are not allowed to develop. It is easy to stop squabbles and arguments in the interests of peace and harmony, yet to do so often prevents us from observing significant behaviour which can give the counsellor invaluable insight into how older people think and feel about themselves, other people and their situation.

In this way, groups can be used to open up many topics for discussion, which can then be used to reverse some of the sociological and psychological factors which contribute to senescence in our society.

Formal group counselling

Groups can be formed by bringing together two, three or more people who share similar problems and difficulties with the specific purpose of discussing those issues. Such groups can also be formed around the issues and situations which arise from informal group settings. Group size is important. Anything over two constitutes a group, but sharing and transference are facilitated better with more people. However, the group should not be too large as this can be threatening, and people may not feel sufficiently relaxed in a large group to make a contribution. Groups of up to about eight allow an atmosphere in which it is easier to share views, and to ensure that group members can get to know each other.

Comfortable seating should be used, set out in a circle so that everyone can see each other. This ensures good eye contact which is very important in promoting mutual trust and confidence between members. The distance between seats should be carefully arranged so that they are not too remote from each other, but not so close that personal space is invaded.

The counsellor has responsibility for starting up the discussion. It is always helpful to try to relax the group prior to commencement, perhaps with a cup of tea. Introductions are important, and to say a few encouraging words about each individual can be helpful. Group members can also be asked if they could give a small life history of themselves, although never without prior warning, and only if they are sufficiently confident to do so.

When this introduction is successfully achieved the topic can be introduced, and the counsellor should try to ensure that the group takes over most of the talking. Throughout the discussion, the counsellor has several tasks.

1. Giving everyone an opportunity to contribute. Some group members will inevitably be shy whilst others will tend to dominate the discussions. The former will feel that they do not want to impose their views and problems on the others, whilst the latter will tend to see their problems or their viewpoint as essential. Such situations have to be handled delicately, without putting down the more extrovert or putting too much pressure on the more introverted to make a contribution.

2. Ensuring mutual empathy within the group. It is important that group members try to see the point of view of other individuals, and are willing to talk about their problems. It is possible to see groups functioning in which individuals are intent on putting forward their own views without listening and sharing their problems with other members of the group. To prevent this from happening, several approaches can be tried. The group can be asked to respond to what one individual has just said; or it can focus discussion on one individual at a time; or the counsellor can ensure that the group discusses general or shared problems, or that it links and compares different problems faced by individuals within the group.

3. The leadership role. There is a tendency for group leaders to interfere too much in the running of the group, often anxious about the group not going well, with too many silences, or not being sufficiently helpful. This should be avoided. Wherever possible the counsellor should leave the group to work out its own solutions, restricting his input to occasional clarification, keeping the group to the point and ensuring fairness. There is also a role for the counsellor to introduce an 'extra' thought or dimension to the topic, perhaps involving a point of view which has not been considered by the group. Where there is too cosy an agreement between the group, the counsellor can sometimes act as 'devil's advocate' by introducing a more controversial idea into the argument.

4. The use of games and exercises. It is often helpful to group dynamics to introduce games and exercises into group discussion. There are many texts outlining group games, often aimed towards children and young people. But an excellent book by Ian Crosby and Jim Traynor (1985) relates specifically to older people, and explains how group exercises can be used to enhance and extend the learning potential of groups.

5. Life cycle group therapy. Butler (1974) used groups of older people specifically for developing individual life histories, and using the sharing of these in a therapeutic group setting. Certainly, such an idea combines and co-ordinates the value of the group and the value of reminiscence in a single setting.

Peer counselling

Groups of older people have the potential to develop as the vehicle for the counselling *of* older people *by* older people, offering mutual emotional support for group members in times of stress. Certainly, it is arrogant ageism for younger people to assume that only they can help older people.

Older people have specific advantages in providing help and support for their peers. There is often a shared pattern of experiences, beliefs and attitudes which have all arisen within their particular generation and which can never be fully shared by younger people. There is no 'generation gap', and often none of the resistance that can exist about discussing their feelings with 'youngsters'. It is a similar attitude to that of children and adolescents who have their secret understandings and life-styles which are often, quite intentionally, separate from those of parents, teachers and others of the 'older' generation. Counsellors who are younger than those they counsel must similarly allow that the feelings of older people can be based on quite different values and assumptions from their own. In recognizing this, the younger counsellor should accept that the peers of an older counsellee might often provide something the counsellor can never offer.

It might be that they can discuss and compare life during the Great War, or in the 1920s and 1930s; or they might want to talk about how expectations, duties, responsibilities have changed since their childhood days. Many topics may arise from such conversations, many happy and formative memories can be rekindled.

Or they may wish to discuss their present lives with each other, and compare how they cope with the problems and difficulties of being old. New ways of coping can be shared, and solutions to problems can be found based on the values and ideas of their generation, not according to the views and attitudes of the modern world.

Self-help, and self-action groups

There is considerable evidence that older people are becoming less passive and more assertive in demanding their social and political rights. Groups such as the Grey Panthers in the USA started the process. Similar UK movements, both within and outside the trade union movement, are now working to improve the condition, status and quality of life of pensioners. These organizations usually consist entirely of older people committed to fighting elderly issues directly. They have been established in recognition of the fact that it is pointless to wait for public sympathy and a change of political will to improve the level of basic old age pensions, and the quality of life for older people generally. Only by being more actively involved in identifying issues, organizing action, and thereby helping themselves by fighting for their own rights, can older people hope to improve matters.

This kind of group can be thought of as having only a minor role within counselling. But when older people form groups with the intention of becoming involved, or rather re-involved, in the wider social context, they raise their own self-image and the status of older people generally by showing society that they are full citizens who have to be reckoned with. They enable older people to be the givers rather than the receivers of help. It also enables older people to challenge what is done for them, and to make provision more in line with their real needs. These should be major counselling objectives, and encouraging an ageing person to be part of such a group would indeed constitute a major counselling success.

The campaigning or action group of committed older people may not be what many people expect from the counselling process, preferring acceptance and contentment rather than possible militancy as the outcome of help and support. It is, after all, easier for us all if we know where our 'old folk' are and what they are doing. We feel 'responsible' (which really means that they are not or should not be responsible), and believe that they should be taking matters more easily, accepting their situation and peacefully 'enjoying' their last years of life.

Age integrated groups

There is an increasing social trend towards age segregation. Retirement sections off the 'elderly' from the rest of the population. Special old age concessions such as travel permits, cheap beef and butter, of which we are so often proud, emphasize that pensioners are to be treated differently. Separate holidays for the young and the old can now be purchased. Special forms of segregated sheltered housing, and ultimately the old person's residential home, ensure that older people are taught to feel that their lives are somehow different and separate from other age-groups. For some older people the establishment of groups for the elderly merely emphasizes age segregation.

Not every older person wants to be in the company of peers, or find it difficult to include younger people among their circle of friends. Many older people prefer to be in groups which emphasize the common experiences and interests of young and old alike. Such groups can lead to valuable exchanges of feelings and knowledge between the generations; many focus on particular interests, hobbies and pursuits, and where appropriate older people should be encouraged to join, and even take a lead in their running and organization.

The role of the counsellor

Whatever the relationship with the individual counsellee, the counsellor can perform many functions in relation to groups of older people. The counsellor can be the 'facilitator' of group formation, or merely provide an opportunity for an individual to enter an already established group. It is assumed here that the counsellor will play an active part in the formation of a group.

The primary task in the early stages of group formation is to create a safe environment which provides individuals with secure boundaries in which they are able to function. Introductions are important, making each group member feel welcome. Thereafter, the use of names is an important element in making everyone feel part of the group. The purpose of the group meeting should be made clear from the start so that everyone knows what they are about, and what is expected of them.

The agenda of meetings should arise from the interests and concerns of the group. No subject should be forbidden, and each individual should be encouraged to raise issues that are of current concern or interest. Similarly, all feelings should be considered valid, despite the fact that they may upset other group members. The group, and individual members of the group, will go through many experiences which the counsellor can use. Observation is therefore very important. As situations arise, the associated feelings can be discussed, enabling group members to share their sorrows, their grief and their loneliness with others who have experienced similar events. Even the anticipation of future loss, and the way it can be handled, can be the subject of conversation.

The role of the counsellor can eventually become self-limiting when this level of sharing is attained, as the counselling becomes part of the process of group interaction. The ability of the counsellor to be part of a group, fully involved and an interested party, but at the same time an 'observer', may appear to be more difficult than it really is. Counsellors should try to limit their direct contributions, but ensure that important issues are fully discussed and that real feelings are expressed rather than avoided.

An agreed time for finishing each session can be an advantage, although this too must be flexibly interpreted. It is important not to go on for too long, or to leave difficult business unfinished.

The major objective of the counsellor, especially the counsellor who actively seeks to combat ageism, is to encourage involvement. It is important that the counsellor, observing the problems and deprivations within the group, does not fall into the trap of being more concerned with what he or she can do for the group than what the group can do for itself. The strategy should be to enable the group, and its individual members, to discover their own strengths and weaknesses. Group members should not only feel that they are contributing to the life of the group, but that their participation is important. Encouraging self-help, self-motivation, self-action leads to feelings of purpose, relevance and fulfillment, and these can in turn lead to new meaning in the life of the older individual.

The best possible outcome of the counselling process is where individuals actually begin to feel sufficiently confident to act on their own initiative, on their own behalf, and to follow the objectives that best match their own ideas about themselves and their lives. In other words, to begin to defy the dictates of ageism, and to follow the philosophy of 'I do, therefore I am'. Counselling should help individuals to see what is possible in old age, and to strive towards achieving it in order to make their lives more complete and fulfilling.

CHAPTER 10

Family counselling and older people

The importance attached to family relationships tends to increase with age. As we approach our own death, children represent both 'our' future in terms of the family line, and an important element of what 'we' have produced in the world. Harmony with our children, even where harmony has not existed before, becomes an important element of our peace of mind. Similarly, children often remain unaware of their debt to parents until too late, and then spend many years regretting their failure to show their gratitude when they were alive. In the counselling process with older people, the importance of working with the family should not be underestimated.

Whilst many families spend a significant part of their lives together, and their needs are usually closely linked, individual members do not always share the same objectives in relation to each other. Often these objectives are mutually incompatible and it is from such incompatibility, and the misunderstandings that arise from it, that many social and emotional problems experienced by older people arise. Where the problems of older people relate to their family, it is often crucial to involve key members or even the entire family group in the counselling process.

Family counselling, or family therapy, began in the USA in the 1950s, underwent enormous expansion during the 1960s and is now a well developed technique with a sizeable literature devoted to it. Normally the principal counsellee is a child; but there is no reason why the process cannot centre upon the problems of an older relative. The methods and techniques which have been developed to cope with the child-rearing process seem to apply equally to families who are experiencing the difficulties and frustrations of caring for an ageing relative. However, the task of transferring the central focus from the child to the older relative has not yet been attempted, and this chapter can perhaps be viewed as a small beginning to such a process.

Systems theory and family constructs

Systems theory developed in the 1940s as a explanation of human behaviour which took account of the important impact other people have on the individual. It focuses on systems, such as the family, considering them to be an entity, a whole, rather than merely the result of a number of contributions from independent parts or individuals. To reverse the same idea, individual behaviour is seen to be strongly influenced by the systems in which it functions. Indeed, the whole is considered to constitute more than just the sum total of its parts. The theory suggests that it is impossible to gain a significant understanding of an individual without first understanding the functioning of the systems within which the individual operates.

The family system is an open one which continually exchanges information, ideas and material with other systems. The counsellor of older people may be bringing together several of these open family systems; the system formed by the older person, and the systems formed by one or more of their children. This makes the counselling task even more difficult to interpret, but even within this complicated network of family systems, aspects of the wider, extended family unit will still be evident, perhaps comprising a number of separate systems which interact upon the way that the provision of care for older relatives is organized. One task of the counsellor is to determine which members of the family are relevant to the processes which contribute to the problems being experienced – who to include and who to leave out.

Counselling within families is based on the idea that many of the problems and difficulties older individuals experience have both cause and effect within the family process. The construct theory of Kelly (1955) (see pp. 61–2) has been applied to the family by Proctor (1981) who proposed a model of family functioning based upon shared constructs. These constructs constrain the individual's view of the world, and whereas everyone is potentially able to make their own choices and decisions, they are restricted by the knowledge that to do so has an impact on other members of their family. These constraints build into a complex family network, which forms patterns of expectations and choices that are shared by all members.

Shared family constructs enable individuals to organize their lives with some degree of predictability and certainty about the likely behaviour of other family members. It produces a state of homeostasis, a mechanism which enables a system to remain in a stable state through time. Each input or interaction upsets homeostasis, but the parts which make up the system are programmed to respond in such a way as to ensure a return to normality. Homeostasis should not necessarily be seen as a fixed state which allows no change, but one which allows change to occur in manageable stages thereby preserving a measure of continuity and security.

Family homeostasis can result in the system, and its individual parts, becoming stuck within patterns of behaviour which produce only failure, unhappiness and insecurity. This occurs when individuals' act in a way they know is destined to be hurtful to other members of the family, who, in response, reciprocate with actions they know will cause even more distress. Families which operate in this way might be expected to break up but they usually do not do so.

An example may be helpful. When ageing parents become increasingly unable to look after themselves, a daughter may assume the main responsibility for caring for them. Perhaps she resents the duty, feeling that other family members should do more, or that the parents do not show sufficient gratitude in return. But by stepping into the role the daughter ensures homeostasis within the family. Owing to what she sees as a lack of gratitude, she threatens to refuse to continue with the caring tasks. The family now has a problem. Perhaps the response of the ageing parents is to become ill, or demonstrate in some other way their dependency and distress. The family combines to make the daughter feel guilty and re-assume her task. Feeling threatened by family hostility, and in danger of being excluded from the family, the daughter re-assumes her caring role, albeit with increasing resentment. This in turn makes the parents feel unhappy about being a burden, and not being loved and respected in the way they had expected. This leads to further guilt, producing a network of family duties and expectations that cause considerable unhappiness and distress, but which produce homeostatic mechanisms which ensure that the situation continues.

This type of family construct can become entirely negative, leading to unhappiness on all sides. The real issues are never discussed, nor do they have to be, for established patterns of family behaviour eventually ensure the maintainance of the status quo, albeit an uncomfortable and unhappy one. But it is important for the family counsellor to remember that even such negative family systems provide individuals with a basis for role allocation, and a security based on certainty and predictability, however unpalatable.

The social background: family care of the older relative

There is a popular perception that the modern family has become a problem, that increasingly the family renounces its former responsibilities towards the care and maintenance of older relatives. Many argue that there is a major trend away from family-centred care towards state provision throughout the western world, and even in the more traditional oriental societies of Japan and

China, and that state provision further enables families to opt out of their former caring functions. This is not a new idea. Gray and Wilcock (1981) trace the attitude back to a Royal Commission on the Poor Law in 1909, but no doubt it is much older than this.

It is important to place this alleged trend in perspective. Contrary to such perceptions, the family still remains the biggest single source of care for older people by a very substantial degree (Means, 1986). It is therefore wrong to assume that there is a widespread move away from the family care of dependent older people. Instead, this increasingly popular element of dominant ideology should not be seen as an expression of social concern for the well-being of older people, but examined for its wider social purpose. By seeking to blame the family for the plight in which many older people find themselves, attention is distracted from the very real problems that structural social changes have placed on the family in providing such care. These include the rise of the smaller nuclear family unit, smaller houses, earlier marriages, female employment and increased population mobility, all of which are encouraged and supported by a variety of social, fiscal and economic factors. These factors contribute to the difficulties experienced by families in performing their caring functions, in turn increasing the likelihood of unfulfilled need and frustration developing within families over the care of older, dependent relatives. These perceptions also serve to obscure the inadequacy of social provision which supports the army of people, usually female relations, who are expected to carry the burden of the caring role, often at considerable personal sacrifice.

The structure of modern social life merely exacerbates the problems faced by families. Some carers will feel imprisoned by the demands made of them, and they will be torn between their desire to care for their older relatives and their own need to lead an independent life. The balance between these two factors has no doubt always been difficult, but is perhaps especially so within the modern family.

The nature and origins of family difficulties

Problems between ageing parents and their now adult and independent 'children' will centre on the system of relationships and the patterns of interaction that have developed over many years. The origins of many of these will be the unresolved issues in the process of children growing older, and growing away from their parents, problems which are the more usual subject of family therapy. Clearly, the family process will have moved on and new issues will inevitably have entered the scene, and perhaps old ones will have become worse. Moreover, this is likely to be the case regardless of whether the children now live independently or the family home is still shared, for in either case there will have been an almost complete role-reversal. Those who were formerly independent and dominant will have become dependent, and vice versa. The role of carer and cared-for will have been reversed. It is easy to underestimate the immense process of adjustment involved in this change. Children find it difficult to come to terms with the responsibilities involved, and parents find it difficult to relinquish them.

Caring for dependent older people can, in any case, be a daunting task, particularly when problems of mental confusion and incontinence arise. Carers cannot make decisions in their own lives without considering their needs. They may often have to forego social evenings and holidays. The sexual lives of carers are often severely handicapped, especially where the ageing relative lives within the home. These problems, and those which surround the major role-reversal, frequently remain unconsidered and undiscussed within families, thereby enabling problems to grow until they reach the stage of 'granny bashing' or 'granny dumping' when care is withdrawn, and even family breakdown occurs.

Family issues

Counselling issues between older people and their families often arise from these fundamental changes of power and status and the counsellor embarking on work with a family therefore needs to ask several key questions.

1. What is the nature and quality of family relationships between the two or more generations?
2. How does the existing pattern of relationships and interaction within the family match the needs and expectations of the different generations?
3. What rights, duties and debts do the various individuals within the family feel they have towards each other? How do these expectations match, and to what extent do individuals feel that family responsibilities are being fulfilled?
4. What patterns of dependence and independence have developed, and to what extent are these accepted or resisted by all parties, pointing to issues of unresolved stress and conflict within the family?
5. What was the nature of the former parental relationship with the children, and what impact do these former patterns of interaction have on current relationships, especially when children have left home and established their own families?

It is when family duties, responsibilities, roles and expectations are confused, uncertain or even mutually incompatible that problems within families arise. No counsellor can assume that 'good' relationships either are or have been the norm within the family, and idealistic pictures of family life as a reciprocally loving, mutually committed and concerned relationship should be abandoned. Family construct theory suggests that it would even be wrong to assume that such 'good' family relationships are wanted by some families which actually rely upon 'bad' family relationships.

The perception of change and development within families can also be affected by problems associated with ageist attitudes, particularly, when younger family members make the assumption that because their parents are growing older they, and the problems which surround their care, will remain forever unchanging (except by getting worse) and unchangeable. This fatalistic ageism can be another reason for failing to discuss the problems and difficulties of caring for ageing relatives as they arise – there is no point, for there is no possibility of change taking place.

Developing self-awareness within the family

The primary task of the counselling process within families is to focus upon the different viewpoints of key members of the family group, how they differ from each other, and why stress in family relationships has developed. The primary aim of family counselling is to facilitate and enhance the ability of individuals to examine their own needs and expectations, and to compare these in relation to the needs and expectations of other members of the family. From such awareness it is possible to increase general family understanding of the main conflicts, misunderstandings and incompatabilities that exist within their group. The primary object of family counselling is to help negotiate new, mutually acceptable and agreed expectations, with each party being aware of what is expected of them, and how much they can reasonably expect from others.

The starting point is to get family members together, and embark upon discussions which seek to define and highlight family problems. This demands not only the skills of counselling previously outlined, but the ability to referee and control the expression of different and conflicting attitudes, to give equal time and importance to everyone's point of view, and to encourage each member of the family not only to explain their own feelings, but to listen to each other.

The counsellor needs to be aware of the wishes and expectations of both old and young alike about the nature of the caring role within the family, and this is particularly so when families live separately. Some older people want to be cared for by their children, others most definitely do not. Some see state support, in all its guises, as a bonus, others as an intrusion. Some will find it a welcome relief, others an indication of personal failure, and the cause of personal guilt.

The possible permutations of these feelings between any two individuals are endless. Within families the complexity and inter-relatedness of expectation and need can appear to be a perplexing and entirely confusing maze. Arising from these complex interactions can come a variety of feelings – guilt, disappointment, sorrow, anger, despair, frustration, depression and many more. The counselling task is not only to understand what each individual is saying, but also to spot the differences, the possible areas of friction and incompatibility that exist within the family, and then to interpret and explain these to the family group.

The counsellor is helped in interpreting this complex situation by the generality of family behaviour. The apparently small and isolated family incidents observed by the family counsellor are often typical examples of family interaction. Walrund-Skinner (1977) describes the family therapy session as 'a slice of real life', providing the counsellor with a 're-enactment of the ongoing patterns of behaviour', 'a microcosmic expression of the family's continuous drama, enacted during the other 23 hours of the day, when the therapist is not with them'. To extract generality from family behaviour is important to the family counsellor. People do not usually alter their feelings, their behaviour or their interactions with others because of a particular situation, or the presence of the counsellor. One apparently isolated incident can vividly illustrate a more generalized pattern of family life.

Impartiality and family power structures

Embarking on family counselling can subtly change the relationship between the counsellor and the older counsellee. It is no longer a one-to-one relationship in which the counsellor concentrates exclusively upon the feelings and needs of a single person, for other people must now be considered. This inevitably alters the nature and emphasis of the counselling relationship, which can often cause some difficulty if counsellees feel that their problems are now being ignored, and that 'their' counsellor is no longer 'on their side'. Some prior preparation aimed at outlining the purpose of family meetings is useful, and the stance the counsellor plans to take should be clearly explained to the counsellee before the start of family meetings.

Counsellors have to be impartial. Often they will enter a family situation where the focus of all difficulties lies with one person, perhaps the ageing parent who has become dependent upon the younger members of the family. Even if the primary focus is the needs of an older person, the counsellor cannot afford to 'take sides', but should instead aim to help the whole family face up to and develop a wider understanding of the problems and difficulties that exist in old age, and in caring for older people. In doing so, the counsellor has to look at the family dynamic with a particular emphasis on those factors which impinge upon the life of the ageing family member, but to be seen as anything other than impartial, particularly when there is jealousy and conflict within the family group, can lead to a lack of trust and the possible withdrawal of co-operation and participation by some family members.

There is perhaps one exception to the rule of impartiality. All families have their own power structure, and usually the position of the very young and the dependent elderly tend to be the least powerful. They have least to offer the family in return for all the help and support they may need or expect in return. There will also be status differences within the family based not only on age but also on sex, and the control of money and other resources. Family negotiations can be delicate in this respect. Family work, as in most social work, is often concerned with balancing the power of the strong with the rights of the weak. Therefore, if the counsellor acts entirely impartially with regard to existing patterns of power and vulnerability in family meetings, the needs of the ageing relative may continue to receive inadequate attention and response. However, if the counsellor seeks to support the position of the older person, care has to be taken over how the imbalance of power is handled.

The existence of power structures within the family cannot be ignored when it is clear that the power of one party is being used to the detriment of another. The usual outcome is that the weaker, more dependent individuals are blamed for family problems. Individual pathology is used to explain family ills whose origins are usually far more complex. This outcome of family power politics has to be avoided. The counsellor should try to achieve a more equitable balance by enabling the weaker individual to present feelings and needs as coherently and forcefully as possible, perhaps by clarifying and expanding on what is said. The outcome may be to highlight the part played by more powerful family members in the problems of the family.

The neutrality of the counsellor, so necessary in order to develop mutual trust and confidence, has to be compromised in such a way that individuals are not annoyed or upset, or that members of the family begin to see the counsellor as partisan. Developing awareness of individual need within the family is the objective, and failure occurs when the counsellor so upsets certain family members, particularly the more powerful, that he or she can no longer have any impact on the family dynamic. Sensitivity to the family, and to the needs of individual members of it, allied with the confidence to tackle issues whilst maintaining an impartial stance, is the task the counsellor has to fulfil.

How such paradoxical objectives are handled will depend upon the individual counsellor. Family therapy is not a precise skill with correct and incorrect approaches. Different counsellors can use different methods in similar situations with equal success. Counselling responses often have to be rapid, based on personal judgement rather than precise theoretical principles. Indeed, the development of family therapy has been highly pragmatic in character, more involved in solving problems than adhering to particular dogmas. The counsellor has to enter into the family dynamic, not intrusively, not demanding compliance with the wishes or even with the needs of the elderly counsellee, but to ensure that the feelings and needs of each member of the family, however weak, are heard.

Openness, honesty and the development of harmony and understanding

Once the family sessions have begun, the counsellor has to ensure that the family group is maintained, despite the many potentially explosive problems and difficulties that might need to be discussed. This is another important paradox that has to be dealt with in family counselling. There are many ways in which the need for openness and honesty can be harmonized with the need to maintain the family group, and to ensure that individuals within the family are not damaged.

The initial focus of family discussion is important. Rather than starting with the current difficulties, it is often possible to begin with the history of the family, perhaps concentrating on more positive, happier times. To do this is most helpful when there is, or at least has been, a genuine basis of care, love and mutual need within the relationship. It enables the counsellor to remind the family that better times did once exist, and raises the prospect that they could exist again if the reasons for current difficulties can be understood. From this more harmonious base the counsellor can attempt to move the family on to consider when family relationships began to falter, what the circumstances were, and how all parties felt about the issues at that time. By adopting this 'historical' approach, misunderstandings can be traced back to their origins, and then linked and brought up to their current situation. It can lead to a mutual re-affirmation of affection and concern between the parties which, throughout the discussions of more difficult issues, can serve as the basis to which the family can return if discussion becomes too heated and acrimonious.

Family counselling does not have to have a historical basis. Indeed, some families will want to talk about the present, believing that what has occurred in the past is of little or no consequence. It is equally possible to use the present as the starting point of work with the family. Indeed, the very first piece of family self-revelation is the way they choose to sit together, for this can show the observant counsellor the existing pattern of alliances and tensions, as revealing as any words. Thereafter, engaging the family in a discussion of the problems they face can quickly indicate the current nature of family relationships and interactions.

In family counselling, regardless of the starting point, difficult issues should be tackled rather than left because it is considered 'kinder' to do so. There is no long-term advantage in avoiding contentious and divisive issues. On the other hand, when the family atmosphere becomes particularly strained or difficult, the counsellor should attempt to bring the discussion around to a more harmonious matter. Whatever the need for honesty, there is little point, and usually no advantage, in allowing discussions to continue on the basis of anger or mutual recrimination. It will be helpful to consider a typical general example, and then to illustrate how a balance between these two considerations can be achieved.

Family hostility often arises when the expectations of older people make quite unrealistic demands upon younger relatives. The usual, if not the inevitable, result is that their expectations are regularly disappointed. Whilst it might cause some obvious short-term distress to tell the older people that they have unrealistic expectations of their children, to fail to do so inevitably leads to more unhappiness in the longer term. Similarly, younger relatives can come to the conclusion that whatever they do nothing is right or sufficient. They begin to assume that their ageing parents are never satisfied, and may eventually conclude that it might be better to do nothing at all for them. Therefore, in this situation any failure to tackle such issues may trade short-term distress for long-term breakdown in the relationship.

Obtaining frankness within families about the feelings and expectations they have of each other can be mutually beneficial. Continuing with the above situation, when young carers do eventually withdraw their help and support from their ageing parent, they will almost inevitably feel guilty. Whilst they may be able to rationalize what they have done, there is usually a strong element of disappointment about the broken relationship. When families place elderly relatives into residential care, a similar feeling of guilt is often apparent.

Disclosure of personal feelings and attitudes within the family group is important. It is better, especially in manipulative family situations, for individuals to talk directly to each other rather than relay messages through a third party. Some people find this kind of face-to-face honesty difficult to cope with, especially if the individual feels in any way weak or threatened within the family group. To avoid doing so, devious messages are often sent, perhaps attributing their feelings to mysterious 'theys' or 'others'. One method of overcoming this is to encourage family members to use 'I' positioning (Bowen, 1978) in which people are expected to use 'I' statements when expressing attitudes and feelings. Yet during family sessions, feelings can rise so quickly that very damaging statements can be made, which may be frank and honest but have a destructive meaning or impact that would not be intended in calmer and more reasonable moments. If they are left entirely unqualified they can do more harm than good to family relationships. 'I don't give a damn about you', 'You can go to hell', 'You were the worst father/mother/daughter/son that anyone could wish to have', are typical of the kind of remarks that can be made. A closer interpretation is necessary in family work, with the counsellor focusing on the statement rather than passing it off or trying to pretend that it was not said, seeking to analyse and ascertain what exactly was being said, why is was said, and what the real message might be. In doing so, it is important that the counsellor tries to extract the feeling within the statement, which was real, rather than the literal meaning of the words, which may not have been.

This highlights one of the main differences of approach between normal communication within the family and the counselling process. Within the family it is usually the words and their literal meaning which take primary importance. In counselling it is the emotions behind the words that need to be pursued. What is important is that the individual understands why someone feels strong enough to say 'go to hell', and not merely to believe that this is an accurate statement of what that person desires. Violent and damaging words are used to express feelings, not intentions. The other person does not want the relationship to end, although this can be the outcome, but perhaps feels subjected to unreasonable demands or expectations, or is struggling with guilt or frustration, or feels neglected and unwanted. It is the counsellor's task to try to move the discussion to these underlying meanings of words used in anger.

A similar technique often used in family counselling is ascribing 'noble intentions' to actions and behaviours which have caused friction and animosity between family members. This involves developing explanations for particular actions or behaviours that have caused problems, expressed in terms that both parties can understand and recognize in more positive and acceptable ways. For example, it is often possible to explain angry and hostile behaviour in terms of an individual's love and concern for the other rather than as a straightforward expression of hostility or hatred. Such a technique can be a useful way of bringing two or more parties together when there have been serious misunderstandings which have led to conflict.

The family counsellor will always meet resistance. It is a normal reaction to the pain and anxiety that discussing difficult issues will bring. Keeping the entire family attending meetings can be a continuing problem, particularly if progress is slow, or problems are particularly intractable. The refusal to attend meetings is one way that key individuals, who feel they have most to fear from change, have of undermining family work. There is usually no way of enforcing attendance, so such threats have to be taken seriously, and perhaps worked through by paying special attention to their particular feelings and needs.

Another typical resistance is met when it becomes clear that despite everything that is being achieved in terms of family understanding and awareness, individuals are sticking rigidly to old patterns of interaction and behaviour. The most recent trends in family therapy have tended to suggest that seeking merely to increase self- and family awareness may be insufficient to bring about effective change within the family dynamic. They stress the importance of achieving structural change within families through the development of family tasks. These more direct techniques have been developed to give the counsellor a more active role within the family, based on the idea that change is more effectively brought about through action rather than the development of self-awareness.

The setting of family tasks

The setting of tasks helps to focus the family's attention on the need for change, highlighting the importance of their own actions, and giving them meaningful and helpful activity to perform between family meetings. Tasks can also help the family define in precise and concrete terms what can be done to improve their situation. The attention of individual members can be drawn to small, practical ways in which they can change the dynamic processes within the family. They enable powerful members to modify the impact they have within the family. They also enable weaker members of the family to point out what is happening to them whilst it is actually happening. How the tasks have been performed, and what members of the family feel about the 'new' way of doing things, can then become the starting point of the next family meeting, leading to new understandings being discussed and new, more subtle tasks being developed.

Family tasks are most appropriate within families which have become stuck in hurtful and damaging interactions, and who seem resistant to or incapable of change. Their aim is to provoke change rather than to enhance awareness. A few examples of some of the techniques which have been developed, and their relevance to work with older people, can briefly be described.

It is often possible to effect change by apparently recommending the continuation or intensification of interactions that are at the root of family problems. Presented with this paradoxical technique the family is placed in a double-bind situation. They can either accept the recommendation, admitting that they are in control of what they do and the situations they create, or more likely they will protest that to take such advice will worsen the situation. An example of this occurred where a daughter's care for her dependent father was continually met with ingratitude and unkindness. This made her feel that she was not doing enough, so she would increase the care she gave him, which in turn increased the unpleasant response. All suggestions for changing this pattern were resisted. Finally it was suggested that if her father continued to be unkind or unpleasant, the only way she could increase the level of care she provided would be to move away from her family and live with him. This led to a heated family argument, the daughter not wanting to leave her family, the husband not wanting to lose his wife, and the father indicating that this was not what he intended. For the first time this opened up an honest discussion of feelings, and started the process of constructing a new pattern of interaction.

Reframing procedures are attempts to place family problems in another, more manageable, context. This technique has already been mentioned when talking of ascribing noble intentions. Another example, using the technique of redefining the problem and using the above situation, may be for the counsellor to suggest that the intention of the father's behaviour was to place the daughter in an untenable position so as to break up her marriage. This may not be an accurate assessment of the family dynamic, but the re-labelling of the problem does enable the family to focus on a problem that might not otherwise be considered, the effect of one caring relationship on another. Straightforward directions can also demonstrate the need for change. In one situation, a younger daughter was being constantly criticized by her older sister for the way she cared for their mother. The allegation was that she did not do enough to help her, and over a period of time this had made the carer extremely angry, and at the same time made their mother dissatisfied about the care she was receiving. Although the older sister lived away, she travelled to stay with her sister occasionally and during one visit, after she made her allegations in a family meeting which she had joined, the counsellor asked her to take over the caring role for the final week of her stay so that her sister could actually see how it should be done. This strategy enabled the various members of the family to see the difficulty of the younger daughter's task, and the part everyone played in making it worse.

There are also a number of tasks and activities which have been developed to illustrate the family dynamic – these include family choreography, role-playing, role-reversal, family drawing, charting, listing, and perhaps most well-known, family sculpting. These are all techniques by which families can be helped to understand the way they interact together by practical, visual means.

Working with families can often appear to be a daunting task because the counsellor has to hold together so many different individuals at the same time. However, it is often not as difficult as it appears, and the process can be fascinating and the results very worthwhile.

CHAPTER 11

Reminiscence and the life review

We are all the products of our history, and the multitudinous influences of circumstance, events and people which fill our lives. Psychology has concluded that the most formative period of life is childhood, and in particular the first five years of life. Experiences in childhood form not only our earliest, but our most enduring and persistent perceptions of the world, our place within it and our relationships with other people. The circumstances and experiences of life create ever more diversity and certainly by the time old age is reached, differences can be expected to be at their most extreme.

Whilst people of all ages reminisce, old age, not unnaturally, is a time when looking back at our lives, reviewing its failures and triumphs, its joys and sorrows, its pleasures and regrets, is of particular importance. Yet this process has not always been seen as important or even helpful, for a variety of reasons. Many pre-eminent people working with older people have considered reminiscence a mixed blessing, particularly for those whose past life experience seems to have lacked fulfillment and purpose. Reminiscence was perceived in the 1950s and 1960s to be an unwelcome symptom of mental deterioration, a failure to maintain contact with the realities of the present, and a potentially harmful process. The idea that older people live in the past, that they are always talking about the 'good old days' is common, and reminiscence has often been devalued as merely the aimless meanderings of an increasingly decrepit mind. This has a reciprocal impact. Older people are inhibited about discussing the past because they sense that no-one is interested. Klein *et al* (1965) found that many older people hesitated to talk about the past because they did not want to meet with rejection, and that many actually needed help and encouragement to reminisce. For many older people this is perhaps a common experience, reflecting the dominant social preoccupation with the present and future, and the dismissal of past experience as either uninteresting, irrelevant or unimportant.

Although these attitudes still persist, the general view has been transformed and reminiscence is now seen as a normal, if not essential, element of successfully growing old. Norris (1986) points to five reasons for its importance. First, reminiscence highlights older people's assets rather than their disabilities. Second, it can enhance their feelings of self-worth and esteem. Third, it can help older people recognize their individuality and identity. Fourth, it can aid the process of life review, and fifth, it is an enjoyable and stimulating experience. Given all these factors, reminiscence should be an extremely valuable counselling aid.

Even so, it is important to examine why there has not always been agreement on the value of reminiscence, and to place the value of reminiscence within the counselling process into perspective. A review of recent research led Coleman (1986) to conclude that reminiscence therapy could not be said to stand on a very solid base, and that it is important not to make generalizations about the value of reminiscence to any particular individual. Each person needs to be considered in his or her own unique way. Research has divided people into 'reminiscers' and 'non-reminiscers', and then divided both groups again. There are reminiscers who find the process helpful and supportive, and those who find it difficult or disturbing. Amongst the non-reminiscers, some find that there is little point or purpose served in looking back at their lives, whilst others do not reminisce because they find it too depressing, often because of the contrast between their past and present life which they find too difficult to contemplate.

The problem that counsellors face is to determine whether reminiscence is a useful tool to use with an individual. They will no doubt be helped in making this decision by counselling itself, and the empathy that should exist between counsellor and counsellee. Clearly, with 'reminiscers', even those who find it difficult, there seems good reason for counsellors to make use of the process. With 'non-reminiscers' there would appear to be less reason to dwell on the past, and it might be more useful to avoid it unless the counsellor feels that there is a particularly strong reason and purpose for doing so. With these general rules in mind, counsellors should carefully assess the potential benefits of using reminiscence in their work with older people.

Empathy between generations

Early formative experiences are powerful factors in establishing personality. For older individuals, these experiences took place in a world which was very different from the one in which we now live. Most of the current generation of older people were born at a time when the motor car was an unusual sight on the streets, aeroplanes were rarely seen in the skies, telephones were rare, radio and television were many years from invention. Further from common domestic experience, medicine had not discovered penicillin or antibiotics, and social and health insurance was an item of political discussion rather than practical reality.

As fundamental aspects of social life have changed, so have the perceptions of the nature of life, its problems, pleasures, responsibilities and duties. When the younger counsellor shares these experiences with the older counsellee they are both doing far more than embarking on a process of recalling the past, they are sharing a common heritage which has been formative for the young as well as the old, although less directly so. They are helping each other understand their different experiences of life, and their different views and attitudes towards it. This should be particularly helpful for the younger counsellor who, if not aware of the potentially vast differences of life expectations between generations, will have difficulty in fully empathizing with the attitudes and feelings of older people. With such understanding, the complaints and uncertainties older people have about the 'modern' world can be more fully appreciated and understood. The sadness about change, the cynicism about so-called progress, the regret for passing values and customs can all be placed legitimately where they belong, within the context of the social realities older people knew and experienced when they were younger.

History as counselling

Autobiography and life history play an important part in our knowledge and understanding of past social life. The great majority of such texts and records, forming the basis upon which history is understood, interpreted and taught in our society centre on the rich, the famous and the influential. These are the people we believe have shaped and moulded history, and the society in which we now live. Yet more recent understanding of historical study has moved the focus away from the centres of power and social influence, and towards the lives of ordinary people. How did these people live their lives? What were their main concerns, difficulties and problems? How did the dominant social, economic and cultural forces affect the way they lived their lives? To use a single but important example, it is the difference between looking at the Great War as an event which centred around the policies and machinations of politicians and generals, or one which impinged upon the lives of ordinary people. Lloyd George and Kitchener have their biographies; yet those who experienced most directly the turmoil, disruption and loss of the war have their information locked within their memory. Historians are increasingly realizing that if the experience of older people is not sought we are in danger of losing a unique individual insight into the times and events they report, and one which will die with them unless recorded (Thompson, 1978).

Both viewpoints are important in a historical context, but not in counselling. Most younger counsellors will have learnt about the war from texts, films and documentaries based essentially on the political view of history. Conversely, most older counsellees will have experienced the war in entirely personal terms. This being so, the experience of older people is not only an invaluable and irreplaceable source of history, it is an essential element of counselling empathy. By concentrating on the value and significance of their experience, the counsellor will generate not only an important historical and social insight, particularly if a physical record is kept, but will learn about the impact of the war on the individual, that is, from the only perspective that has relevance to the counsellor. In order to do so, the counsellor may have to 'unlearn' some of the more conventional understandings she or he might have about the nature of the war.

Reminiscence can provide the counsellor with an initial point of contact with the counsellee. Taking the time to talk about the past, focusing on the experience of the counsellee in all its detail and complexity, can help to establish the counselling relationship. At the same time it can reverse completely the power/information balance that can often be a problem in counselling. The counsellee is the teacher and expert, the counsellor the pupil. It can also help to emphasize to the counsellees the value and significance of their lives, and the part they have played in the history of their times.

The counsellor as 'historian' is perhaps an unusual view, but by travelling through an individual's life history, and especially when making a physical record through family albums, scrapbooks, memorabilia, and genealogies, the counsellor is in effect producing an important autobiography which serves both functions.

Life history as a source of insight into the individual

The importance of a 'lifetime perspective' on ageing is being increasingly recognized. This perspective states that in order to understand an individual in later life, it is important to know something about his or her past experience. Reminiscence can provide the counsellor with invaluable insight into the nature and quality of the counsellee's early formative years which can, to a large extent, determine the way people live their later lives. Early experiences shape the way we face up to and deal with problems and crises; the way we cope with disappointments; the way we form relationships; the way we construct personal aims and objectives; the way we develop strategies for fulfilling needs and desires; and the way we build a system of social and moral values and attitudes. It is these that provide our basis for living, life scripts upon which we base our responses to all new situations and circumstances. And although such scripts are potentially modifiable, they more usually remain essentially intact throughout a lifetime.

General personality traits emerge from this, which will tell us whether we are dealing with individuals who will tend to cope with problems optimistically or pessimistically; whether they are hopeful or depressive; whether they are extrovert or introvert, and so on. It will tell us about the individuals' ability to make and maintain new relationships. It will tell us about former hobbies and interests which may be important in future plans. It provides us with information which can suggest not only how individuals came to be in their present position but the way they are likely to respond to new difficulties and choices.

The individuals' personal history, what they have done, who they have been, what has been important to them, makes them come 'alive', helping them emerge from the 'elderly' or 'dependent' or 'infirm' stereotypes. Understanding individuals in the context of their past can help us understand the present-day person. This is important when dealing with older people who in many cases are not now what they have been, making the counselling task different from that of any other age group.

Locating the origins of current problems

Older people often find it easier to talk of their childhood and early years than their current problems. As reminiscence naturally proceeds from the past to the present, it can often give the counsellor an indication of where, and at what period, to focus attention in the search for the origins of the counsellee's particular mental state or circumstances. There comes a point when reminiscence is blocked, or when there is resistance to proceeding further. Such periods will often be found to correspond with times of particularly stressful social change for the individual. The counsellor may often find that this period also coincides with the onset of a depressed or confused state of mind, suggesting that it is the problems and difficulties which occurred around this time that require counselling attention. In such circumstances, the counsellor will often find that invaluable help and information can be obtained from relatives and friends, who may have been aware of the personal circumstances, but perhaps unaware of their full significance at the time.

The counsellor must also recognize that in returning to past experiences, there will be regrets and disappointments as well as joys and successes. The life review may lead to unresolved and perhaps painful conflicts. Some older people may be pre-occupied with these negative aspects of their lives, where the counsellor will be dealing with a lack of personal satisfaction and fulfillment, failed relationships, unfulfilled hopes, and even perhaps with events that elicit feelings of disgrace and shame. Reminiscence can be a means through which such matters can be re-examined and resolved. If such unresolved conflicts are successfully addressed, if individuals can begin to forgive themselves for their failures and indiscretions, it can bring them a renewed meaning and significance for the remaining part of their lives.

Yet here the counsellor faces the problem of whether to delve into the difficult past, or to leave it alone. The decision rests on a balance between helping individuals to come to terms with what has happened in their lives at difficult times, risking the possibility of taking them back through stressful and disturbing memories, and leaving the past alone, risking the possibility that counsellees will never come to terms with what is disturbing them. Such a decision should not be taken timidly. The view that upsetting issues should be avoided is one that has already been addressed. Providing counsellees can be coaxed into exploring these more sensitive areas, and counsellors feel that they have the time and the ability to cope with any resulting distress, then the eventual outcome can be, more often than not, extremely valuable.

Reminiscence can play an important part in ameliorating personal distress, and can be adapted when counselling older people through such matters as retirement, dependence, depression, ill-health, as well as coming to terms with bereavement and death. This will be dealt with in more detail in the chapters relating to these subjects in Part 2.

The life review – making sense of our lives

Young people lead their lives with an eye on the future, and with a sense of the potential for further work or achievement. Nothing is yet complete or whole. It is only when we reach old age, whenever that is, that we can experience and reflect upon an almost entire life cycle.

An important objective in counselling is to help the older individual live for today rather than for an uncertain tomorrow. Counselling should encourage reflection on the past, and use the life review as a positive, formative part of growing into old age. When older people think of the past they are not just taking stock of their lives but trying to decide what to do with the time that they have left, and trying to do so in relation to concluding or making sense of what has gone before. They are checking on the legacy they want to leave behind them.

This can be seen to coincide with the characteristics of an 'ideal' old age outlined by Erikson (1965) (see page 40–42), concerned with identity and generativity. The life review can help to address the problems of the place of older people within existing social life. As both personal acquaintances and known physical landmarks disappear, and their personal role and integration with society declines, older people experience a reducing familiarity with current social organization. Their experience becomes increasingly alienated from the life they have known and loved. The life review can provide a means of re-establishing and confirming individual involvement with current reality, and linking their past work and efforts with the social change that has occurred, for in a variety of subtle ways they will have been part of the changes and developments that they are witnessing.

PART 2

The employment of counselling skills in the problems of old age

CHAPTER 12

Introduction

The subject matters dealt with in Part 2 are artificially separated. It is unlikely that the older counsellee will experience difficulties in just one and not other areas. Indeed, problems in one area are likely to lead to difficulties in another. Similarly, solutions to problems in one area will help resolve difficulties in others. Nor can the counsellor set himself the task of dealing exclusively with one area. People and their lives are whole, and need to be considered and treated as such.

The order and the organization of the chapters is sequential, in that they begin with the earlier problems of old age, taking a preventative stance, and move thereafter through to deeper, more pathological experiences of old age. Each begins with a consideration of the nature of the area being discussed on the basis that greater understanding of the nature and origin of the problems of old age, dispelling some of the myths surrounding them, can help the counsellor in his task, and help the counsellee to prevent some of the more avoidable pitfalls of ageing. Particular attention is paid to ageism, and the part counselling can play in combating its effects. Counselling is concerned with maintaining the quality of life of older people for as long as possible. It looks at the ageing process with optimism and hope rather than despair. It does not seek to change physical laws, only to delay them. Neither does it deny the ageing process, or the ultimate destination of life itself.

Part 2 begins with retirement, the time 'old age' is usually thought to start, and the problems that the loss of productive employment brings. Then consideration is given to the importance of maintaining social involvement through keeping up personal relationships in old age. After a special consideration of alcohol and older people, the next four chapters deal with perhaps the most important areas older people face, ill-health, dependence, depression and mental confusion. The unchanging inevitabilities, bereavement and personal death, are recognized in the final two chapters.

Clearly, whatever the problems it is important that they are dealt with as early as possible. It is perhaps too idealistic to suggest that the process of ageing should be dealt with during childhood, but it is certainly during these years that the basis of ageism becomes rooted in us and thereafter affects the way we approach our own old age. Problems which are ignored are generally made worse with time, and consequently take much longer to deal with effectively, and also require more confidence and expertise on the part of the counsellor. However, the counsellor will have to work with older people whose lives have already been deeply affected by the problems of ageing, and this will require all the skills and insight of looking into individual feelings and attitudes already outlined in Part 1.

For counsellors to know the the limits of their competence is clearly important, and calling in specialist help is always something that should be done in good time. But it is also emphasized that professional competence is not something that can or should be taken for granted, and that the intimate knowledge of the carer–counsellor can often be as useful as the most vaunted professional.

CHAPTER 13

Preparation for retirement

Old age is considered by many to begin with retirement. The ability to be 'productive' is a powerful element of individual status within our society; according to our particular scale of values, to work and contribute to the national wealth is the largest single contribution anyone can make to their society. Therefore, retirement constitutes for many people the end of an important element of life.

This has not always been so. Prior to the implementation of state pension schemes at the turn of this century, older workers did not retire. They might often be forced, through declining health and strength, to take on low-paid and unskilled work, but for most people the idea of giving up work was not possible, short of the desire to risk starvation or enter the workhouse. So the concept of retirement is still comparatively new, particularly amongst the poor. In Britain, it has been estimated that 73 % of the male population over 65 were occupied in 1881, but by 1981 this had reduced to only 11 % (Johnson, 1985). Moreover, the International Labour Office has found this to be an international trend (Townsend, 1981).

The reason for this increase in retirement is interesting to ponder. Popularly, it is attributed to social philanthropy, and to successful campaigns to relieve people from the need to work in their old age. They have earned their rest from work. Retirement, in this sense, is considered to be a natural and inevitable period of peace and dignity, fully enabled and recognized by both law and social provision. But there are less philanthropic reasons that can be forwarded for the growth of retirement.

Economic policy and retirement

Despite the seeming social compassion for ageing workers, it is important that the counsellor of retired and retiring people is able to see the reverse side of this apparent concern. One view sees retirement as no more than a form of compulsory unemployment within an economy which can no longer offer full employment. In many subtle ways, retirement is considered an increasing burden upon the rest of society, with retired people joining children in becoming major 'consumers' of resources but who, unlike children, have no future productive value. They are seen increasingly as an economic liability.

Retirement is viewed in two quite distinct ways, with the ascendent viewpoint at any time depending upon the prevailing needs of the national economy. Phillipson (1982) described these two views as they relate specifically to manpower policies.

> One outcome of this process has been the emergence of older people as a reserve of labour. In periods of slump, for example, they may be drawn out of the labour market more quickly than other groups (particularly unskilled and semi-skilled older workers); in periods of labour shortage, the justification for retiring and becoming a 'non-producing consumer' may be questioned as part of a campaign to call back or retain people in the labour force.

This correlation between retirement, idleness and economic liability is particularly damaging to retired people. Old age becomes an economic burden on younger, more productive people.

> In the 1950s, the elderly were described as 'passengers', threatening to pull down the standard of living enjoyed by society as a whole; they were a regressive element, dampening the 'initiative of youth', and playing a conservative role in social and political life. In this period, the elderly experienced the tension of being 'non-productive' in a society which demanded that everyone should work and be productive. (Phillipson, 1982)

The first attitude has been witnessed in the 1930s and during our more recent experience of high unemployment. At these times, the scarcity of employment opportunities has led to the view that older people should give up their jobs in order that younger people can benefit from the experience of work. Demands to bring forward the age of retirement come to the fore; for older people to continue working is seen to be selfish, depriving younger people of opportunity. Different attitudes confront older people; they are seen to be too slow, too set in their work practices, or possessing skills which have become or will become redundant.

This disparity in social attitudes is certainly reflected in the ambivalent feelings held by retired people. Whilst some welcome the opportunity of early retirement, others see it as an unwanted imposition on their lives. Rather than a blessing, retirement becomes a period of crisis, depriving older people of the status and role of work. Clearly the counsellor will come across both attitudes, with retiring people requiring counselling support both when they have to continue working when they would wish to retire, or when they have to stop working when they wish to continue.

Despite these views being diametrically opposed, both exist simultaneously in attitudes to retired people. Either they are doing the work that younger people could and perhaps should be doing; or they are part of a growing population of retired people whose idleness is creating social and financial difficulties for the rest of the productive population. To work is wrong. To retire is wrong. The result is that older people can be attacked from either direction regardless of what they decide to do. Pressure to work and pressure to retire is placed on older people in proportions which can be both confusing and callous. Counselling can play a vital part in helping retired, or retiring, elderly people to cope with the many dilemmas and pressures such attitudes place upon them. Perhaps it is the results of such non-philanthropic attitudes that are more clearly seen than the actual attitudes themselves. Retirement usually brings with it not only the loss of the largest single activity in which people have engaged, but also a massive drop in income, standard of living and social status. Whilst this may appear an extreme and pessimistic view, it is the reality of retirement for many retired people. The more palatable impression of retirement peacefully spent in the warmer climes of retirement homes on the south coast (or now the more exotic coastline of southern France and Spain) is available only to a privileged few. For most people, retirement does not offer such vistas; for many it represents a grinding poverty, and the monotony of a life-style structured by the meagre levels of state pensions. It is groups from such backgrounds that will have the greatest need of counselling.

Dominant social attitudes and individual need

Whilst counselling before and at the point of retirement is becoming more widely practised, these wider aspects are too rarely considered. Yet when it is placed within the wider social and economic context, retirement counselling assumes a breadth and an importance that far transcends the encouragement of useful and meaningful interests and hobbies to fill the 'idle' hours of leisure. Dominant social attitudes towards retirement place the personal needs of older people in a subservient position to the perceived social and economic interests of the wider society, and it is this that causes many older people problems, bringing into question their personal value and worth, and placing them under considerable social stress.

Counselling should place the needs of individuals, their situation, feelings and attitudes, into a position of primacy. The effects of retirement can only be understood on an individual basis, its significance depending upon a personal interpretation of the value and importance of work, and what the individual wants and expects from the rest of his or her life. It is this subjective evaluation that determines whether retirement results in personal satisfaction or emotional stress.

Atchley (1976) proposed that retired individuals have a 'hierarchy of goals' which give rise to their expectations, their behaviour and their sense of well-being. When the achievement of these goals is frustrated, for whatever reason, individuals have to make one of several choices. Either they can maintain their expectations and seek new ways of meeting them. Or they can modify or substitute new goals which are more readily obtainable. The third outcome is to fail to reconcile the discrepancy between personal goals and achievement, and it is often this failure which leads to retirement becoming a problem.

The role of the counsellor is to help the individual in this process, first in understanding and determining his or her particular goals, making sure they are realistic or indeed, sufficiently ambitious; second, to help decide how best they can be achieved; and third, to help the individual come to terms with retirement, and to play a more active part in its outcome. Only if this is done will older people be able to make choices and reach decisions about retirement which are appropriate to them, and which they can thereafter justify both to themselves and their social critics.

The social impact of retirement

However and wherever retirement counselling is undertaken, these wider implications of retirement, brought about largely by dominant social attitudes, cannot be ignored. Indeed they should feature strongly in any retirement counselling programme. It is the failure to do so that often makes such programmes both unrealistic and ineffective to participants both during and certainly after the event.

The development of retirement counselling in recent years has arisen from the significant numbers of retiring people who soon encounter severe personal problems. This can happen even to those who have a positive attitude towards their retirement years. The losses involved in retirement are often either not foreseen, or not recognized as a problem. The experience often leads to depression and serious illness; indeed many people die shortly after retiring. It is important to be aware of the various hazards of retirement so it can be understood and interpreted in terms of the individual's own feelings and priorities in life.

Despite this, the problems of retirement should be kept in perspective. Recent analysis of the impact of retirement on personal adjustment suggests that it is less aversive than many have assumed. Braithwaite and Gibson (1987), reviewing the literature, came to the conclusion that the belief that retirement was a major crisis of old age was not substantiated. This suggests that many older people will experience few problems as the result of retirement. But some will, and it is at such times that counselling can play an important role.

1. The loss of activity

Work will have usually occupied a considerable part of an individual's life prior to retirement. The need to work for a living is widely recognized, but the necessity to do so may have often been bitterly resented by many people over the years. This is particularly so for those involved in repetitive, unskilled manual labour. Evenings, weekends and holidays would have become the 'highlights' of life, much treasured but all too brief. The prospect of retirement appears to offer the 'highlights' of life on a permanent basis, and, at least from a distance, this can seem very alluring.

Yet even those people who have regarded work purely as an economic activity will discover that the workplace, and/or work itself, has become a central feature of their lives. Even the most monotonous work will have occupied the mind and body for long periods of the day. Travel to and from work may have been combined with other activities, or with a knowledge of other activities going on around them. Lack of thought about what is going to replace all this is a common mistake.

The problem is worse for people who have not used their spare, non-work time for 'constructive' purposes. Constructive activity can be considered as that which provides the individual with an interest. It usually has a definite purpose and a particular or planned outcome. Its successful pursuit will usually lead to a sense of personal fulfillment or pride. Often, and particularly with those individuals who have spent long hours in heavy manual labour, there has perhaps not been the time or energy to develop such interests or hobbies. More passive, less constructive activity with little or no end result, will have been the norm, like watching television or having a pint at the local pub. Such pursuits might be sufficient for short periods, but by their very nature are an inherently inadequate base for full-time retirement.

The result is that retired people too often become bored, dissatisfied and unfulfilled. They begin to look back rather than construct a future for themselves. Perhaps work was not so bad after all. Instead of seeking to replace work with constructive leisure, its loss becomes the subject of 'grief', made worse when the individual comes into contact with the retirement-idleness attitude within social life.

Alternative activity is an important factor in successful adaptation to retirement, and whilst counselling does not have a direct role in its provision, it should encourage the individual to seek it.

2. *The loss of social companionship*

The place of work also provides us with a base for social interaction. Working people probably spend more time in the company of their workmates than with their marriage partners, and almost certainly more than with other friends and relatives. Most work situations provide people with a social network that is often taken entirely for granted, and which is missed only after retirement.

Companionship at work for many people is the most important single source of new friendships. This becomes more important with increasing age, when people can expect to lose long-standing friends at an ever-increasing rate. Retirement combines these two aspects of companionship, on the one hand an increasing rate of loss, and on the other, less social opportunity to replace them through the place of work.

3. *Loss of income*

Whereas the counsellor can hope to point retired people towards new activities and new sources of friendship, the loss of income associated with retirement is a matter over which counselling can have little direct influence. Old age and retirement have been associated with poverty throughout history. Despite the political rhetoric of the modern welfare state, which has created popular images to the contrary, the reality is that the basic state retirement pension continues to provide an income between a third and a half of average earnings. Rates are fixed according to officially designated subsistence needs which are much lower than net earnings during the period of paid employment. The result is that poverty and retirement are usually close allies. Townsend (1979) found that the risks of poverty were highest amongst older people, particularly those over 75 years. Whilst social provision allows retired people to exist, there is little scope for them to grow or make full use of their later years.

The reality that many pensioners face is concerned with basic life-choices, such as choosing whether to spend their money on food or heating. The absence of any prospect of being able to do more than survive on the finances available to them can be deeply depressing. Those who live on basic pensions have little spare cash for the continuation or commencement of the leisure activities or social contacts discussed above. For most pensioners their income excludes any social involvement which depends upon a significant level of expenditure.

4. Health and retirement

Unemployment makes many people very unhappy, and has been found to have serious effects on both mental and physical health. Depression and suicide are not uncommon. Argyle (1987) concluded that the effects were worst for people who were committed to the work ethic. Braithwaite and Gibson (1987) found that good health is one of the strongest factors correlated with the ease of adjustment to retirement. Good health increases good adjustment to retirement, and enables the individual to take advantage of the opportunities it provides. Conversely, good adjustment is more likely to ensure the maintenance of health during retirement. The contrary also applies. The failure to adjust to retirement can form the background to future poor health, and many other age-related problems. This indicates that if the possible hazards of retirement are not adequately discussed, the seeds of ill-health, depression and other problems can be sown.

5. The maintenance of social integration

The counsellor has to avoid the simplistic but often convenient idea that older people withdraw from social activities and friendships because they no longer want them, or because withdrawal is inherently part of the nature of old age. Often, withdrawal is a straightforward but tragic response of older people to their inability to finance social integration. Moreover, this enforced withdrawal from social integration can quickly cause the kind of demoralization so often associated with old age. The economic difficulties of older people are probably a far stronger cause of demoralization than other factors more closely associated with elderly morale, such as illness and pain.

6. Retirement and gender

There is a popular assumption that it is men rather than women who feel the full effects of retirement. Even Simone de Beauvoir (1972) suggests this when she wrote:

> ... the elderly woman adapts herself to her stage better than her husband. She is the person who runs the home, and in this her position is the same as that of the peasants and craftsmen of former times – for her, too, work and life merge into one another. No decree from without suddenly cuts her activity short. It does grow less from the time her grown-up children leave the home and this crisis, which often happens quite early in life, often disturbs her very badly; but still she does not see herself thrown into total idleness and her role of grandmother brings her fresh possibilities.

If such an assessment of the impact of retirement on women can be made by such an eminent female writer, it is perhaps not unnatural that the idea is very much part of our dominant social attitudes. Yet women have been part of the world of paid employment for many years. Indeed, poorer working women have never been able to leave it. More recent changes in female employment, and the increasing 'liberation' of women from a life centred entirely around the home and the family, will make such an assessment increasingly outdated. It is entirely wrong to assume that older women, who have been involved in employment during their lives, should experience retirement as any more or less significant than it is for older men.

7. Retirement and social class

The different access that people from different social class origins have to resources in retirement is a major determinant of who can and who cannot provide for themselves in old age. Professional, managerial and skilled workers will have had many advantages over semi-skilled and manual workers. As already mentioned, it is likely that their life-styles will have involved more constructive and fulfilling leisure activities. They are also likely to have more savings, extra pensions and insurance income which will enable them to maintain their life-style, their status and to pursue their interests without as much regard to cost. And they are also likely to be healthier in old age, and have better access to good diet and medical assistance.

Post-retirement counselling

The counsellor will meet problems associated with retirement at many different stages. Clearly it is better if some consideration is given to the potential hazards of retirement prior to the event. Pre-retirement courses are becoming more common, organized by such bodies as the Pre-Retirement Association and the Workers Educational Association in conjunction with employers. Phased retirement schemes are also now making a small, but important contribution. People approaching retirement should be aware of the possibilities of putting pressure on their employers to provide such courses for their staff in association with these bodies.

However, the majority of people will still retire without any formal support, and it is likely that the counsellor will be involved with those who are experiencing problems in the post-retirement period. The task at this stage will be to ascertain the feelings and problems which exist on an individual level, and to discuss them. This may involve dealing with depression, disappointment and many other feelings that have arisen since retirement. It may be necessary to get the individual to look at alternative ways of approaching and coping with the circumstances of life without work, perhaps trying to 'wipe the slate clean' and start the process all over again, but with an increased awareness of the problems and difficulties that are involved.

Counselling should seek to present a positive view of retirement, but one which stresses the need for individual commitment and effort. Too often retired people will say that retirement did not turn out to be as they had expected. Often this arises from the absence of any realistic concept of the practical implications of retirement. Most people recognize the negatives; that it represents the end of work, the end of paid employment, the end of having to rise early from bed. Many retired people expect to slow down, expect their health to deteriorate; in fact, their expectations are so low they do little to make their lives full and interesting.

Retirement should be seen as the start of a new phase of life, not just the end of an old one. The opportunities available to retired people should be stressed, particularly in the context of the need to maintain personal commitment, involvement and activity. Weir (in Phillipson *et al.*, 1986) distinguishes between *reassurance*, warning against 'the bland, cosy suggestion that our troubles are all illusory and will melt away with little or no intervention on our part', and *encouragement* in dealing with retired people. Counselling has to be rooted in practical reality, with the dangers and opportunities of retirement being presented side by side, and with the understanding that personal decision and volition will determine a large part of the eventual outcome.

CHAPTER 14

The maintenance of personal relationships

Human life is gregarious, the quality of our lives depending to no small degree upon the relationships we have with other people. Social relationships are a major source of happiness, particularly those which come from marriages which are close, confiding and supportive. No individual has the ability to live totally without other people. Solitary confinement is recognized to be one of the most psychologically damaging punishments that can be imposed upon any individual and if, like Robinson Crusoe, we are subjected to an enforced exile, whilst some people will no doubt cope better than others, few will willingly choose isolation or loneliness as a favoured way of life.

Attachment theory

The need for humans to make strong social and emotional attachments to other people is strong. Bowlby (1980) describes attachment behaviour as that which seeks to maintain strong affectional bonds. This arises from strong and ongoing security and safety needs, and not just to fulfil certain biological needs such as food and sex, as others, such as Lorenz, have suggested. Attachment behaviour develops in childhood and endures throughout life, usually directed towards a few specific individuals. The presence of an attachment figure is considered to be vital to the emotional and social survival of the individual, and when attachments are threatened or removed in any way it can lead to intense forms of attachment behaviour, such as clinging, crying and extreme grief.

Yet old age within modern society appears to be closely associated with an increased experience of isolation. Everywhere older people can be seen living alone and, in many cases, apparently suffering the recognizable effects of solitary confinement – apathy, depression and ultimately self-neglect. At certain times, such as periods of festivity or spells of excessively cold weather, this is recognized as a problem. However, it is increasingly accepted as 'the norm', something that older people have to expect, a 'natural' element in the process of growing old. What is more, current social work and health policy seeks to move away from institutionalized forms of care provided by elderly persons' homes and hospitals, concentrating instead on maintaining ageing people within their own homes. Whilst these 'community care' policies are soundly based on principles which seek to maintain elderly independence, they can also lead to, and exacerbate, social isolation.

Aspects of social organization have contributed to the increasing isolation of older people. The decline of the extended family network, and its replacement by smaller 'nuclear' family groups, has meant that valuable networks of support and care have to a considerable extent disappeared. Moreover, traditional family networks not only offered the elderly relative a place, but one which gave them an important and respected role within the family group. The rise of the nuclear family has created an expectation and desire for independence and privacy by younger members of the family, often quite separate from former family ties, and this can often leave little room for the care of older relatives. However, whilst it is important to recognize this trend, we should not forget that the family unit still performs most of the caring functions for the majority of older people in modern society.

The change in family organization has been structurally confirmed by the size and design of modern housing. Homes are now small, compact and designed principally for two adults and their children. There is often no provision made, or considered adequate for elderly relatives without causing gross inconvenience to all parties. Such inconvenience pre-disposes young and old alike to decline both the offer and acceptance of joint occupancy.

Increased social mobility has further added to the isolation of older people. Not only do children live in separate houses, they often move many miles from their parents in order to follow work or careers, and the mutual support they could formerly give each other has been accordingly diminished.

Whilst not wishing to create visions of the past as a 'Golden Age' (it was certainly not), it cannot be denied that the main social trends in family organization, particularly since the Industrial Revolution, have increasingly served to isolate ageing people. This has led to feelings of abandonment in older people, and of considerable guilt in younger relatives. In turn this has resulted in the need to develop explanations to justify why younger people have ceased looking after the needs of their elderly relatives.

The theory of disengagement

The loneliness many older people experience has been given respectability by certain social theories which either seek to give, or are interpreted as, an explanation for the isolation of older people. The theory of 'disengagement' promulgated by Cummings and Henry (1961) has been popularly received in this way. Disengagement is explained as the process by which older people gradually relinquish roles and activity within their society. It arose from observations of old people who appeared to welcome and initiate increasing isolation as a release from the problems, pressures and difficulties of life. Cummings and Henry interpreted this as a 'natural' process arising from the individual's loss of skill, energy and determination in coping with the pressures of mainstream social life. Through disengagement, elderly people are believed to transfer their remaining time and energy to matters more restful and congenial – to reflection, reminiscence and rest.

These explanations and justifications for the loneliness and isolation of older people are socially attractive and emotionally convenient for those who feel some guilt about their situation. Far from seeing the loss of elderly social roles and status as 'a problem', the theory presents it as a necessary social and psychological mechanism. Disengagement is not something that should be avoided, but is part of the natural process of ageing which can be readily accepted. The theory provides the younger relative with a convenient explanation for any guilt they may feel about their role with ageing relatives. Rather than recognizing our feelings there is a tendency to submerge them beneath suitably comfortable ideas about the nature of old age, such as   older relatives' diminishing needs, lower expectations and contentment with the loneliness and idleness of their lives.

The problem with disengagement theory is that it fails to ask whether such observable characteristics of older people are attributable, at least in part, to cultural expectations. Is withdrawal initiated by the individuals, and their needs? Or do the institutions of retirement, the social norms of limited activity and poverty, and expectations of ill-health and disability suggest to ageing people that they are expected to do so?

Certainly, older people learn to play the game according to the dominant social rules. They do not wish to make demands. They do not want to be heard to complain. They do not want to put pressure on younger relatives who, after all, have their own lives to lead. Some disengagement is clearly socially enforced, for example, when older people are obliged to retire from work against their wishes. Yet there are more subtle factors. Dominant social attitudes play a large part in suggesting to older people that 'disengagement' is what is expected of them – and ultimately it becomes what they themselves expect from old age. To a considerable extent, older people have learnt to respond appropriately to the dominant social expectations of old age, but often entirely inappropriately to their own feelings and needs. Whilst for some the experience of ageing does bring with it a degree of social disengagement, it is far from being a 'natural' or inevitable event.

Disengagement is just one of many social theories which underlie what Phillipson and Walker (1986) call 'Acquiescent Functionalism' – 'a body of thought about ageing which attributes the causes of most of the problems of old people to the natural consequences of physical decrescence and mental inflexibility or the failures of individual adjustment to ageing and retirement, instead of to contemporary developments of the state, the economy and social inequality'. These factors are dismissed as inevitable or unalterable, or not considered at all. But they make an important contribution to the problems of many older people.

The counsellor's task is to try to unravel these separate strands of cultural norms, social theory and individual need, and to discover the real feelings and needs of the older individual. In doing so, the counsellor has to be careful not to be beguiled into believing the more comfortable initial reactions that many older people might present. The counsellor should seek to question the assumptions made about elderly withdrawal by both the older individuals and their carers. If such assumptions are correct, if ageing is an inevitable period of withdrawal from the social process, why should we intervene? Such theories lead logically to leaving older people alone rather than attempting to improve the quality of their lives through continued social engagement.

The focus of counselling with older people should be to encourage continued engagement in the processes of socialization. Old age generally involves the loss of two crucial social roles, highly regarded by dominant social values, and it is essentially the loss of these valued roles which associates increasing age with diminished social status and prestige, and with disengagement. These are the loss of the productive, or work role considered in the previous chapter, and the loss of the nurturing, or parenting role.

The loss of the parental role

The loss of the parental role is of crucial importance in understanding the life and problems of many older people. The crisis that many married couples face when their last child leaves home is well known. For many people, much of the previous 20 to 30 years has been closely associated with the issues and problems of bringing up their children. The growing independence of their children, at each successive stage, can be a matter of concern rather than joy for those who over-commit and over-identify their lives with the nurturing of dependent children. When the children are gone, and no longer require parental help and support, how is their time to be filled? And what of the marital relationship, how much meaning and importance does this still have for the partners? A new life, with new relationships, has often to be found if this new stage of personal development is not to seem meaningless and empty. Many fail to make such a transition, and become embittered by their apparent abandonment by their children. Many relationships begin to fail at this stage, and are often allowed to do so by default because the difficulties of living through this stage of life are insufficiently understood.

Counselling help and support at this stage can be vital to the way that individuals learn to face up to their lives as post-generation parents. The counsellor can perform two functions; first, to help former parents accept and come to terms with their new situation, and second, to encourage them to fill their lives where necessary by developing different interests and pursuits. The end of parenting is usually the first shedding of an important social role, and if a successful redirection in life can be achieved at this point, many of the problems and difficulties of later adjustments to old age can be more successfully faced. The transition will demonstrate to individuals the importance and value of periodic re-direction in their lives. It will help to make them more aware of their own personal needs, and the importance of dealing with those needs as former roles and responsibilities are shed.

However, this opportunity is often missed. The end of the parenting role rarely corresponds with what we consider to be 'old age', or even an age when people require any particular help. Indeed, the loss of the parenting role is often something that is noticed only by the parents themselves. Other people are as likely to assume, and indeed make jokes about, how lucky they are to have so much spare time on their hands without the problems and responsibilities of children. Unlike the problems which surround retirement from work, the loss of the parental role has not been widely discussed as a social issue, and certainly not in terms of the problems and difficulties it might bring in its wake.

Perhaps it is true that 'life begins at 40' (or 50) for those who recognize the opportunities available to them after parenting ceases, and are prepared to take advantage of them. If this is not the case, then opportunities are not only missed, but advancing years can be seen as synonymous with increasing loss, increasing isolation and increasing boredom. This is often the life-attitude more obviously held by many older people who are in need of counselling support. They see their lives as becoming progressively more empty and meaningless, and this essentially pessimistic outlook on their lives is reflected in all that they do, or perhaps more accurately, in all that they fail to do.

The loss of social involvement

Many older people will have failed to develop and maintain an adequate network of friends and social activities. The origins of this failure may go back to early parenthood. When young children have to be looked after it reduces the opportunities that parents have to take part in the social round. Visits to the places where they once met their friends decline. Friends also have children so they no longer attend. Social groups are thereby disbanded, and they are not necessarily reconstituted in other forms, or replaced by other groups. The greater part of social life is involved with child-minding, in all its many forms, and staying within the family home. There is nothing intrinsically wrong with this, but with life revolving almost exclusively around young children the potential for later social isolation is obvious.

More often than not, social disengagement will not have been intentional, and certainly not brought about simply by the process of ageing, but rather by a failure to maintain an adequate level of social life beyond that of being parents. After many years, when children no longer need the same amount of time and attention from their parents, many find that their lives are no longer full of interesting social contacts and experiences. They will have failed to maintain an adequate level of expectation about what life can be as non-parents. This pessimism is only confirmed by many dominant social attitudes about the crucial importance of the parenting role, particularly for the mother. Add to this the pessimism and fear of becoming old, and the result is too often that many older people can become non-participating social individuals, who feel increasingly isolated and cut off from all that is happening around them.

The counsellor has to discover to what extent these feelings are present within the individual, at what point such feelings have arisen in his life, and to persuade him to re-consider his real needs and feelings, as opposed to socially induced attitudes about the quality and extent of his involvement in social life.

The decline of the marital relationship

The marital relationship always undergoes considerable strain with the arrival of children. The once exclusive partnership has to be shared, and this sharing can often unbalance even the closest of relationships. Marriages are increasingly breaking up at or soon after this point. Within some relationships, the two partners can begin to move in opposite directions. The husband can feel abandoned, and expend more of his time and energy in his work. It is quite common for the husband to assume that being the 'bread-winner' is his main or only contribution to family life. However, this attitude can also represent a response to feelings of rejection by his wife who now has other things to occupy her, or an unwillingness to play a full part in the parental role. The new mother will often throw herself into motherhood so fully that she forgets to give time to the marital relationship, which can suffer considerable damage as a result.

By the time the children have grown up, the marital relationship can be very empty, often extending little further than sharing the same house. When the children leave home the problems of re-adjustment are considerable. It is certainly not uncommon for counsellors of older people to find marriages which have followed this broad pattern of decline. Rather than being long-standing relationships which have been strong enough to stand 'the test of time', as we often assume, they are little more than empty shells which are no longer of any significant mutual support or value. Often, partners can be depressed by the disinterest that each shows towards the other, and this indicates that such marriages have lost the ability to meet the needs of the individual for companionship.

Sexual relationships

The myth of declining sexual potency and need with increasing age is now being actively questioned. Research indicates that ageing people continue to be sexually active, and that age itself does not undermine either the need or the capacity for sexual activity. (See, for example, Thienhaus *et al*, 1986.) When sexual response in older people is reduced it has more to do with social factors such as the absence of a partner; health problems, particularly relating to cardiovascular disease, diabetes, multiple sclerosis and prostrate troubles; drug side-effects (many drugs prescribed to older people can have adverse effects on sexual functioning); and the intolerance of social attitudes towards sexual activity in older people, which consider sex to be the province of younger people and that older people make rather ridiculous lovers.

Masters and Johnson (1966) found that, apart from these social factors, there was no age limit for the enjoyment of and participation in sexual activity. As far as women were concerned, they found that there was no significant loss in their capacity to enjoy sexual intercourse. Yet women have very particular problems, with which the counsellor might have to contend. The menopause is an experience which causes many women considerable anxiety. Many of these anxieties arise because women do not understand and cannot control the physical changes which they experience at this time. This has been reinforced by the idea that the menopause is a 'deficiency disease', indicated by the reduced level of oestrogen in the body. This view, in its more extreme form, has described post-menopausal women as 'castrates' (see Wilson and Wilson, 1963). Small wonder that women worry about the menopause, and that their anxiety is then influenced by social factors such as attitudes about the sexual attractiveness of their ageing bodies, the changing status and role of women as children leave home, and the risk of loneliness and poverty if their marriages should fail as a result. The prevailing view, however, is less extreme, seeing the menopause as a natural life event, and that the problems women experience in middle age stem from external social causes.

> These causes include role strain or loss, devaluation associated with the loss of stereotypical sexual-youthful attractiveness and reproductive capability, economic disadvantage, or medical exploitation. The

> menopause may be a marker event, signalling to women that their social
> desirability is terminating. (Berkun, 1986)

Women suffer from male-dominated ideas about sexual attractiveness,
being brought up to conform to the idea that they should be sexually attractive
to men, and that sexual attractiveness is associated with the youthful, attractive bodies of the pin-up. Women lose this image of attractiveness with ageing,
a process that men do not experience to the same degree.

But men are not entirely without their problems. Masters and Johnson
(1966) investigated the causes of impotence in older men, and found that it is
caused as much by anxiety about possible physiological change as by the
ageing process itself.

> The fear of performance reflecting cultural stigmas directed toward
> erective inadequacy was that associated with problems of secondary
> impotence. These fears were expressed, under interrogation, by every
> male study subject beyond 40 years of age . . . Regardless of whether the
> individual male study subject had ever experienced an instance of
> erective difficulty, the probability that secondary impotence was asso-
> ciated directly with the ageing process was vocalised constantly. The
> fallacy that secondary impotence is to be expected as the male ages
> is probably more firmly entrenched in our culture than any other
> misapprehension.

This would indicate that the expectation of impotence in old age can play an
important role in actually bringing it about.

The disassociation of sexual activity from old age, despite these modern
advances in our understanding, is still strong. Dominant social ideology,
reinforced by traditional Christian teaching, makes the assumption that sex is
primarily for procreation and not recreation, and this places sex outside the
moral boundaries of many older people, for whom there is still a strong and
widely held link between sex and immorality, the belief that sex is wrong or
indecent. Closely connected with this is the idea that sexual activity and love
are concerned with youth, and that it is somehow undesirable, or even an
object of mild amusement, for ageing people to indulge. Such attitudes can
prevent older people fulfilling their sexual needs. When marital relationships
have declined, or have been lost altogether it becomes far easier for older
people to suppress their sexual needs, to feel that they are unnatural and
unwanted. Sex can therefore remain a personal need, but the difficulties of
fulfilling that need can lead to the acceptance of dominant ideas about the
unacceptability of sex in old age. This attitude can lead to older people
believing that they cannot seek advice about their sexual needs and feelings.

Older people often give up sexual intercourse because it has become painful. The rate and amount of vaginal lubrication does decrease with age. Where
this is the case, counselling can offer simple advice, such as the use of lubri-
cating jellies. Yet, sex is more than the act of sexual intercourse and penal

penetration. It is close physical contact with another individual, involving touching, stroking and caressing, and mutual stimulation using both hands and mouth. Sex therefore is ideally suited to fulfill the human need for close body contact. Even physical disabilities caused by illnesses such as strokes and arthritis need not signal the end of sexual activity of this kind. Indeed, much depression in older people, which is at the root of many illnesses, can be caused by the lack of this essential physical contact. Perhaps we have again mistaken cause and effect in the nature of old age. Even without a sexual partner other forms of sexual fulfillment can be found. Masturbation can be a source of considerable pleasure, once it is removed from traditional ideas about immorality, and its adverse effects on health. It can help to relieve sexual tension when there is no other way this can be done.

Counselling can play an important role in enabling full and frank discussion of sexual matters. Sex is a taboo subject for both young and old, and many of the restrictive and repressive attitudes might have to be overcome by both counsellor and counsellee. Certainly, the counsellor should be able to discuss sensitively such topics as sexual feelings and need, masturbation, oral sex, etc., whenever it is relevant or necessary to do so.

Several tasks have to be undertaken. The first is to ascertain whether the individual wishes to talk about sexual activity. This can often be difficult to determine as attitudes towards openly discussing sexual matters have changed only in very recent times. This may make it difficult for the counsellor to know whether, and to what extent, to pursue the issue. Failure to talk about sexual needs may mean that the individual does not consider it to be a problem, or that he or she finds it embarrassing to discuss such matters. Sex may not be a topic which the individual wants to discuss, and this feeling clearly has to be respected. Many older people have never had a satisfactory sexual relationship, for a variety of reasons, and if this is so there is no reason to believe that the period of old age is likely to see new beginnings in this respect. Moreover, many older people may feel too embarrassed or morally outraged to discuss the subject, especially with younger people, and if so, the subject is often best left alone. Certainly, there would need to be sound reasons to pursue it under such circumstances.

When sexual matters are discussed, there may be a need to talk about feelings of shame and guilt. What is 'normal' and what is 'abnormal' sexual behaviour in older couples, or for individuals living alone, may be important issues. Developing an understanding of sexual need lies at the heart of the counselling process. Many ageing people need to understand and accept the changes in their sexuality in order to continue enjoying it to the full. This is where counsellors can often take the opportunity of expressing some of their own thoughts, feelings and experiences as a means of legitimizing the subject for discussion.

Talking with their age peers may also be important, and small group counselling can be a useful means of both enabling elderly people to realize that their sexual needs are not unusual, and putting them into contact with others who may have similar or even corresponding needs. The maintenance of social relationships is a crucial element in counselling. If older people can maintain reasonable social involvement, with satisfying contacts with other people, the quality of their life-styles can remain as fulfilling as at any other stage of their lives.

CHAPTER 15

Counselling and health

The concept of health used in this chapter is not the narrow medicalized term meaning merely the absence of disease. Good health is as much to do with being in good spirits, being happy and content, coping with the problems and difficulties of life, but enjoying life to the fullest extent possible. So it is used here in the wider sense defined by the World Health Organization as a 'complete physical, mental and social well-being and not merely the absence of disease or infirmity'. It has often been observed that, whilst old age is not an illness, it does bring with it an increased susceptibility to illness and disease. Yet because the old are seen to be more ill, more often than other age groups, illness and old age have become closely associated in our minds, leading to the belief that the old have to suffer and bear an unavoidable amount of pain and discomfort. In turn, this can lead to an acceptance of physical ill-health that would not be tolerated by younger people.

Knowledge and the maintenance of health

Alongside income and social relationships, health is one of the three issues older people consider to be the most important in their lives (DHSS, 1983). Yet, the medicalization of health within our society has left people generally unaware of what they can do to maintain their own health. Moreover, conventional medicine has concentrated mainly on the treatment of chronic and acute illness, and until recent years the role of preventive medicine has suffered comparative neglect.

Older people are probably the largest consumer group of health provision, yet they are generally less informed about matters relating to their own health, and more deferential to medical authorities than any other group. Gray (1982) has indicated that programmes of health education amongst older people 'can make a significant contribution to the promotion of a healthy life'. A Pensioners Link initiative in Barnet (Meade, 1986) has undertaken a local campaign to promote health activity for and with older people, with promising results. It came to four main conclusions. First, that health education sessions with older people had a significant impact on them. Second, it highlighted the importance of active participation by elderly people themselves in all aspects of course planning. Third, it pointed to the necessity for critical preventive work to be recognized as a priority. And fourth, it recognized the need to challenge the traditional patterns of health education, with one-off talks on broad topics to groups of older people.

These findings indicate something of the importance of counselling in the health of older people, and this chapter outlines the way this might be achieved. The prevention of ill-health, and to some extent the treatment of existing health problems, could improve if older people had more accurate and relevant information about the factors which contribute to good health.

Health and ageism

The general health of older people might be improved if they were able to rid themselves of the many ageist attitudes that surround the issue, and were able to feel more positive about their health prospects. The attitude that 'you must expect this at your age' is something that is heard all too often. Counselling should challenge such attitudes by encouraging older people to examine the myths that 'elderly ailments' are inevitable. Gray (1982) states that the 'good news' about old age is that most enjoy a healthy life, untroubled by incontinence, dementia and other disorders that receive so much publicity. It is nearly always possible to treat the diseases and disabilities that older people experience. There is no reason why anyone should assume that disease in old age is untreatable, although we often do.

It is sometimes difficult to differentiate between illness and natural ageing processes. This often provides the excuse for ageism, it being simpler to assume that the problem is old age rather than a treatable condition. One significant difference is when an 'illness' has a starting date, or when the decline in energy or function can be pinpointed to a particular time. If so, it is more likely to be disease rather than old age. Chronic illness develops slowly. Decline due to ageing is nearly always imperceptible, noted only when comparing present ability with that of many years past.

Ageist assumptions connecting old age with ill-health can often arise from the extreme social isolation and withdrawal experienced by many older people, the self-neglect that this can cause, and the illness that then arises from this neglect.

This chapter does not ask counsellors to pretend to be doctors, but to question whether ill-health is not more concerned with social/emotional factors, such as poor diet and lack of fitness, than with normal ageing. The prevention of ill-health and the successful treatment of chronic and acute illness in older people could result if they felt more positive about their potential for good health in old age, and had access to relevant information.

Health and mental attitude

There is a strong connection between health and mental attitude. This has been demonstrated in conventional medical circles in the study of psychosomatic illness and the placebo effect, and in certain alternative medical practices such as faith healing and yoga. Argyle (1987) concluded that health is linked with happiness by preserving the immune system and encouraging good health habits. Martin (1987) suggests a link between psychology and the immune system, based on the idea 'that the brain influences the immune system and, therefore, our resistance to disease'. He discovered that many studies had found small but statistically significant correlations between life events which had forced individuals to alter their life-style, such as bereavement, loss of job, etc., and the frequency, severity and duration of illness. All this indicates that a positive mental attitude is as important to good health as a negative or resigned attitude is to illness and disease. The links between the mind and health are not yet fully understood but there is sufficient evidence to suggest that physical illness is not a straightforward matter of bodily components breaking down or wearing out. If we expect to be ill, the likelihood is that we will be.

Yet to acknowledge this is to recognize that our health is under our own personal control to an extent far greater than is currently accepted. Given the ageism that abounds within our medicalized social attitudes, this is an understanding of crucial importance. It suggests that matters of health should not be left entirely in the hands of the medical professionals, particularly if they share and perpetuate the dominant belief that good health is purely a 'mechanical' process which can be remedied by drugs and surgery. The counsellor can clearly play an important part in challenging ageist assumptions about health, and in promoting more positive but realistic states of mind. In particular, the counsellor can counter the belief that pain and illness are the natural and unavoidable consequences of growing old.

Older people can quickly become dispirited and depressed by chronic illness. When they can see no end to it they begin to assume that their condition is ongoing and immutable. This serves only to confirm and reinforce the illness. It is important for older people to look more positively at their physical condition and, whilst accepting the reality of it, resist feelings about the hopelessness of recovery, or the inevitability of further decline. It is too easy to become resigned to what we feel to be inevitable. Even stroke victims have some mobility so the message should be to use it, exercise it, find new and interesting things to do and try to get back as much mobility as possible. Don't give up.

Good health is a combination of many factors, most of which reside within the individual. Helping the older individual deal with such matters is therefore within the competence of the counsellor. Social factors, such as the experience of loss, bereavement, depression, social isolation, lack of exercise and poor diet, can determine the way they think of themselves, their expectations of life, and ultimately their health. Where counselling is able to discuss some of these feelings it can have a more positive potential effect on elderly health than the tranquillizers and sedatives which are too readily and too frequently dispensed for older people who are sick.

Health, exercise and fitness

Lack of fitness results from not keeping our muscles, organs and joints working. Disease and lack of fitness are closely related – disease causes lack of exercise, but more importantly, lack of exercise increases susceptibility to disease. Moreover, joints become stiff, muscles become weak and organs become progressively more inefficient.

Fitness arises from regular exercise. This does not mean embarking on extremely vigorous pursuits, although people in their 70s and 80s still run marathons! Walking, swimming, gardening and even general housework are all good exercise. It is quite sufficient to do a little exercise, often. What is important is to become breathless, to raise the heartbeat, to stretch all parts of the body. There are three aspects of fitness. Stamina relates to the efficiency of the heart and lungs and their ability to sustain effort without becoming tired and breathless. Strength is concerned with the muscles and their ability to lift, move and carry. Suppleness is concerned with the muscles, ligaments and tendons and their capacity to allow freedom of movement. All are important elements of life in old age, and in maintaining both independence and freedom from ill-health, yet older people often avoid taking exercise because of the widespread ageist assumption that it is dangerous for them to be too active. To take light exercise is not usually dangerous, but if anyone is uncertain it might be wise to consult a doctor.

The importance of good nutrition

Good nutrition is a vital factor in good health, but is often a neglected area in the care of older people, especially those who live alone on low incomes.

Ageism intervenes here too with the common assumption that older people do not need as much food. Again this has little foundation; the food requirements of elderly people are associated more closely with the level of individual activity than with chronological age.

What is certain is that inadequate diet can lead directly to ill-health. A variety of factors has been associated with nutritional problems in old age (Davies, 1981; DHSS, 1979; Exton-Smith, 1971), and many of these are the legitimate subject of counselling.

Poverty can lead to inadequate diet for a number of reasons, notably an inability to purchase an adequate, balanced diet. Older people who have fewer than eight main meals each week, or who go for long periods of the day without food, are considered to be especially at risk.

Personal neglect, perhaps arising from social isolation, loneliness or depression, can lead to elderly people who cannot be bothered to prepare good food, relying on quick and easy foods, thereby getting an unbalanced diet.

An inadequate knowledge of what constitutes a 'good diet', particularly regarding the essential protein, mineral and vitamin constituents of food, can also contribute to poor diet. The diets of older people will often consist of foods favoured in their younger days, but which are now known to be deleterious to health. Eating the wrong sorts of food, drinking insufficient milk and the virtual absence of fresh fruit and vegetables from the diet are common problems.

Illness is a major cause of loss of appetite, often compounding existing health problems. Clearly, there is a circularity here which is often confused. Poor health does lead to a loss of appetite but, perhaps more importantly, poor eating habits can play a major part in causing ill-health.

Physical disability or mental disturbance can lead to difficulties shopping for food, and in its preparation and cooking. Poor dentition and the absence of teeth can affect both what is eaten and how well it is masticated and absorbed.

Alcoholism, smoking and the side-effects of drugs can all affect both the eating of food and the absorption of nutrients. Smoking, for example, reduces the absorption of vitamin C.

Poor diet and elderly health

It has been found that the intake of nutrients in the diet declines markedly in old age, and whilst it is difficult to determine to what extent this is caused by, or is the cause of, increased physical disease, the connection with elderly health is known to be significant. A fuller consideration of the relationship between nutritional factors and elderly health can be found elsewhere (Davies, 1981). What follows is a consideration of a few vital food elements, outlining their importance to the health of older people, and looking at the effect that dietary deficiency might have on what have hitherto been considered normal factors in the ageing process.

1. Vitamin C deficiency can ultimately lead to scurvy, but in less extreme form can be the cause of listlessness, weakness and a general lack of energy. The body becomes readily subject to bruising, sometimes spontaneously. Wounds heal only slowly. There is greater vulnerability to infection. All these are symptoms of a simple dietary deficiency but often are mistaken for normal ageing processes. Many older people have been found to have low levels of vitamin C, and by increasing the dietary intake the problems can be overcome. Oranges and other citrus fruits and fresh vegetables are a ready source of vitamin C, although it is easily lost in the process of preparation and cooking. Vitamin tablets are also available.

2. Vitamin D assists in transporting calcium to the bones, and a deficiency can cause both muscle weakness and bone disorders. One effect of vitamin D deficiency is a loss of bone density and strength. Again, such disorders can be mistaken for normal ageing, but can be readily rectified by eating liver, eggs and 'fatty' fish, although perhaps the best source is exposure to normal sunlight.

3. Potassium deficiency can also cause muscle weakness, but is perhaps more significantly linked with its effect on the mind, and in particular with both depression and mental confusion. Although most foods contain potassium, especially potatoes and green vegetables, it has been shown that a high proportion of elderly people select a diet low in potassium (Davies, 1981). An additional problem is that some drugs, notably diuretics which are commonly used with older people, cause a loss of potassium.

4. Calcium deficiency can lead to osteoporosis, common in older people, which resembles the loss of bone that appears to be a universal phenomenon of ageing (Exton-Smith, 1971). Calcium is found most abundantly in milk.

The principles of good eating have arisen from many years of evidence and research. There is now a reasonable level of agreement of what constitutes a 'good diet' and this has recently been outlined in the BBC Food and Health Campaign (Tudge, 1986; Rogers, 1986). Foods to be avoided or reduced are those which are high in fat, such as fatty meats, sausages, pies, polyunsaturated margarines and oils; those high in sugar, as in many processed snacks, soft drinks and sweets; and those which have added salt, and other additives used extensively in processed foods. A healthier diet is composed of natural foods, such as vegetables and fruit, lean meat and fish, dairy products which are low in fat such as skimmed or semi-skimmed milk, and those which are high in fibre such as wholemeal bread, brown rice and pasta, and potatoes. Bad diet is now closely connected with most of the main illnesses associated with old age, and attention to these details may be very important.

If dietary deficiency seems to be a factor, the counsellor should be able to help the counsellee ascertain which factors in the diet might be contributing to poor health, perhaps in consultation with the books mentioned above, or with a nutritionist or dietitian. Where this is the case there will be a need to remedy the deficiency as quickly as possible, and thereafter to seek to improve the individual's eating habits by careful discussion and support.

It is important to stress that ill-health in old age is not just the result of physical and mental wear and decline, or that the only effective action is to call for the doctor. Good health resides in areas under more direct personal control, and those with time to investigate such matters as exercise and nutrition may be in a better position than a doctor to arrive at an accurate understanding. Counselling sensitivity and insight can often be of more value than strictly medical knowledge.

Monitoring conventional medical practice

Conventional medical practice is generally held in high esteem by society and the medical profession represents one of the most powerful, high-status bodies in the country. There is no doubt that many older people and their carers will look towards their doctors when illness and poor health intervene. This is probably correct, but conventional medical wisdom need not be accepted entirely at face value. Indeed, in my experience many doctors welcome, and benefit from, the interest and advice other informed people can give about their patients, this often enhancing the accuracy of their diagnosis. Other people can also help by noting the more subtle effects, both beneficial and adverse, of treatment.

Modern medical practice, particularly with older people, has many shortcomings about which the counsellor needs to be aware. Certainly it is not always correct to assume that older people are 'safe' in the hands of medical professionals. There are many reasons for this, outlined here, but given in greater detail elsewhere (Illich, 1977; Thunhurst, 1982; Doyle, 1983). As has been mentioned, medicine has traditionally been more concerned with treatment than prevention. The modern obsession with transplantation takes precedence over finding the causes of organ disease. The effects of stress in modern life-styles, the impact of environmental pollution, the benefits of simple dietary guidelines and the importance of exercise all take second place in terms of status, expenditure and publicity.

Many doctors reflect the ageist attitudes of the society in which they work, feeling that the medical problems of older people are a lower priority than their younger patients. Consequently, they are often more hurried in their diagnosis, more likely to deal with symptoms than the underlying causes, resorting to palliatives rather than cures. In extreme cases of ageist practice, certain forms of treatment might be refused purely on the basis of age, and on a cost-benefit assessment of treatment being 'wasted' on older people with a low life expectancy.

The iatrogenic (or drug-induced) effects of modern medical treatment are well known and understood by the medical profession, but less well known by the general public. Drugs often produce effects far worse than the original problem for which they were prescribed. The side-effects of some drugs regularly used by older people can lead to mental confusion, incontinence, diabetes, loss of mobility and balance, and even death.

The vulnerability of ageing people to iatrogenic desease is greater than with any other age group. They are more likely to be subject to polypharmacy and the harmful interactions of potent drugs. Their reduced renal function makes the build-up of drugs within the body more likely, and their tolerance of high doses lower. Forgetfulness may lead to unintentional self-overdosing. Repeat prescriptions, allied to the low priority given to older patients, can lead to drugs being prescribed for periods which are longer than those recommended as safe. It has been estimated that as many as 10% of old people admitted to hospital are there as a direct result of drugs prescribed by their GP (Age Concern, 1977), and Phillipson (1982) suggests that much over-prescription of drugs is a conscious attempt to control the medical demands on the health service by older people.

Complete reliance upon medical professionals can therefore be dangerous. As with all professions, medical and pharmacological competence cannot and should not be taken for granted, as evidenced by the frequency with which new drugs are introduced and then withdrawn from the market after proving to be harmful, even fatal in continued use.

The counsellor can play an important part in monitoring the quality, effectiveness and possible iatrogenic effects of medical treatment, and can do so without necessarily bringing into question medical authority or competence. However, questioning the medical professional is a difficult and often a daunting task, given their present high social status. Even other professional groups, such as social workers, have traditionally adopted a passive, even a subservient role, more usually limited to obtaining client acceptance of medical decisions, helping clients come to terms with them, and finding meaning and satisfaction with what has led to their current situation and state of health. Yet, the intimate knowledge of the sick individual often places them in an ideal position to link illness with iatrogenesis, and the better doctors will see such insight as a welcome assistance rather than interference, and make full use of it.

This does not suggest that good medical advice and treatment is not often essential. In stressing the social, psychological and nutritional factors which underlie elderly health, it is the dominance and exclusiveness of medical answers that need to be questioned. Moreover, it is the doctor–counsellor as much as anyone else who needs to ask these questions, for often spending time considering these aspects of ill-health might be more helpful than a prescription for drugs.

Links with alternative medical practice

The counsellor can also suggest the intervention of non-conventional or alternative medical practitioners, especially for those problems for which conventional medicine appears to have little or no answer. This is particularly relevant to conditions such as arthritis, to which the traditional medical response is to prescribe pain-killers which, whilst relieving pain temporarily, do not pretend to treat the causes of the disease itself. The subject of alternative medical care for older people has been entirely unexplored. Given the claims that many alternative therapies make for the treatment of 'incurable' conditions, many of which are suffered mainly by older people, it is perhaps time for those responsible for the care of older people to investigate the potential of such treatments as homoeopathy, acupuncture, chiropractic, osteopathy, herbalism and many others.

I have had two experiences in which the mental health problems of older people have been successfully treated by a homeopath. One was suffering from deep depression, the other believed he was beginning to lose control of his mind. Both had conditions to which conventional medical practice had no solution (except for unacceptable levels of drug treatment and ECT), and both showed signs of considerable improvement within a week, the latter recovering control of his mind completely. In situations where there seems to be little acceptable alternative, advice from an alternative practitioner can do little harm, and has potential for considerable good.

The counselling role with sick people

Counselling the ill is more difficult than counselling the well, not least because of their reduced ability to think clearly, to make judgements, to arrive at sound decisions, to determine on a course of action and generally to fight their own battles. Much has been made of the need to question the impact of elderly medical care but it is clear that, unlike other areas of counselling, it is the counsellor who has to do this rather than the counsellee. It is often less appropriate to involve counsellees to the same extent, and the counsellor may have to take more direct action in their interests, much in the way that any friend would do in similar situations. In such circumstances, the counsellor is acting on behalf of the counsellees rather than directly according to their wishes. Wherever possible, however, the counsellor must take into consideration what the counsellees might themselves have wanted had they been sufficiently well to have made the judgement themselves.

Where ill-health is concerned, the counsellor should seek to defend the interests of the individual, and not be subservient to the wishes and dictates of any other authority. The counsellor should become fully acquainted with as much relevant knowledge and information in as many professional spheres as possible, and use that knowledge in an attempt to ensure that the best possible treatment and care for the counsellee is obtained. This is not to set themselves up as nutritionists or as medical experts – but to use the knowledge available to them from every quarter sensibly, and to ensure that others are using their knowledge and expertise in the best interests of the counsellee.

Whilst this might appear to make the counsellor a 'jack-of-all-trades', a more positive interpretation is that the counsellor is in the privileged position of seeing the older individual as a whole or entire person. This holistic outlook is extremely important, and potentially very powerful. The counsellor's task is not just to understand only one facet of the counsellee's life, but to know something about the totality. It enables the counsellor to focus upon the changes brought about by changing diet, medication, or social and psychological circumstance. In this way the various inter-relationships between all the many factors which make up an individual's life can be seen as contributing to that individual's health, or ill-health. This role gives the counsellor a threefold task.

1. The counsellor should seek to assess the various factors which might be contributing to the ill-health of the older individual.
2. The counsellor should discuss the significance of these factors with the counsellee.
3. The counsellor should help the counsellee decide on the most appropriate response to the main factors contributing to ill-health.

In situations where the mental state of older counsellees appears to be important, for example in depression, extreme social loss or grieving, and excessive emotional stress, counselling can be a means of determining the origins of this mental state, and seeking to help the individuals to face and come to terms with their feelings.

Even matters such as immobility may have emotional rather than medical origins. In such cases, illness can leave not only a physical inability to cope, but an emotional fear of doing so. The reluctance to resume walking after a series of falls, or the unwillingness to return home from hospital to an independent life are two examples of this. Counselling can have a direct role in attempting to encourage and renew confidence, both through dialogue and through practical assistance and support. Even conditions such as frailty can be assessed in this way. What is the nature of frailty? Is the loss of body weight the 'natural' consequence of old age? Or is it an illness with nutritional deficiency at its root?

Even with physical illness or disease, the counsellor can play an important part by asking several questions. Is the doctor treating the condition rather than the symptoms? Has the doctor diagnosed accurately or have 'ageist' considerations clouded medical judgement? Is the prescribed medication or treatment safe, and what are the likely side-effects? Is the current illness the consequence of side-effects from medication or treatment prescribed for former illnesses? Are there safer or less extreme treatments which might be more effective? These questions require some knowledge of medical treatments and their potential iatrogenic effects, and it is not the purpose of this book to go into this at any length. A comprehensive outline of drug side-effects is available elsewhere (Blair, 1985; Turner and Volans, 1987; Parish, 1987). You can also ask doctors for an old copy of the British National Formulary, and MIMS which they receive regularly, free of charge.

The aftermath of illness

The emotional and psychological impact of many illnesses, particularly those serious enough to leave the patient weakened or incapacitated, can be enormous. This is particularly so when mobility, speech or hearing have been impaired, perhaps after a serious stroke. Heart failure and illnesses such as pneumonia can be equally traumatic. Some older people suffering from these and other major conditions can undergo a significant change in personality which can be distressing to people close to them.

Counselling can often deal with the personal anger, frustration and eventual depression caused by the losses such illness brings. It should aim at helping individuals to assess the cost to their former life-style, and either to fight the consequences realistically, or to accept and come to terms with them, whichever seems to be the most appropriate. It can further help individuals to re-assess what they are able to do in future, and where necessary to find alternative ways of coping with the tasks of life. Where the disabilty is permanent, counselling can help individuals to decide how they are to maintain their social involvement in future, and obtain personal fulfillment from their lives.

Where illness leads to loss of sight, speech or hearing it diminishes an individual's ability to make use of counselling assistance. Too often, the loss of these senses results in older people being treated as if they were mentally impaired, with people talking to them as if they were slightly silly, or as if they had reverted to infancy. There is nothing more annoying to older people, for their need and desire to communicate, at an adult level, is likely to be as strong as ever. In such situations, counsellors have to be innovative. For the deaf and asphasic, they will need to employ pen and paper in addition to speech, and make more use of bodily and facial cues than might otherwise be necessary. For the blind, more physical touch may be required. In every case, the need for empathy and positive regard is greatly increased. All these matters will be considered in more detail in the next chapter.

Recovery from illness is sometimes avoided by older people, particularly when they feel lonely and neglected. Being sick can bring with it a degree of sympathy and attention that is greatly valued by more isolated individuals, and they may believe that if their health improves they will lose out on the time and attention that is given to them on the basis of their illness. The counsellor may therefore come across many older people who do not want to overcome their illnesses and disabilities. If this is the case, an incentive to improved health might be for the counsellor to talk to them about ways and means of increasing their social contacts and involvement when they get better.

CHAPTER 16

Alcohol and older people

In the USA, it has been estimated that approximately 10–15% of the general elderly population suffer from alcoholism – over two million elderly Americans (Price and Andrews, 1982). There are few statistics relating to the extent of alcoholism and ageing people in this country. Certainly, it has not as yet become an issue of widespread social concern, despite the increasing problem with younger age groups. Yet, the incidence of alcoholism in the older population is said to be increasing too. Certainly, it would seem reasonable to believe that a problem affecting society generally will also occur in an age group which, as we have seen, faces a multitude of social and emotional difficulties.

There is a popular view that if an older person has a drink, 'it will do them no harm'. This is not only untrue, it is probably less true than for any other age group. Ageing livers and kidneys lose their ability to cope with alcohol, and older people are therefore more susceptible to its effects. But this is not the only way that ageist attitudes patronize, and indeed endanger older people. It is often said that alcohol is 'the only little pleasure that old people have', which may be true to an extent, but if drinking becomes a problem then it is for the individuals to decide how much of a pleasure drinking is, and whether they want help to stop. Taking these ageist attitudes one stage further, Price and Andrews (1982) state that 'diagnosed alcoholism frequently is not referred for alcoholic treatment because of health professionals' beliefs that the alcoholic is too old to benefit from treatment'. This is also entirely without foundation.

The causes of alcohol abuse

There are two types of ageing alcohol abuser; those whose drinking started in much earlier years, and those whose drinking habits have started or become excessive in old age. The problem is that it is often difficult to determine how long an individual has been drinking. Rosin and Glatt (1971) differentiated between primary factors which caused chronic, long-term alcohol abuse, chiefly pathological personality characteristics such as neuroticism, and what they called reactive factors which were particularly relevant for late-onset drinkers. The latter are usually factors such as retirement, bereavement, loss, loneliness, depression, anxiety and other major life changes which cause disruption in older people's lives. It has been found, for instance, that widowers comprised the largest proportion of late-onset elderly alcoholics.

This indicates that drinking is often a response to an inablity to cope with the many losses of old age. It is used as a means of temporary escape from circumstances that the individual finds unbearable. Alcohol serves to deaden feelings which the individual cannot manage, or wishes to avoid. It is often, at least initially, a response to social distress, and in turn, this indicates that counselling responses to problems of excessive drinking should not concentrate on the drinking alone, which can be regarded as a symptom, but on the deeper underlying social and emotional causes which have given rise to it.

The physical effects of alcohol

Many people believe that alcohol is a stimulant because most drinkers seem to become more outgoing and friendly in social settings. It is said to 'cheer people up'. The fact is, however, that alcohol depresses the nervous system, including the part of the brain which inhibits behaviour. What many people believe to be stimulation is actually a loss of inhibition that normally controls their social behaviour. The main 'benefit' of depressing the nervous system with alcohol is to dull the pain and losses associated with old age. The benefits are transitory, wearing off as the alcohol is filtered out of the body. As the underlying problems have not been tackled, more alcohol is required to continue dulling the pain, and consequently the desire to drink can become continuous.

There is also a belief that alcohol has certain other benefits. It is popularly assumed that it has medicinal benefits, but there is no evidence whatever to support this, and much evidence to the contrary. It is said to help people in sleeping, but whilst it may get people off to sleep more quickly it can lead to waking later at night. Alcohol is also supposed to have a 'warming up' effect, when in fact alcohol actually speeds up the loss of body heat, and can aggravate the problems of hypothermia.

With prolonged heavy drinking, the effects of alcohol on health can be drastic. Appetite is lessened, resulting in weight loss and dietary problems. Absorption of vital minerals can be affected with many consequences to both physical and mental health, notably through vitamin deficiency. It can lead to cirrhosis of the liver, hypocalcaemia (a deficiency of calcium in the blood) leading to osteoporosis, cardiomyopathy (a chronic disorder of the heart muscle), and many other disorders. It can also lead to certain cancers, notably of the mouth, pharynx and oesophagus.

There is also the danger of alcohol causing unpleasant interactions with drugs commonly prescribed for older people. If alcohol is taken with sleeping tablets and painkillers, excessive drowsiness can result, and severe stomach upsets can be caused when alcohol is taken with drugs used for arthritis.

These consequences of over-drinking are not confined only to those with a recognizable drink problem. With older people, problems can result from continuing to drink the same amounts they became used to consuming when they were younger, then apparently without effect. As the ageing body loses its ability to cope with alcohol, the amount that can be consumed has to be reduced. Alcohol Concern (1987) suggests that older people who have been regular drinkers may need to reduce by half the quantity of alcohol they consume.

Detecting excessive alcohol use

The effects of alcohol on the social behaviour of older people can be severe because of their reduced kidney and liver functioning. There is a loss of both physical and mental co-ordination, judgement is weakened, reaction times become slower, falls and accidents increase, sleep patterns are disturbed and sexual interest and performance declines. Incontinence is another problem that can begin by excessive alcohol intake. Alcohol can also lead to poor memory and an apparently confused state of mind which can then be wrongly interpreted as the onset of senile dementia. Indeed, the symptoms of alcohol abuse are similar to those of Alzheimer's disease. Similarly, the effects of alcohol abuse are often mistaken for depression, again because the physical and mental symptoms are similar. The effects of alcohol abuse, seen as a major social problem at other ages, can unwittingly be accepted and dismissed as the outcome of 'normal' ageing.

Social distress and alcohol abuse

The fundamental causes of alcohol abuse are to be found within the social and emotional lives of the individuals, and it is not wise for the counsellor to view alcohol abuse separately from these more basic causes. Excessive drinking is often caused by negative self-images, which indicate to individuals that they are unable to cope with the stress and unhappiness existing in their lives. Consequently, alcohol abuse should be dealt with not as a problem in itself, but as an individual's reaction to social distress.

The counsellor should first be alert to the possibility of heavy drinking amongst older people, and be aware that the symptoms of excessive drinking are often mistaken for signs of normal ageing. This means that there is a need to search beyond what may at first appear to be a case of depression or senility. When faced with these symptoms, and certainly before the diagnosis of depression or dementia is accepted, the counsellor should check whether an individual has an alcohol problem. This is particularly important when it is felt that ageing people can no longer look after themselves at home and some form of residential care is suggested.

The task of discovering whether an ageing individual has a drink problem requires considerable tact and sensitivity. Denial is a major factor in alcohol abuse, both over the amount the individual drinks, and whether it is a problem. Many older people retain a strong sense of the social stigma attached to heavy drinking and may consequently be unable or unwilling easily to volunteer the information. On the other hand the counsellor may be assisted by many physical signs which suggest that alcohol is a problem, such as finding lots of empty bottles around, or when an older person is found to be drinking at all times of the day, often alone and not as part of a social occasion.

The attitude of the counsellee

There are two important questions that need to be asked where alcohol abuse is suspected. The first is whether counsellees recognizes their drinking to be a problem. In this respect there is sometimes a need to dispel some of the myths which surround alcohol. Many well-intentioned people, including some doctors, still recommend alcohol, albeit in moderation, for a variety of conditions and complaints, giving the impression that there might be positive advantages in a small drink, and tacitly suggesting that there are no dangers. However guarded such advice might be, this reasoning is often expanded by lay people and used to justify increasingly heavy and more regular drinking.

Consequently, there may be a need to educate the older person, family and friends, and perhaps even the doctor, about the potentially harmful effects of alcohol within the ageing body. 'Once given this information and guidance on how to drink more safely, many people manage to cut down without needing special treatment or counselling' (Alcohol Concern, 1987). The reassurance and encouragement of the counsellor can often be sufficient for an older person in this situation. Controlling the source of the drink is another important consideration, and this may involve persuading well-intentioned friends and relatives to discontinue supporting and justifying their visits with alcoholic presents.

The second question is whether counsellees want to give up drinking, or at least to reduce the amount consumed. Often they will not, which makes the situation more difficult for the counsellor to deal with. Individuals may see alcohol as an acceptable way out of their problems. They may be unwilling to face their feelings and emotions, preferring to drown them in continuous drinking. When told about the consequences of excessive drinking, their attitude may be to welcome death as a more permanent solution to their problems.

When the counsellor faces this situation it is often more appropriate to leave the subject of drinking, and to try instead to focus on the nature of the social distress that the individuals are experiencing. Often, the counsellor will need to assure them that it is acceptable for them to grieve over their loneliness, their losses and bereavements, and to explore their feelings about life generally. It is often important to discuss their feelings and fears about their own death. Often, all that is required is for individuals to feel that there is someone willing to be supportive and understanding of their feelings, willing to listen to their problems, and to discuss alternative strategies for coping with their social distress.

Planning withdrawal

Whatever the setting, the counsellor should stress that alcoholism is a curable condition, particularly when the social distress underlying the need for alcohol is openly discussed and the problems tackled. In taking this positive stance, it is important that the counsellor tries to emphasize the personal strengths that are available to combat the problem, and not the weaknesses which led to the problem in the first place. The establishment of specific, graded and realistically achievable goals for the elderly drinker is important, goals which will hopefully result in eventual abstinence. It must be understood that such a programme of withdrawal requires a high level of support, from the counsellor, the counsellee's family and friends, and from any group to which the counsellee is attached. In losing the 'support' of alcohol there may be a need to fill the gaps left in a person's life by the process of withdrawal. New activities, new relationships and new supports may have to be found to re-engage the ageing individual with mainstream society.

Since most older people who have a drink problem tend to be lonely, retired and out of the mainstream of social life, some form of social group support may be helpful. The group can consist either of other elderly people, or special groups for people of all ages with an alcohol problem. Every effort should also be made to involve the family in giving support, particularly in breaking the pattern of denial that often surrounds cases of alcohol abuse.

Post-withdrawal support

There is also likely to be a continuing need for support after alcohol withdrawal has been successfully achieved. Just as it was important to consider the problems of alcohol abuse in conjuction with the underlying social distress, it is now important to realize that after the withdrawal from alcohol, those more fundamental problems will still exist. Coping with life in old age without drink may require an entirely new and improved self-image. Feelings of worthlessness, hopelessness, grief, lack of purpose and depression may still have to be dealt with, or the individual may again resort to an alcoholic solution.

Other drugs and older people

A very similar approach can be taken in the case of dependence on and abuse of other drugs. The reasons, consequences and approach taken remain essentially similar, regardless of the type of drug used. With older people, who have lived through the period when new 'miracle' allopathic drugs have appeared to offer a solution to all pain and ill-health, it is these prescribed rather than proscribed drugs that will be the main problem. Their side-effects can be different from those of alcohol, and are considered in more detail in Chapter 15, but similarly they can be mistakenly classified and thereafter dismissed as part of the normal process of growing old. Older people will often take drugs to relieve the pains and griefs of old age, rather than attempt to come to terms with them intellectually and emotionally. As with alcohol, social acceptance encourages their use, and ageist attitudes about the depressing nature of old age permits their abuse.

CHAPTER 17

Dependence: The emotional and social impact

What does it feel like to be old? In particular, what does it feel like to be considered 'old' in a society which values youth more highly than age? The fear that many people have about old age is becoming dependent, and having to rely on other people for the normal processes of living. The effect of dependence is to add a further element to the low status society assigns to older people. The double handicap of being old and dependent is common amongst older people, but the concept of dependence itself needs some consideration. Although many people believe that old age and dependence are inseparable, this is far from being a universal truth.

Structured dependence

Dominant social attitudes appear to see older people as 'handicapped', incapable of living their lives without considerable support, and dependent upon the assistance of younger people. This link between old age and dependence is structured by social laws and organization, by institutions, and by the dominant ideas about the nature of old age.

> The condition of dependency of the elderly is not the inevitable outcome of a natural process of ageing, but is socially structured, and hence potentially open to change. In this process the state plays a large part, by determining the events in the latter half of life which result in the dependence, poverty or isolation experienced by many elderly people. By the state is meant not just the elected government of the day, but that ruling complex of central administrative, legal, economic and political institutions which have become established over a long period of time, and

which govern the scope and, in large measure, the nature of everyday social acitivities. (Townsend, in Phillipson and Walker, 1986)

Ageist thinking is quite indiscriminate. Some older people do become dependent, but many others do not and indeed remain quite capable of leading their lives independently. Restrictions are placed even on these able individuals by common social attitudes which, for example, consider that old people should not engage in hard physical activity, either as work or recreation, should not travel alone or go swimming, should not scrub floors or stand for too long. They have earned their rest, and should now allow others to provide for them. Old people should rest, and be at peace.

This constitutes 'disablist' thinking. For many older people it is successful in its disabling effect; they stop doing things not necessarily because they are unable to do them, but because it is not expected of them. Social expectations become internalized. For younger people, 'disablist' thinking is the safer option. Old people are more susceptible to illnesses of all kinds, many of them fatal, and so excluding certain activity from their daily lives is considered to be the less risky, more acceptable option in most cases. The fact seems to be forgotten that people of all ages take risks all the time as part of normal life.

When people become frail or incapacitated it is easy for carers to assume rights and responsibilities in their lives which are not justified and are often deeply resented. This is taken a step further when physical disability is mistaken for an inablity to think, reason and make decisions. Frail and handicapped older people are often treated like children in this way, although the comparison with the dependence of children is entirely without foundation. The emotional impact of, say, toileting an elderly person is quite different from the toileting of a child because of the pride and dignity which most older people have developed throughout their lives. Yet carers often embark on this necessary physical task without considering the emotional impact on the older individual.

This means that many older people not only have to come to terms with their loss of ability, but also have to deal with the patronizing insensitivity of some of those who 'care' for them.

Yet when fit and mentally alert elderly people talk about their age, their feelings and viewpoints are illuminating. Many older people express their surprise at being old. They have recognized their age, but never really believed that they would become old themselves. Moreover, they do not feel 'old', or perhaps more accurately they do not feel 'old' in the way they have been led to expect. As one 70-year-old put it to me:

> I do not feel any different in my mind now than I did when I was a child.
> It's not the mind that gets older, except perhaps that it gets more forgetful,
> it's just that the body will no longer do the things it would once do, and
> the mind would still have it do if it were possible.

Alex Comfort expressed the same view when he said 'Old people are in fact young people inhabiting older bodies and confronted with certain physical problems' (Crosby and Traynor, 1985). J.B. Priestley said succinctly that 'Behind the appearance of age I am the same person with the same thoughts as when I was younger' (Crosby and Traynor, 1985).

This is a common insight in old age. It is not the mind that ages but the body, and it is this divergence between the things which the mind is still capable of contemplating, but which the body has become incapable of doing, which is the most difficult process for an ageing individual to accept. It is the reverse process to childhood, where the mind and body become progressively more able to co-operate to do the things that were once impossible, thereby achieving more independence. In old age, the mind stays able and pride wants to maintain personal independence; but the body increasingly and progressively lets us down.

The emotional significance of dependence

If this is so with able-bodied and able-minded people, what is the emotional impact on those who, through illness or other circumstances, have lost the ability to cope with life independently? Older people do gradually lose their ability to look after themselves, and would do so even if structural factors did not hasten the process. Tunstall (1966) asked what it was that triggered an older person to become housebound. He concluded that ageing people were usually aware of how they were 'expected' to behave as old people, but that they did not consider themselves to be old until a 'turning point' was reached. What constituted a turning point varied with the individual. For some it was a bereavement; for others a significant fall, for others having other people helping them with household tasks. These events triggered their acceptance of being 'old', with all its implications, and hastened their decline into dependence.

When I started social work with older people, the failure of many otherwise caring people to understand the emotional impact of dependence was instantly striking. They had failed to think beyond the facts of the situation – that these people could no longer perform a task, and that as a caring person they would do it for them. Yet if, as carers, we can see no further than the physical need to care, we ignore the entire emotional significance of acts of caring on the dependent individual. An act which we intend as 'caring' can seem to be no more than an imposition on personal pride and dignity.

It is not possible to counsel older people without coming face-to-face with those who are struggling with their pride, based upon a lifetime of independence which is progressively coming to an end. Carers who do not appreciate that the very act of caring for older people diminishes them and emphasizes that they are no longer masters of their own lives, are working under a delusion. Often, the more dependent older people become, the more reluctant and ungrateful they can be when receiving the support and assistance they increasingly require. Failure to understand the full emotional significance of dependence can lead to apparently irrational behaviour, such as anger and violence against carers, who are then surprised that their care does not receive the gratitude they expected.

Even those who appear gracefully to acknowledge and receive support from carers can still feel secretly diminished, their pride and independence deeply hurt. Care can easily lead to feelings of hopelessness and despair. It is not surprising, given this, that so many older people feel depressed. They have lost not only their role and status in life, they now have to look forward to years of dependence, often on their own children which for many makes matters far worse.

The inadequacy of caring

The process of physical care can often prevent discussion of the problems of increasing dependence. We fail to acknowledge that dependent people may have needs other than for practical help. Perhaps we do not want to discuss such an obviously distressing subject as dependence, preferring instead to concentrate on physical acts of care. Our failure to recognize the need for counselling can then be compounded by counsellees who, sensing our unwillingness to talk, repress their feelings. Losing the ability to be independent is a form of personal bereavement and, as in all bereavement, feelings of anger, fear, grief, depression and denial may all need to be acknowledged before individuals can come to terms with their situation.

It is not sufficient merely to 'care' for ageing people, particularly when they are becoming progressively more dependent. Indeed, the more care offered, the more dependent the individual is likely to feel. The more that is done the less useful or valuable the individual feels. Caring by 'doing', which is often the only care offered to older people, is by its very nature debilitating. It is likely to be either rejected, or else accepted with resignation.

Handicap, and the dependence and emotional trauma which arise from it, affect the individuals in terms of how they see and assess the losses involved. This is confirmed by Shakespeare (1975):

> Reaction to handicap acquired in adulthood is not proportionately related to the objective severity of the handicap. A comparatively mild handicap can cause a severe emotional reaction and a more severe handicap much less reaction. The causal factors in the degree of reaction seem to be what the acquired handicap means to the person in terms of his life style, his job and his interests.

Shakespeare was writing of handicapped people generally, but there is no reason why the gradual decrease in the coping ability of older people should be viewed any differently. Indeed, as the dependence of older people may be a gradual process, it may make the problem significantly worse. At least the handicapped individual has either had to cope with disability since birth, or has had to come to terms with it over a period of years. Disabled people also receive greater social sympathy and understanding, for their disability has perhaps occurred through accident or misfortune. Older people receive less consideration. They have lived their lives, so their dependence is often seen as part of the 'natural' process of ageing which they should readily recognize and accept.

Counselling and gradual dependence

So what does the carer do when it becomes increasingly apparent that older people really can no longer manage on their own? Merely to insist that they continue to fend for themselves can be counterproductive, for to demand that someone perseveres when this is no longer possible merely leads to increasing levels of frustration and anger, and this frustration serves to enhance their growing feelings of hopelessness.

Neither is it sufficient for carers to begin doing everything for the ageing person, stating as we so often do that, 'I don't mind doing it for you', or 'You did it for me long enough'. These comments do not address the central problem of coming to terms with dependence. It is not how *we* feel about offering help that matters, but how *they* feel about having to accept it. Indeed, in an albeit well-intentioned way, comments such as these actually tend to dismiss such feelings because we are saying implicity that what they feel is unnecessary, even foolish.

The dilemma can be overcome through a counselling process which attempts to determine how individuals feel about their dependence. Whether they prefer to persevere, often painfully and slowly, or whether they are ready to accept an offer of assistance. The individual should be engaged in a discussion about his or her feelings, on the basis of 'I feel that you are reluctant to let me do this for you. Why is this so, when I am quite willing to do it for you?' This approach is more likely to lead to a discussion about how they feel about their newly acquired dependent status, and how they want practical help to be provided. It also demonstrates our willingness to help, but allows individuals to respond by describing their feelings, which in turn can help them come to terms with their dependence. Moreover, when the counsellor becomes more aware of the troubled emotions involved, both parties may together be able to come to some idea of how feelings of worthlessness can be overcome, perhaps involving ways in which older people can give some practical assistance in return for the care they require. In this way, the counselling process can lead to a more mutually acceptable provision of care.

Each stage in the progressive pattern of dependence can be discussed openly and fully. There is a tendency for carers, when they feel that an ageing person requires additional caring tasks, to merely add them to the list without comment or discussion. Often no comment is made so as not to cause unnecessary upset, but such well-intentioned secrecy can cause more rather than less anguish. Carers should never assume that just because they 'do' more, they are being more helpful.

Sudden dependence and counselling

Similar considerations apply to older people who have become dependent because of some sudden or single event, such as a stroke. Whilst there is normally an initial stage when there is a ready acceptance of illness as an explanation and justification for our caring input, if recovery is slow or if permanent dependence is likely to result, then counselling can be beneficial to someone struggling to accept such a situation.

Sudden illness and disability can be devastating. It can quickly lead to disorientation and bewilderment, followed quickly by frustration and anger, and/or tears and depression. There has been no warning, no preparation for dependence. It can be a bereavement as sudden and unexpected as any death. Moreover, it is a bereavement which affects the individual and his or her own personal life. All the many implications have to be internalized quickly, and many find this too difficult to handle. Drastic personality change, with the docile becoming demanding and the reasonable becoming unreasonable, is not uncommon at such times.

Such situations need to be handled with great sensitivity and forbearance by the counsellor. Above all else, time is required for individuals to come to terms with the new realities of their lives, during which they require understanding and sympathy. When carers provide physical care, it is always important that such provision of care is openly discussed, as mentioned above.

Reactions to dependence

It is not unreasonable that the loss of former abilities should cause depression and anxiety in the older adult. Even a period of denial, especially after sudden dependence, is quite common, probably being part of the normal process of self-protection from the shock involved. However, all such reactions are a matter for concern if they become excessive, or last too long. Other reactions which might accompany increasing handicap are outlined by Shakespeare (1975):

— regression, where people behave like someone younger, perhaps becoming overdependent;

— increased egocentricity, when they become demanding and intolerant of others' needs when they conflict with their own;
— withdrawal from contact with other people;
— increased use of fantasy, again as an escape from facing the reality of the handicap;
— projection, where feelings of inadequacy are deflected onto others and reversed, so they believe that others regard them as inadequate;
— new identifications, such as buying expensive possessions or joining groups felt to be of high status, in an effort to restore damaged confidence by new and impressive associations.

All these reactions can be seen as an expression of the social distress which results from declining physical abilities. Whilst none of them is necessarily damaging, they are expressions which call for counselling attention. Eventually it is healthier for the individual to recognize and come to terms with his real circumstances. The counselling process seeks to enable this.

Considerable tolerance and understanding may be necessary when caring for dependent elderly people, as it is often difficult for others to appreciate the position such individuals are in. This has been well expressed by Comerford (1986), a quadriplegic adult, in describing the effect that even small caring functions can have on someone who is entirely dependent upon them;

> These are only small things, and to most people probably irrelevant, but when you depend on another person to perform these tasks then, believe me, the most insignificant detail can become a huge factor in your life, especially if you want to retain your individuality . . . I know only too well how (residential care), and indeed disabled life in general, can lead to demoralisation and apathy and can cause even the most active bodies and minds to become stagnant and indifferent to all but their own immediate needs. I am no different myself.

Incontinence

For older people, there is no more depressing and shaming dependence than incontinence because of all its many associations. The social and emotional trauma this can cause an individual is deeply and painfully significant.

There is an ageist tendency to believe that incontinence is an inevitable and irreversible part of growing old, and something that has to be accepted when it arrives. Incontinence should never be accepted as a normal part of old age, or that the only response is regular toileting programmes, incontinence aids, and the task of tidying up after 'accidents'. One result of incontinence is often the breakdown of family care, often because insufficient support is given to carers, or is given too late.

The first counselling task with an incontinent person should be to investigate carefully the individual circumstances. Often incontinence can be remedied by simple measures. Incontinence can be caused by poor diet, lack of exercise or poor mobility, perhaps allied to a fear of falling or poor eyesight. Illness, such as disorders of the bladder and urethra, can cause incontinence, as can constipation. Drugs can also be a contributory factor, particularly night sedatives which suppress the normal signals from bladder to brain, and diuretics which increase the frequency of urination. Social and emotional problems, personal worries and anxieties can also precipitate bouts of incontinence. In turn, incontinence adds to personal worries, anxiety increases, and incontinence worsens.

If incontinence has a more permanent cause, it can be managed by a wide variety of measures, including toileting programmes, the use of pads, the proximity of toilet facilities, especially at night, etc., whilst more drastic circumstances may require bladder retraining, medical treatment and even surgery. All this does not directly concern counsellors, except that they may have to put pressure on agencies to act and give support.

Dependence and leisure

Dependence often means that old hobbies, pastimes and interests have to be reduced, or even abandoned. Even the ability to get out to see friends may be restricted. The counsellor should be aware of the losses of dependence, and seek to discover from the counsellee what they most miss in life. This is particularly important in the case of gradual decline when older people can stop, or be prevented from, taking part in meaningful tasks and functions without other people being aware.

How and with what are such activities to be replaced? What is available to the older adult that will involve a lively mind in constructive and satisfying activity? Counselling has an important part to play in this; indeed, it is an essential feature of the caring role which seeks to avoid the development of feelings of helplessness and boredom experienced by so many dependent older people.

Loss of hearing and speech

The main attention so far has focused on physical dependence. However, loss of speech and hearing can also create dependence with similarly drastic results. Clearly it has particular implications for counselling which is a skill which relies almost entirely on the ability to communicate. Many older people will have difficilties in hearing; a few in expressing themselves verbally.

Hearing loss

Loss of hearing can create considerable frustration, both for the individual and close friends. It can lead to people becoming unco-operative and antagonistic. It can lead to feelings of being cut off, isolated and not totally aware of what is going on around them. As hearing deteriorates, many activities and interests have to be discontinued – visits to the cinema or theatre, going to parties and pubs, bingo and much else. Hearing impairment often prevents the enjoyment of activities that people around them are enjoying, whether this be ordinary conversation or the television. The annoyance of turning up the volume is well known, as is the frustration of older people not answering the doorbell or the telephone.

In this way, hearing impairment constitutes a disability which is suffered by everyone, carers included. It leads to irritation and impatience, to carers becoming exhausted. They may tire of repeating themselves, even to the point of ending any real attempts to communicate, except when it is absolutely essential. Hearing loss also tends to embarrass some younger people, whilst others 'play them up' by talking softly, or talking behind their backs. Carers can also become over-anxious – perhaps worrying that the older person will not be able to hear traffic on busy roads.

Acknowledgement of disability is an important step towards coming to terms with it. Yet many people will try to avoid this, and hide the fact from others. Many older hearing impaired people dislike wearing hearing aids, or will go to considerable lengths to hide them. This means that hearing impairment is not always obvious to other people.

Loss of speech

Loss of speech is usually the result of a sudden illness, such as a stroke. Its onset can therefore be sudden and traumatic, and can be either partial or complete, but the results for both counsellee and counsellor are obviously of the utmost significance. Aphasic older people are particularly prone to assumptions about their intelligence, and even their adulthood. The assumption that physical handicap signifies a handicapped mind is common with all forms of handicap, but is one that the counsellor cannot afford to make. Indeed, the counsellor should initially make the opposite assumption, that the counsellee is an intelligent, sensitive and feeling individual for this is not only more likely to be correct, but if it is incorrect the mistake is more easily remedied.

Individuals who have speech difficulties are often very sensitive to and frustrated by their inability to communicate, and they need someone who is willing to take time to understand rather than someone who pretends to do so. Perhaps the biggest potential barrier to communication with aphasic people is the anxiety and embarrassment of many carers who feel that they 'ought' to be able to understand, and that failure to do so reflects upon them rather than the difficulties of the situation.

Often, such assumptions constitute a form of embarrassment about the carers' inability to understand what they are being told, or asked. Carers may feel embarrassed that they have to ask aphasic people to repeat what they are trying to say, or they are perhaps unwilling to admit that they do not understand. The result, too often, is that carers pretend that they can understand, or they jump to wrong conclusions. There is a tendency in such situations for carers to assume that they are being asked to provide physical or practical help, with the result that many older people are brought more cups of tea, or taken to the toilet more frequently than they desire!

Counsellors should be aware of their own feelings in this respect. To avoid this kind of situation, it is important that the counsellor does not pretend understanding. It is better to ask for numerous repetitions, and seek many clarifications. One useful technique is to ask if the older person can use different words to explain what is meant. It may also be possible to ask if a relative or friend more used to the older person's communication can be present in the early stages. Most aphasic people prefer an honest approach for they realize that someone is genuinely trying to understand them accurately.

Alternative communication with deaf and aphasic older people

The problems of counselling aphasic people underlines the importance of listening in the counselling process; aphasia merely means that the listening process is more lengthy, more difficult, and requires not only additional time but additional skills. It is important, for instance, that difficulties of communication are not compounded by outside disturbances, whether this be extraneous noise or any other distractions which might hinder the counsellee's attention.

Where speech is not possible, word or picture books can be developed which contain key words and information. These enable counsellees to point to the words they wish to communicate. Micro-computers can also be of assistance, utilizing their ability to construct, store and recall words and phrases at the touch of a button. These methods can also be used for practising and developing speech skills, if such improvement is possible, for example after a stroke.

Arrow questioning is another technique that the counsellor can use. Only questions which require a straightforward 'yes' or 'no' are asked, so it is a technique which can be developed for those who are completely unable to communicate verbally, as nods and shakes of the head, eye movements or squeezes of the hand can be used for communication. The skill of the technique is in framing questions that require only affirmative or negative answers, and whilst this takes a little time to master it eventually becomes relatively easy.

Arrow questioning means that the counsellor has to play a much more active role within the relationship, both in putting forward the possible meaning of behaviour, and interpreting the needs of the counsellee. Whenever a tentative hypothesis is made, the counsellor should ensure that the counsellee realizes that it is just that, and that it is quite acceptable to reject it if it is not accurate. The extent to which a hypothesis is accurate can also be ascertained by techniques which indicate how close or far away, 'warm or cold', the counsellor is.

More sophisticated systems of alternative communication also exist, such as symbol systems like Blissymbolics, manual signing languages and synthetic speech. Those wishing to find out more about these systems can write to the addresses given in the Directory on page 207.

Whatever means of communication is employed, the counselling skills required are identical to those used when working with people who are able to communicate verbally. The counsellee's need for establishing communication may often be greater. It is important that the counsellor remembers that a warm, reassuring manner, free of patronizing attitudes, remains the best counselling technique with aphasic older people. When they are aware of our concern, our willingness to spend time with them, and when we empathize with their inability to communicate, they will often relax which itself may release abilities which were previously restricted by anxiety, unhappiness and a lack of opportunity for communication.

Counselling older people with speech impairment can be a frustrating and time-consuming business; but it can also be an extremely rewarding one. Often they are more cut off from other people, less likely to have the opportunity of talking about their condition and their feelings with others, and therefore more appreciative of the opportunity to do so with someone who is not only willing, but has sufficient interest to develop the appropriate skills for doing so.

CHAPTER 18

Depression, loneliness and loss

Depression in older people is essentially no different from any other age group. Depressed individuals develop a negative self-image, viewing themselves as inadequate or defective personalities, unable to cope with the situations which face them. They will tend to see the problems and difficulties in their liveš as primarily the result of personal defects, and these defects, allied with an inability to cope with their lives, increasingly make them feel unable to achieve an adequate level of fulfillment, happiness and contentment. They begin to see every event and circumstance in their lives in a negative and pessimistic manner. They become defeatist in their outlook. Everything becomes too much for them to cope with, the entire world seems to be putting insuperable obstacles in their way. They feel themselves increasingly isolated and lonely, rejected by everyone.

Such feelings can paralyse the individual, who can feel that he or she has no power to change the circumstances of his or her life. This belief becomes self-fulfilling. The acceptance of incompetence ensures inability to alter or modify personal circumstances, thereby deepening the apparent hopelessness of the situation. The future seems to hold only more problems and pain. Current difficulties, which are believed to be insoluble, are consequently projected far into a future which seems filled with continued hardship, failure and frustration.

Depression and older people

Gurland (1976) investigated research into the frequency of depression in various adult age groups, and found general agreement that the highest rate of depressive symptoms was in the 65 + age group. Depression in older people is usually associated with loss – loss of status and function, loss of important friends and relations, loss of mobility, loss of independence, loss of personal strengths and abilities, loss of home and familiar surroundings, and so on. Associated with these is often a loss of purpose and will, and often an increasing sense of being alone. Old age can be time when the reasons for living seem uncertain. Prospects for future fulfillment, even enjoyment, seem remote, not just on the basis of how older people view their condition, but also from dominant social ideas about the inevitability of future decline.

Loneliness is another vital factor in depression. Townsend (1963) found that the most isolated older people tended to be unmarried or childless people with few surviving relatives, who reinforced their isolation by either refusing or being unable to participate in outside activities, by joining clubs or forming new friendships. Yet everyone needs the company and stimulation of other people. There is no truth in the belief that attachment needs decline with age. The social isolation of older people is a situation from which many feel there is no escape. Loneliness lowers morale, reducing hope that they will be able to fill the gaps in their lives. The horizons of life are reduced and a vicious circle of loss, loneliness and depression tightens. Moreover, for older people loneliness is a double or mutual loss, meaning not only a reduction in companionship, but a reduction in their capacity to care for other people.

The effects of depression

Depression in older people can lead to increasing debility, dependence, mental confusion and even death. Depression presents itself in a number of ways: general apathy, even towards those areas of previous interest; loss of appetite accompanied by weight loss; irritability and prolonged bad temper; over-tiredness and a continual desire to sleep. Or it might manifest itself through failure to sleep; a permanent state of sadness; an inability to see the brighter side of any situation or event; lack of activity; feelings of physical and mental weakness, and much else. These symptoms might be recognized as abnormal with younger people, but with ageing individuals they can be too readily accepted as part of growing old.

Depression is experienced at many levels. Perhaps the starting point is a feeling of not being hopeful or optimistic about the future, or disappointment that something has happened or not happened. When depression is mild, the individual is able to look at the situation with some degree of objectivity. It is often cyclical and time-limited, linked with a 'bad period' of time which passes when events are placed in better perspective. Some people are prone to recurrent periods of depression throughout their lives, and as they grow older these can become deeper and more frequent. Such depression often responds quickly when apparently insuperable problems are counselled. The time and concern that the counsellor can give, and the alternative perspectives that can be brought to bear on a particular issue, can help reassure the individual that not everything in life is bleak and hopeless.

Mild, temporary depression is something that we all experience at every stage of our lives. It is perhaps true, however, that ageing people become more susceptible to severe, debilitating and long-lasting depression. After all, dominant ideology suggests that there are few prospects in old age, leading many older people to refrain from involving themselves in social activity.

In deeper depression, the individual becomes more obsessed with negative thoughts and ideas, and this negative outlook feeds the original causes of depression. Pre-occupation with current problems makes it more difficult to focus counselling on other perspectives, or even to engage in reasonable discussion. Some depressed people refuse to eat or drink, or to take part in any kind of activity, staying within their homes, probably fixed to a favourite chair or bed for most of the day. This depression is concerned more with despair than disappointment, with the feeling that there is, and can be, little hope. In extreme cases, individuals can appear totally unresponsive to anything which does not confirm their negative feelings, intent only on feeding their depression, oblivious to the people around them and the help that they can offer.

Depression in old people can ultimately lead to mental stress which is commonly mistaken for the early signs of senile dementia. Many people can feel that they are losing control of their minds, becoming anxious and worried and suffering from a series of fears and delusions. Depression at this level is obviously serious and can indeed be life-threatening.

Suicide

The potentially lethal effects of depression cannot be accurately gauged. Annual suicide figures indicate that a significant proportion of older people take their own lives, but beyond this it is difficult to know how many people facing the prospect of old age lose the will to live, and thereafter refuse to eat properly, abuse their medication or in other subtle ways contrive to terminate their own lives.

The possibility of suicide at the extreme end of depression, when the individual decides that he or she no longer wishes to continue living, is a very real one. Yet to become over-aware of the dangers of suicide amongst older people is to risk becoming too defensive in our approach. Only a small proportion of depressed people try to commit suicide, and it is usually possible to provide help and support long before this stage.

It is when life appears to the individual to be without worth, value and significant meaning that thoughts of suicide arise. It is common for older people to feel that they are a burden, and that they do not want to be a nuisance to anyone. It is also common for older people to look forward to dying, perhaps in order to be re-united with loved ones.

The threat of suicide is often a cry for help, a threat without serious intent. Nevertheless even a threat of suicide constitutes a strong signal of social distress which should always be treated seriously. Suicide threats can often reflect a series of emotional and social events which have led to feelings of social alienation and isolation. A number of studies have shown that a high proportion of older people admitted to hospital after an attempted suicide had actually told someone of their intentions. When older people talk about 'ending it all', or 'doing away with themselves', they should be taken seriously. It is when such remarks are ignored that threats can develop into active suicide attempts.

Unfortunately, denial is a common response to the suicidal feelings of older people. Their social distress is too often met with attempts to persuade them that there is 'someone or something for them to live for', even when they themselves are convinced that there is not. Such a denial of feelings is not only futile, but dangerously counterproductive. Such feelings have to be addressed, it is no time for side-tracking or for putting discussion off.

Yet in dealing with depressed older people it is important to distinguish between those who are expressing strong feelings of resignation and those who are actively intent on suicide. There are dangers in both over-reacting and under-reacting. The person who is genuinely thinking of ending it all requires immediate help, but the counsellor should ensure that such statements are not a means to attract attention, or threats obscuring other hidden messages. One such message, common in threatened suicide, is revenge, representing to others in the strongest and most extreme way how futile their life has become. They seek to blame and punish other people for the things they do, or fail to do to make their lives empty. Where this is the case, direct attention to the threatened suicide can miss the real point and purpose of what is being communicated. The desire for revenge needs to be confronted directly. Why are they trying to punish other people, what have they done to deserve such a response? Such enquiries can sometimes reveal significant information.

The medicalization of depression

Depression in older people is too often seen primarily as a medical rather than an emotional and social problem. Depression is considered a mental 'illness', a link often reinforced by the tendency of depressed people to complain of some form of physical ailment. Indeed, many older people prefer to present physical rather than emotional reasons for their state of mind. This can be taken to extreme lengths, individuals being certain that they have contracted some form of terminal illness, such as cancer, when there is often little physically wrong with them.

Yet the depressed mind can have a devastating effect upon the functioning of the body. Psychosomatic illnesses are real enough. The depressed individual may indeed have aching limbs, but the depression itself may either be highlighting the pain, or actually giving rise to it. Too often we fail to reach a correct diagnosis by focusing upon ailments, real or imaginary, and not on the psychological causes of those ailments. The implication is that many physical ailments of old age are best treated not by physical or medical responses, but by spending time looking at the economic, social and emotional factors which give rise to depression.

Anti-depressant drugs can often appear to be helpful in the treatment of depression. There has certainly been an enormous development in their use during this century. We have been led to believe that there is no need to feel depressed; whatever the underlying causes, a course of tablets will make us well again. This idea is being increasingly questioned, regarding both the accuracy of claims about drug effectiveness, and the detrimental side-effects anti-depressant drugs are now known to have. Moreover, their effect is transitory, lasting only until the body is able to rid itself of the drug.

Reliance on drugs has other consequences. It reduces the need for people to look at the causes of their depression, and develop from their inner resources methods of dealing with it. So in addition to the habit-forming tendency of the drugs themselves, people can be led to feel that they cannot live without them. Counselling should seek to free depressed individuals from any such dependence, and place the emphasis on developing their personal coping skills.

The causes of depression

An important part of counselling is to discover the underlying, non-medical causes of depression. The first task is to ascertain whether the behaviour and attitudes of the individual represents a depressed state of mind. This can be done by establishing links between behaviour, physical ailments and the wider background problems faced by the individual. Initially, the counsellee might want to talk about physical and medical problems, but the counselling process should seek to shift attention away from this, moving towards other more relevant and legitimate areas.

1. The iatrogenic causes of depression

Far from being the solution to depression, conventional medicine can often be the cause. Many drugs commonly prescribed for older people for other medical reasons can have a depressive effect. These include analgesics, pain killers, anti-arthritic drugs, antibiotics, anti-Parkinsonian drugs, anti-psychotic drugs, anti-hypertensive drugs, and anti-convulsant drugs. Indeed, what all these 'anti-' drugs have in common is an ability to cause or worsen depression. Blumenthal (1980), whilst listing all these drugs, also includes other drugs, such as corticosteroids, cardiovascular drugs, appetite suppressants, and other substances, including alcohol, oral contraceptives and organic pesticides. Blumenthal's list includes most of the common forms of medication prescribed for older people. The list is not exhaustive; nor does it include all the brand names available on prescription, so the counsellor who suspects that drug side-effects might be a possible cause of depression should consult a doctor who is prepared to check the medication. Where drugs might be implicated, doctors should be asked if they consider them to be vital, and if not whether they can be reduced, stopped completely, or an alternative prescribed. The effect of reduced or changed medication on depression can then be monitored.

2. Illness

It is also worth checking with a doctor whether particular illnesses or conditions might give rise to depression. Many painful and debilitating diseases are probably a significant cause of depression in older people. Blumenthal (1980) mentions certain cancers, hypoglycaemia, rheumatoid arthritis, Parkinson's disease and cerebral arteriosclerosis, amongst others, as causes of depression. There is also increasing evidence that virus infections and hormonal imbalances can cause some forms of depression and should be investigated, particularly where there has been no previous history of depression (Petty and Sensky, 1987). Where illness appears to be a possible reason for depression, medical attention to these ailments can often produce good results.

3. Nutrition and depression

Nutrition is another factor that the counsellor should consider. The link between depression (and other mental states) and the food we eat is now well established. Petty and Sensky (1987) link depression with food sensitivities or allergies, and although they conclude that it is probably not a particularly common cause, others have claimed that it accounts for a considerable amount of all depression.

They point more strongly to evidence linking specific forms of depression with deficiencies of several vitamins, to the importance of a balanced diet, and the potential effectiveness of vitamin tablets. Thiamin (vitamin B_1) deficiency can cause irritability, emotional instability, apathy, poor appetite and tingling in the fingers and toes. Thiamin levels in the body can be affected by drinking too much coffee (and coffee is known to cause depression). A deficiency of niacin (nicotinic acid), which is readily available in fish, poultry or brewer's yeast, is another known cause of depression. Pyridoxine (vitamin B_6) deficiency is associated with explosive and hysterical episodes in otherwise shy people. Pantothenic acid is plentiful in a wide variety of foods; it is easily destroyed in processing, but has been used successfully to treat people with depression. Vitamin A deficiency, which causes tiredness and difficulties in sleeping as well as depression, is readily treated with cod liver oil. High levels of copper can also cause depression,and this trace element is obtained from industrial pollution, cigarettes, and from copper water pipes. Petty and Sensky (1987) present vitamin tablet treatment as an effective way of dealing with depression, whilst advocating caution about taking too many.

Depression can also be a consequence of low potassium intake, and several studies have found that older people tend to choose a diet which has a low potassium content (Judge and Cowan, 1971; Dall and Gardiner, 1971). The loss of potassium in older people is closely associated with diuretic drugs.

Weinberg (1972) sought to widen this biochemical appreciation of the importance of food, and linked eating with our state of mind. Food represents our first human contact, involving an exchange of love and affection as well as nutritional sustenance. Thereafter food becomes an important 'symbol of personal security'. Weinberg also saw food as a key factor in social life and personal pleasure.

> In our efforts to provide the aged with a proper diet, we often fail to perceive that it is not what the older person eats but with whom that will be the deciding factor in proper care for him. The oft repeated complaints of the older patient that he or she has little incentive to prepare food for only himself is not merely a statement of fact but also a rebuke to the questioner for failing to perceive his isolation and aloneness and to realize that food eaten by one's self lacks the condiment of another's presence which can transform the simplest fare to the ceremonial act with all its shaded meanings. (Weinberg, 1972)

For the same reason, both the refusal to eat and eating to excess can have powerful manipulative effects on carers, and can be used to worry and draw attention to personal needs. These again should be tackled so that feelings are expressed openly and not by such devious devices.

Davies (1981) also points out that a vicious circle of depression, non-eating, poor nutrition and therefore deeper depression can occur.

4. Social and economic causes of depression

Whilst it is important for the counsellor to check for possible medical and nutritional causes of depression, a high proportion of depression amongst older people undoubtedly centres around their economic and social life. Brown and Harris (1978) suggested that all depression has its origins in psycho-social factors, establishing that events which had severe, threatening and long-term implications, usually associated with loss, played a major role in bringing about depressive disorders. The life events they associated with the onset of depression include;

(a) separation, or the threat of separation, involving death or a spouse leaving home,
(b) an unpleasant revelation about someone that forces a major re-assessment of the person or relationship,
(c) a life-threatening illness in someone close,
(d) a major material loss or disappointment, or the threat of this,
(e) an enforced change of residence, or the threat of it,
(f) other crises involving loss, such as redundancy.

Murphy (1982), relating the work of Brown and Harris specifically to older people, also found that there was an association between severe life events, major social difficulties, poor physical health and depression. Yet because loss suffered by older people appeared to be more irretrievably hopeless than with younger people, he concluded that the outcome of severe life events becomes more serious the older we grow. Yet not all life-threatening events cause depression, and in order to explain this Brown and Harris (1978) suggested that these events are mediated by four 'vulnerability factors'; that is, factors which make it more likely that depression will be the result. It is interesting to look at the specific relevance of the first and third of these in the lives of older people:

(a) the lack of a confiding relationship with a spouse or similar partner,
(b) the presence at home of three or more children under the age of 14,
(c) the lack of employment outside the home,
d) separation from one's mother before the age of 11.

The potential social agendas which lead to depression are clearly numerous involving many complex inter-relationships between personality factors, life history, recent events, loss and current life expectations. Brown and Harris (1978) considered that social class and related issues of poverty and life on lower income produce additional pressures and strains which increase vulnerability to depression. Those from lower socio-economic classes often have to make basic choices of spending money on food or heating. They live in poorer, more overcrowded housing, and are consequently more likely to be socially isolated, suffer from physical disability, more prone to serious illness, less mobile and more dependent. But other factors not related to class are also important, such as cumulative loss, social isolation, incapacity and dependence, illness and pain.

The primary counselling task is to discuss those life events and social

factors that might be contributing to depression, raising them with the counsellee and judging from the responses received whether they are significant.
Disinterest often indicates that any such link is incorrect. Conversely, a refusal
to enter into discussion often indicates that the topic is relevant, and the
counselling task is then to gently and compassionately open up that particular
area for discussion.

According to Petty and Sensky (1987), empirical links are now being found
between social trauma and the biochemical and hormonal changes in
depression discussed earlier. They mention two recent studies which link
significantly high levels of the hormone cortisol with people whose
depression followed a severe life event. If this link is established, it suggests
that counselling the emotional effects of social trauma may be of considerable
value in treating depressed people.

A counselling approach to depression

The counsellor should see depression as a particular response to personal
circumstances. It is a state of mind largely determined by the way an individual has learned to interpret his or her life. It is primarily involved with present
thoughts, feelings, wishes, attitudes, assumptions, inferences and conclusions. We saw when considering Kelly's theory of personal constructs
(pp. 61–2) that individuals assume a social role based on certain assumptions
made about themselves and their circumstances. Depression often arises
when individuals arrive at understandings which are either not their normal
viewpoint or not related to the real facts. The counsellor's task is to try to
uncover such personal constructs and so develop a better understanding of
how individuals are currently interpreting their situations, and then help
them modify their current distorted view of their world, and their entirely
negative self-images.

It is therefore important that the counsellor emphasizes that depression is
both a response to certain specific features of the counsellees' life and, equally
important, to their particular mental attitudes towards themselves. Grief over
a recent bereavement may be quite normal and understandable, yet if it per-
sists for an abnormal period of time, it might be appropriate to challenge the
counsellee about whether the grief still concerns the event in question, or if it
has not instead become a chosen, or preferred, state of mind.

In fact, depression is a state of mind that rarely corresponds entirely to one
event or situation alone. Whilst depression has real roots in feelings with
which we can no longer cope, feelings that life is unfair, that there is no further
point in continuing to deal with life's struggles, depressed states arise only
when the individual gives in and declines to battle further. Initially, we might
do this in order to obtain help, or to demonstrate to others how badly or
unfairly we have been treated, and the hurt and pain we feel. In effect, we ask

whether everyone would not give up when faced with such odds? But there comes a point when depression becomes a way of life, a state of mind looking for sympathy rather than resolution.

Ultimately this has to be put to the counsellee, for conquering depression will ultimately depend on the individuals themselves wanting to do so. Whilst the lives of many older people in our society are depressing enough to warrant sympathy, sympathy alone does not necessarily lead to effective counselling. Overcoming depression requires a personal commitment to struggle, to accepting reality, to facing problems, to accepting that matters can improve, and in determining to do something about it. Negative moods produce negative thoughts, and negative thoughts deepen depression in a circle that only the individual can break. Ultimately, depression is overcome only when the causes have been honestly faced, and the individual has determined on a positive and active personal response. The counsellor should seek to discuss with depressed counsellees how they can cope better with their depressed feelings, how they can clear their minds of the depressing events of the past, and fears about the future. In extreme situations, the counsellor may need to deal with depression by resorting to techniques for physical and mental relaxation.

Given the depth of some depression, the counselling task is not normally easy or straightforward. The counsellee can be confused, preoccupied and distracted. Moreover, depressed individuals often have little motivation to do anything constructive about their situation, and will often reject offers of help on the basis that no-one can make their problems easier. Depressed people can even relinquish their responsibilities towards other people whom they once treasured. Even 'normal' human drives for sleep, sustenance and survival may seem to disappear.

The depressed individual will present many other difficulties within the counselling process. These can include a lack of concentration, an unwillingness to discuss feelings and an inability to place them into an ordered or realistic context. All this can make the process of counselling extremely difficult. The counsellor needs to be able to stimulate the counsellee into active engagement, and this is often best achieved by a more direct involvement on the part of the counsellor. When the counsellee finds it difficult to talk, the counsellor may have to take more initiative in clarifying the issues and problems which are making the individual feel depressed, and opening them up as areas of legitimate discussion.

There is often a tendency to react against the negativity of the depressed counsellee. Clearly, the counsellor cannot afford to do so and has at all times to seek empathy with counsellees, trying to feel how they feel, and understand better what is causing them to behave in the way they do. Counselling seeks to help the depressed individual discover some kind of hope, expression and meaning in life. This is something that we all need in our lives, however old, or however empty our lives might appear.

CHAPTER 19

Confusion

One of the most feared perceptions of old age concerns mental infirmity, confusion, or senile dementia. These terms, and others, are used to describe those older individuals who do not have full control of their mind in everyday life. It has been estimated that between 5% and 10% of those over 65 suffer from confused mental states, and that the numbers are increasing. The problem with such information is that it can lead to a belief that confusion has become a common feature of old age, and ageing people can be made to feel particularly vulnerable. So it is important to stress that mental confusion is an aberration, not a feature of normal ageing. Instead, what needs to be stressed is that whilst a very limited physical decline does occur with increasing age, this does not normally have a dramatic effect on either personality or mental functioning.

When mental functioning and personality are affected, it can be the result of an illness or disease. There is little doubt that the figures and trends in elderly confusion contain within them the unavoidable truth that there is a devastating clinical illness called 'dementia'. Ageing people, in this sense, are correct in their concern, particularly as the causes of the illness are still largely uncertain or unknown. This chapter seeks to place the concern of older people into context for the counsellor, to offer a wider definition of the possible causes of confusion, and to suggest that there is a role for counselling in both the prevention and treatment of the condition.

Confusion has a variety of effects. The individual becomes disorientated in both time and space; there is a decreased ability to concentrate; behaviour changes through an inability to control impulses and a failure to make judgements about commonly held norms; wandering and aimless behaviour becomes common; the memory fails to register, store and retrieve information, often involving failure to recognize familiar people; speech can become incoherent, or coherent in the wrong context; and the ability to express emotion, in all its forms, gradually disappears. Marples (1986) describes a typical pattern of a person who is becoming demented:

> In the early stage, anxiety increases as he observes himself coping less successfully. His often inconsistent awareness of failings heightens his confusion and frequently results in paranoid ideation. His anxiety results in decreased flexibility and heavy reliance on coping skills that are no longer effective. Then regression occurs and denial and depression deepen.
>
> In a later stage, he begins to deal less with external factors and more with internal sensations, which results in increased feelings of vulnerability to past and present hurts. Past emotional pain is resurrected and projected onto the current situation. He may call his wife 'Mother' or act as if she were his sister. This process leads to further disorientation.

The medical view of dementia

Research into the mental problems of ageing has not unsurprisingly centred on a 'medicalized' view of the problem, defining and approaching the condition in purely neuro-pathological terms. As such it is seen as an illness affecting the brain, leading progressively and irreversibly to brain death. There are two main types of brain death, or dementia, which have been identified. The first is caused by the narrowing of the arteries of the brain, reducing blood supply and causing blockages which in extreme cases lead to strokes, but which can also cause smaller failures in parts of the brain. The onset of this, the least common form of confusion, is sudden, and the course it follows is unpredictable and patchy, depending upon the regions of the brain which are damaged. The second form, in which brain cells degenerate gradually, and which is generally referred to as Alzheimer's disease, is what is primarily described as dementia. It is still medically unexplained, and the causes remain unproven. Its onset and progress is gradual, and the condition is currently considered to be irreversible.

These medicalized descriptions of dementia are important. They describe the symptoms of confusional states, look minutely into the biochemistry, and investigate the condition of confused brains. But they are limited in that they fail to consider the wider conditions and circumstances which can give rise to this pathology. Without denying the existence of the disease, it is important to question the predominance of the medical view, and to introduce a wider appreciation of the many social and emotional factors that may give rise to confusion in old age, and even lead to the disease(s) which cause brain death or dementia.

Questioning medical orthodoxy

Is confusion a psycho-medical condition which is a likely, if not an inevitable, consequence of old age? Psychological theories of senile dementia point to no single agreed definition or cause, and certainly none which is either entirely adequate or proven. Whilst there is no doubt that some dementias have been caused by disease, for example the death of brain cells through thrombosis, haemorrhage or embolism, post-mortem examinations have failed to prove any significant differences between 'confused' and 'normal' brains. Many studies have attempted to find a link with neuropathology. Many post-mortem examinations of demented brains have shown the deposition of neuro-fibrillary 'tangles' that accumulate within cells, and so-called 'senile plaques', which are patches of degenerating nerve terminals. The problem is that links between these features and dementia is not consistent; many demented brains do not show them when they should, and many non-demented brains do when they should not. Verwoerdt (1976) confirms that 'There appears to be no consistent relationship between intellectual deterioration and organic brain changes (especially in the milder cases)'. In any case, even if research did find a consistent neurological pattern, it would still not ask how or why some people develop dementia whilst others do not, and so begs an essential question.

There is other evidence which raises questions about linking 'brain death' with confusion in old age. Cohen and Faulkner (1984), comparing the memory of different age groups, found that memory varies according to what is being remembered. Over matters such as birthdays and anniversaries, answering letters, and so on, the old were significantly better than younger people. It should also be noted that there are many younger people who have developed the features of confused behaviour, and whose brains have been found to have developed 'senile plaques'. Moreover, those who work with confused elderly people will know that not everything they say and do, for every minute of every day, indicates a confused state of mind. Even the most confused individual can display flashes of lucidity which indicate that they are more aware of what is happening around them than we assume. All this indicates that the link between old age and confusion is far from straightforward, and needs to be carefully examined.

Psychiatric medicine is itself deeply split over how it sees mental illnesses, including dementia. For orthodox psychiatrists the existence of definable 'mental illness' constitutes their main claim to legitimacy in the conventional medical world. For others, 'mental' illnesses, such as confusion, are subjective value judgements made about deviations from normal behaviour, which in turn serve only to encourage both staff and patients to expect and accept unnecessarily the role of 'mental' patient (Goffman, 1963; Scheff, 1966; Szasz, 1973). They have described how definitions of mental illness are more vague than with physical illness, but these definitions nevertheless imply that cures are to be found in a clinic rather than seeking prevention through wider social and environmental understandings and reforms.

These questions do not deny the existence of a physical disease called 'dementia', but they should at least raise doubts about whether confusion is always a psycho-medical condition, and whether there are not other equally appropriate and accurate alternative explanations, perhaps based on social and environmental experiences. Again, it is important to emphasize that most ageing brains do not suffer decline leading to confusion, and that this would indicate that a wider understanding of the origin of confusional states is vital.

Why do the arteries of the brain narrow, and why do some brain cells deteriorate but not others? Are there environmental, social and emotional causes which have led to the significant increases in dementia we have witnessed this century? The potential role of counselling in elderly confusion depends crucially upon the answers to such questions. If confusion indicates either a disease entity or the normal and inevitable decline of an ageing mind, then counselling will have little significant part to play. But there is sufficient reason to doubt that this is the whole story, or even an adequate explanation of just part of it. Monsour and Robb (1982), in a review of the literature, concluded:

> that old age is basically a reflection of an aging person interacting with and reacting to the psychosocial and environmental demands. Because the exact mechanism of biological aging remains in doubt and because brain changes do not necessarily result in mental impairment, the assumption that organic causes give rise to wandering in old age must be questioned. It is, therefore, reasonable to assume that manifested behavioural patterns in old age, whether intact or distorted by illness, are, to some degree, rooted in the previous years of a person's life.

Why do we remain so selective in the observations we use to explain confusion despite the conflicting evidence that has been known for many decades? The concentration on neuro-psychological factors is a classic example of the 'medicalization' of a problem, reflecting the dominant pursuit of medical science of seeking 'treatment' or 'cures' for the things that go wrong in the human condition. The tendency to study and transform human problems into disease entities mirrors both the dominance of the medical profession and society's unwillingness to consider environmental and social causation. This has two main outcomes.

Firstly, the disease 'dementia' whilst it certainly exists, becomes the explanation for all confusional states in older people. Facts are selected, in this case that brain cells die progressively through life and that older people often become forgetful and lose their memories, and these are then combined to try to explain matters that do not follow – namely that the normal process of brain cell loss leads to senility.

The second outcome is that the onset of even mild confusional states are seen as essentially a medical problem, best treated medically. An alternative approach would be to clarify the complex network of social and environmental factors that can produce medical pathology, and thereafter seek prevention by a wider understanding of the nature of the problem.

The social creation of confusion: A tentative alternative

The medical view of dementia was first challenged by Meacher (1972) who, after outlining the literature of the 1950s and 1960s, concluded that confusion was a complex matter, involving a number of possible causes, none of which was conclusively proven. He adopted a classification which explained confused behaviour as a *logical reaction* to the emotional stresses of social isolation, powerlessness and segregation. This alternative view sees 'mental illness' arising largely from the problems of living in society. Whereas most people can cope reasonably well with the demands and problems of social life, others cannot; and their discontent and unhappiness generates behaviour which is then labelled as inappropriate, unacceptable or antisocial. Such behaviour is classified as an 'illness' merely because it is not considered to be 'normal'. It is this view of confusion that needs more attention, and which provides counselling with a potential role.

When the counsellor is confronted with what appears to be confusion, there should be an effort to discover whether the behaviour denotes some form of coded but meaningful communication, rather than assuming it to be the beginnings of a mental condition. Counselling should seek to find which of many factors have contributed to an individual becoming mentally confused. Has it occurred through normal ageing processes, resulting in organic mental impairment, which is certainly one option? Or is it the result of social, emotional or environmental factors which have made the reality of life intolerable?

The belief expressed here is that the origins of confusion can be rooted in social and environmental aetiology, and that this can lead to the medical conditions outlined earlier. This would indicate that skilled counselling can provide a valuable preventive, and even perhaps curative, role in dealing with the problems of confusion. In searching for the origins of a particular confusional state, the counsellor, perhaps in association with a concerned medical practitioner, should first consider all the potential causes of the condition.

1. Illness

The brain, especially the ageing brain, is a sensitive instrument which can be affected by a variety of external influences. Mild confusional symptoms can accompany an illness at any age, and is a well-known feature of illnesses which produce fever. Acute confusional states can arise from certain specific illnesses, perhaps the most common being infections of the chest, heart failure, high blood pressure, pneumonia and urine infections. Indeed, any illness which causes constant pain, even constipation, can bring about confused states (Wattis and Church, 1986). Verwoerdt (1976) adds many others, including epilepsy and liver disease, whilst Gray and Wilcock (1981) describe the effects of hydrocephalus and syphilis.

2. Hormonal imbalance

Older people are particularly susceptible to metabolic disorders which can cause confusion due to an imbalance in the body of hormones produced by the endocrine glands, or by malfunction in the kidney or the liver. A lack of thyroid hormone, hypothyroidism, produces tiredness, constipation and an intolerance to cold, as well as a confusional state that can be mistaken for Alzheimer's disease (Wattis and Church, 1986). Pernicious anaemia causes confusion when the amount of oxygen carried by the red blood cells to the brain is significantly reduced. Insulin from the pancreas, calcium from the parathyroid gland and urea from the kidney have also been mentioned (Gray and Wilcock, 1981), as has prostate gland trouble and weak kidney function.

All these potential causes of confusion indicate that when older people appear to be developing signs of confused behaviour, it does not follow automatically that they are beginning to develop senile dementia. They may recover quite normally with the help of sympathetic medical attention to these and similar factors.

3. Iatrogenic medical intervention

There is a considerable number of drugs, commonly used with older people for other conditions, which are now known to produce confusional states. Sedatives, antidepressants, tranquillizers, the long-acting benzodiazepines, sleeping pills, drugs based on digitalis, and anti-Parkinsonian drugs being the worst offenders. Wattis and Church (1986) have outlined some of the drugs which have been reported to cause or increase confusion in older people. These include digoxin, barbiturates, the Benzodiazepine group of drugs, tricyclic antidepressants, steroids, non-steroidal anti-inflammatory drugs, antihistamines, diuretics, and anti-Parkinsonian drugs. Yet, in fact, any drug can cause confusion because of the potential interactions with other drugs, including alcohol, and by drug misuse. All these factors make older people particularly susceptible because their kidneys do not eliminate drugs so efficiently from the body, making a build-up of toxicity more likely. The counsellor should check the medication currently being prescribed, and where this causes concern a consultation with a sympathetic doctor, with a view to withdrawing or changing the offending drugs, should be organized.

4. Nutritional factors

The link between nutrition and confusion has long been suspected. Thiamin (vitamin B_1) deficiency, according to Gray and Wilcock (1981), can cause rapid delirium associated with changes in the nerves, and a profound and relatively sudden loss of memory. Along with Wattis and Church (1986), they also mention that vitamin B_{12} deficiency can be mistaken for Alzheimer's disease, and that thiamin deficiency can result in the permanent loss of short-term memory and confabulation. Folic acid, potassium, vitamin B_6, protein, iron and calorie deficiencies have also been linked with confusion. Recent research at Southampton University has linked Alzheimer's disease with aluminium in water supplies in certain areas. If this is correct, the drinking of tea is likely to be an important contributory factor.

Statistics relating to social class indicate that the poorer social classes suffer most from confusion, and this in turn suggests that nutritional links with confusion might be a profitable area for future research. There is also evidence that the consumption of certain foods, such as liver and fish, is helpful in preventing the onset of senile dementia (McDerment and Greengross, 1985), and more research might also be undertaken in this area.

5. Social factors

The primary contention here is that when people suffer from social distress, perhaps arising from bereavement or severe social isolation, they can exhibit features which can be mistaken for confusion, and which can thereafter lead to a confusional state. It is already known that depression is often diagnosed as confusion, but it is also true that biochemical and hormonal factors which lead to those psychological disturbances are often linked to social trauma (Petty and Sensky, 1987). From such a position it is a logical progression to link confusional states, and the biochemical changes found in the brain, with stress arising from social circumstances.

Within ageism, there is a set of powerful social expectations about older people losing their memories, becoming forgetful and losing control over their minds. These attitudes, as we have seen, can become self-fulfilling. Yet however important ageism may be in establishing resignation, older people do not become confused just because they expect to, or we expect them to. Although we need to de-condition people about the limitations of old age, there are many features of social life which might be instrumental in creating, developing and reinforcing confused mental states. Their impact is to make the lives of many older people unbearable, so unbearable in fact that they become unwilling to retain contact with the present realities. Living has become too difficult, too painful for them to bear, so they withdraw mentally from experiencing it. They refuse to cope any longer, they disengage and enter a world of their own which they fill only with what they want to have there.

If confusion is a response by older people to current social practices and values, a reaction to the ravages of grief and time, to low income, poor housing, low morale, low social status, and to neglect, counselling has an important role which has barely been recognized as yet. The first step must be to examine some of the social processes which might contribute to a confused old age. Bergmann and Jacoby (1983) looked at the research evidence and found that six groups of older people seemed most vulnerable to developing confused states.

1. Older people over 75 years of age, and living alone.
2. Older people recently suffering bereavement.
3. Older people recently discharged from hospital.
4. Older people requiring home help and community services.
5. Older people requesting residential care.
6. Older people who are planning to give up their homes.

The association of these factors with confusion is noteworthy, for living alone, bereavement, the loss of independence and the effects of medical treatment have all been central to the overall argument in support of counselling for older people. This indicates that effective counselling undertaken at the time of crisis might be a powerful preventive tool.

Confusion has a strong social class component. It is older people from the lower socio-economic groups that more usually become confused, and this might give a firm clue to one of the social origins of confusion – the struggle against poverty and hardship that many older people have fought throughout their lives. The burden of poverty is a heavy one which eventually takes its toll on the human condition. It is not necessary here to go into detail about how this happens. The stress of day-to-day management on insufficient money, poorer dietary and health care, unhealthier working and living conditions, and so on, create the circumstances which encourage mental stress and eventually, perhaps, psychological withdrawal and confusion. Similar links have already been made between poverty, social neglect and other forms of mental illness, such as schizophrenia.

Yet confusion does not only occur in the poorer classes. Stress, anxiety and worry are classless social phenomena, playing a part in all our lives regardless of income and social status. Poverty merely brings an important additional dimension. A well-established response to high levels of stress is to withdraw, to seek solace elsewhere, even at times in our own company. Stress-induced behaviour is not always entirely rational. We do things we would consider untypical and foolhardy in more relaxed times. We let ourselves down. We feel sorry for ourselves, wallow in our troubles, and consider the world to be an unfair place. We become anti-social. One 'advantage' of being old is that such behaviour has acquired a label which, whilst stigmatizing and uncomfortable, provides an opportunity for older people to withdraw legitimately. Whilst the desire to die may not be a practical possibility, the demise of the mind, a kind of mental suicide, might be an easier objective. Whilst confusion should not be seen as a voluntary state, consciously chosen by the individual who can no longer bear the realities of life in the wake of intolerable social distress, it may nonetheless provide a convenient means of escape. Allied to this is the social isolation of old age. The spectre of living alone is a daunting prospect to many people, especially when the importance of attachment is considered. The ability to communicate and share with other people is an important factor in our continuing sanity. Social communication in all its many forms, dialogue, argument, debate, disagreement and so on, serves to engage our bodies and minds. It helps to keep us active, involved and lucid. In contrast, the harsh effects of solitary confinement on prisoners is well known, and the outcomes can perhaps be legitimately related to confusion in older people.

Yet there is another form of 'isolation', even for those older people who have regular contact with other people. This is the isolation which arises from a perceived lack of understanding and concern, when their complaints are brushed aside as trivial, their feelings discounted as unnecessary or silly. What they say appears to be unimportant, they feel ignored, no-one seems to take the trouble to discover how they feel. They sense that they are too much trouble, a burden, and perhaps begin to feel that there is no-one who cares whether they live or die. This is not how life used to be, when they had people who cared about them. The 'old days' are remembered with fondness. Usually, confused people choose first to forget the more recent, unpleasant realities. Social isolation in old age can also arise from deafness, blindness and aphasia, and the effects these conditions have on the individual should never be under-estimated.

The growing dependence of older people can also play a part in the social creation of confusion. We have seen how the loss of independence signifies for some a damaging blow to pride and morale. Each successive loss in coping abilities necessitates an emotional adjustment, and this can cause some older people the deepest distress.

Fear can be another factor. The ageing process can be frightening, particularly when allied with growing dependence and increasing loneliness. Fear has many irrational impacts on the mind. Fears can become obsessional, leading to obsessional behaviour, panic, and can eventually break our confidence in coping with problems of everyday life. Older people can be afraid not least because they live in a world that has changed out of all recognition from the one in which they were nurtured. Add to this the fear of illness and death, the fear of burglary and mugging, the fear of falling, and there is good reason for older people to be afraid, and to experience all the effects this has on both mind and behaviour.

The relocation of home, or an unwanted move into hospital or residential care, can also contribute to confusion. Social upheaval happens more frequently to older people after they lose control of their lives, through greater dependency and the relinquishing of the right to make decisions for themselves. One consequence of this may be for older individuals to relinquish total personal responsibility for their lives. Confused behaviour may also be induced, maintained and perpetuated by the institutional care of hospitals and residential homes. The loss of independence, unfamiliar surroundings and the stress that these changes can bring often lead to the onset of confusion in older people.

Little wonder then that some older people, having gone through a variety of these circumstances, should 'refuse' to stay mentally lucid. When people are unable to resolve their own difficulties there is perhaps an understandable tendency to withdraw. The 'confused' mind can be a more comfortable state in which to live than the world of social reality. It becomes easier to allow other people to assume responsiblity for their problems, for they feel that they can no longer cope with them. In this sense, the drift into confusion might be considered a rational decision by the individual. Whether these factors, illness, hormonal imbalances, medicines, nutrition and social factors, then lead to brain death or dementia, or the narrowing of the arteries in the brain, is a matter for conjecture, only supported by circumstantial evidence. Yet they would explain why some older people become confused whilst others do not, and offer a wider, more acceptable basis for the medical examination of the ultimate disease condition.

The role of the counsellor

There is no proven method of counselling confused or demented people, perhaps because our current state of knowledge has been held back by the medicalization of the problem, and by ageist attitudes which have assumed the condition to be an inevitable part of growing old. Immediate intervention is probably vital. The more developed the condition becomes, the less likely it is to be reversed. Even the limited idea that counselling may have potential in preventing or containing confusional states is not proven, but this should not stop concerned individuals attempting to use counselling approaches towards this end. Three factors in counselling confused older people need to be considered.

The first is simple caring, which should underlie counselling work at every stage of confusion. No-one can know for certain what dementia feels like, for those who suffer from it are unable to give an explanation, and they do not recover an ability to do so. So we know very little of the personal experience of confused individuals and how they feel about the reactions of other people. Yet it is likely that some of the basic principles of human relations taken for granted when dealing with other people apply equally when working with confused individuals. Spending time with them is crucially important, not rushing them or taking over from them because of their inability to think concisely or logically. It is important to communicate normally with confused individuals, avoiding the tendency to agree with everything they say, or to dismiss what they say as garbled or meaningless. Marples (1986) states that:

> Throughout the course of dementing illness, the individual remains sensitive to the attitudes of those around him. He detects insincerity, along with the irritation and impatience caregivers try to suppress. Although the senile person may not be in sufficient control of his behaviour to act willfully, he is able to respond to others' feelings and act out his frustration.

Confused individuals have the same feelings and needs as other people, and should not be patronized, as so often happens. Their need for love, affection and consideration remains undiminished. The counsellor should be able to offer the security and ongoing support of the counselling relationship, for ultimately this will provide the individual with a sound basis from which he or she may feel sufficiently 'safe' to renew contact with the world of difficult and uncomfortable reality.

The second task involves recognizing the symptoms of confusion quickly, and assessing the possible causes, whether these be ill-health, nutritional, iatrogenic, or arising from social factors. If it is suspected that confusion might arise from any of the first three factors, these should be investigated immediately, enlisting the help of those people who are able to offer an informed opinion. It has been found in some studies that dementia proves to be treatable in 15% to 30% of cases (Ropper, 1979). In this respect it is fortunate that the changes in early dementia are gradual, so that time is available for finding and enlisting support.

Dealing with the possible social causes of confusion should be the third task in the counselling process. Confusion often arises from social circumstances of extreme unhappiness. Despite such origins it is important that the counsellor does not believe that confusion is a happy state of mind, best left alone. The main premise underlying the counselling of confusion should be that the individual's social and emotional problems have not always been faced and resolved in the past, and that a withdrawal from reality has resulted. It follows that a confused state can only be dealt with effectively if those same problems and difficulties are re-engaged and tackled within the counselling process.

Reality orientation and reminiscence

Reality orientation (RO) and reiminiscence are two approaches to working with older people suffering from confusion. Reminiscence has already been discussed regarding its general application to counselling older people, although its value in this respect has been less well developed. RO has been more specifically designed for its application to confused people, and has been used to a far greater extent.

Reality orientation is a major approach to working with older people with mental confusion. As its name implies, the technique seeks to maintain the confused individual in the existing world of reality. More often, the technique is used with people who are already seriously confused, and it is based on an essentially behaviourist methodology. This begins with the recognition that the mind of the individual is no longer functioning in the real world, but in an unrealistic and confused world of their own. It continues by interpreting confused behaviour as inappropriate, seeking to rectify the situation by insisting on behaviour which is more in line with reality. It makes use of a variety of techniques to draw attention to reality; the correct day, month and year; the correct time; the nature of the weather; the place where the individual is, and who he or she is with. It focuses on common, well-known objects, asking the person simple facts about their colour, their shape, their feel, their use, and so on. Attempts are made to maintain attention and concentration for as long as possible. Correct responses have to be made, or the questions are repeated until they are. Rewards are given for appropriate responses, and sometimes punishments are used for inappropriate responses.

Reality orientation can be performed individually, or in small groups. It is considered to be more effective the more frequently it is done. Twenty-four hour reality orientation is considered ideal, usually undertaken in hospitals or specialized homes for confused elderly people where the living environment can be entirely devoted to reality. However, it is perhaps more often performed as a regular series of sessions, undertaken as frequently as time and energy permit. RO recognizes the need regularly to confront individuals with reality, refusing to accept that their confusion is either a happy or a necessary state of mind. This is in contrast to the tendency to leave confused individuals alone in their own world, and not to bother them beyond tending to their most basic needs.

However, in counselling terms, the concept and practice of reality orientation should be considered with some reservation, and its limitations and drawbacks well understood. All behavioural techniques assume that behaviour is learned and not actively chosen by people in making sense of their lives. It disqualifies the idea that the individual might modify their behaviour in response to their particular social circumstances. Behaviour is inappropriate because it does not respond to reality; as such, it is not to be understood, but changed. RO also focuses almost entirely on the present and, like all techniques based on behavioural theories, it tends to discount the idea that the problems of the past and present have contributed to confused and depressed states of mind.

Reality orientation is usually practised with a system of rewards for correct and appropriate behaviour. The correct response gains some form of standardized reward, whether this be a physical gift or an emotionally warm reaction. Incorrect behaviour is punished, or at least certainly not rewarded. Whilst it is reward rather than punishment which is stressed, this assumes that the rewarding of appropriate behaviour, by its very nature, involves the punishment of inappropriate behaviour; withholding rewards in itself can be seen as a punishment. As such, RO can be seen to be trying to cajole or force often unwilling minds back into the present. Standardized rewards and punishments are what make reality orientation a 'scientific' technique, and this makes the technique particularly attractive to some people. Yet by presenting itself as a scientific method, RO is provided with a justification for what can be seen as an impersonal technique of control and coercion.

Behavioural techniques also assume that there is a general consensus on what constitutes acceptable behaviour, interpreted of course by the dominant norms and values of society. These tend to discount the presence of 'meaning' in 'abnormal' or non-conventional individual behaviour. The structure of behavioural techniques does not allow individuals an opportunity to communicate their feelings and wishes, nor does it help them to describe the meanings they attribute to their own behaviour. Yet when counselling confused older people, it is particularly important to reach an understanding of why an individual is unwilling to face up to present-day realities. However, to do so would interfere with the 'scientific' basis on which much RO work is based, in which both behaviour and the responses given to behaviour should be standardized. The fundamental difference between RO and counselling is that, whereas the former sets out to change or modify behaviour considered to be inappropriate, the latter seeks to discover *why* that behaviour has become inappropriate. Certainly, the counsellor should be attempting to do more than alter behaviour in order to make it conform to accepted social norms.

The result is that RO can be a narrow technique whose practical impact on the individual can often be cold and impersonal, concentrating solely upon those very issues and situations of current reality which are most difficult for the individual. It says, in effect: 'We notice that you have rejected reality; and we, who believe that reality is all-important, are going to insist that you live in the real world'.

However, the technique of RO cannot be entirely dismissed, either in its own right or as an integral part of a counselling programme. Indeed it can be argued that, because of its problems, the use of RO with confused elderly people can only be justified if it is part of more personalized and supportive methods of care, such as counselling.

Reminiscence work with confused older individuals is a more recent development (Cook, 1984; Norris and Eileh, 1982). Although its value has not been quantified, reminiscence work does have several advantages over RO. Coleman (1986) suggests that reminiscence may be a means for older confused people to communicate feelings which, if expressed directly, would be difficult for them (and/or their carers) to handle. To support this, he asks whether confused older people often speak as if their parents were alive because of their personal needs for security, and to maintain a sense of their roots. This would certainly be in harmony with the concept of the social creation of confusion.

Reminiscence also tends to focus on times when individuals were in full possession of their skills and abilities. Thus, unlike RO, the counsellor can begin with the pleasant experiences of the past rather than the pain of the present, and therefore engage in a joyful rather than a sad exchange. This is clearly a better starting point for the counselling process.

The material used in reminiscence sessions with older confused people has to be carefully chosen. In selecting this, help from friends and relatives can be invaluable. Norris (1986) uses three criteria for the selection of material. It should be clear and unambiguous; it should be relevant to the past and the experience of the individual; and it should involve the stimulation of as many senses as possible. It should also be sparingly used, with care being taken that it does not overwhelm the individual, and thus lead to more rather than less confusion.

Through reminiscence, the counsellor can often gain access to the skills and abilities that are retained by the confused individual. Often they can be skills which were previously believed to be lost. It is often possible to elicit positive responses from the confused individual, however irrelevant or inappropriate these may be. Thereafter the counsellor can seek to stimulate further, more accurate social interaction. Counsellees may be unable to use words to describe their feelings, but smiles and other gestures can give the counsellor a powerful indication of how they feel. Such interactions can often demonstrate that the individual does retain skills and abilities, however limited these may be in more extreme cases of confusion.

Reminiscence can bring older confused people back into meaningful and enjoyable communication with another individual. From this point of contact the counsellor can try to extend, slowly and with care, towards the reality of the present, perhaps initially switching to mundane events such as eating and toileting, and then to more meaningful discussion of present circumstances. Such transfer from matters past to matters present is usually difficult, and often has to be done slowly and imperceptibly.

The animation that can arise from such experiences between carers and confused people can be considerable. This is particularly so in relationships which have become very sad and one-directional. Reminiscence can help to transform and rekindle for carers the purpose of their caring task, which can be a particularly wearing and thankless one in normal circumstances.

Some general considerations when counselling confused people

Counselling should seek to make sense of present realities, the aim being to help individuals come to terms with their life, to accept it, and where possible to help individuals re-assume personal responsibility for it. In doing so, they need to face up to and resolve the problems which beset them.

Communication is a vital consideration. Throughout the counselling process, it is important to be clear and concise in conversation. The more confused people become, the more difficulty they have in responding to what is said to them. This does not necessarily mean that they do not understand what we say to them, or that they do not appreciate our attempt to communicate meaningfully with them. The counsellor should not be afraid to repeat questions, kindly and gently, or to insist upon focusing attention on the crucial matters at issue.

There are a variety of simple aids which can be used with confused people, especially in the early stages of confusion. Diaries, note pads and scrapbooks have been used to stimulate memory in reality orientation programmes, but they can also be used in a more casual way, and can be helpful in improving performance and reducing frustration. A life history book can be constructed which contains basic information and facts, photographs and other memorabilia from the life of an individual. This can then be used both as a source of ongoing reminiscence work, and to remind confused people of the reality of past events, particularly the death of former loved ones.

The encouragement of activity, and especially activity which gives rise to social contact, is also vital. Too often, confused older people are left to sit in one place for most of the day, often on the basis that they appear to be content doing so. The somnolence of confused elderly people is both caused by confusion and, if allowed, can further deepen the confused state. Where possible it is important that the counsellor tries to get counsellees involved in doing those things which both interest and occupy their minds. Above all, attempts should be made to get people involved in the kind of social contact which provides intellectual stimulation. The absence of social companionship is one possible cause of confusion, and to be involved in the argument, discussion and debate of normal relationships may provide individuals with the intellectual 'exercise' they require to resist further decline.

Any work with confused individuals is time-consuming, and progress can be slow, often imperceptible. Those who expect rapid results and measurable progress will be disappointed. There are no easy solutions to confusion, and there will be none as long as our approach to confusion is so one-dimensionally medicalized, and negatively fatalistic. Counsellors have to be patient, their expectations realistically moderate, realizing that even stability can constitute success, especially with an individual whose drift into confusion had previously been rapid. The rewards are usually limited, but nonetheless real enough for those committed to the well-being of the individual. Considerable work is required before anyone will know whether some of the problems of confusion can more positively be overcome through conselling, reminiscence, reality orientation, or any other technique.

Caring for the carers

The frustration and despair of carers of confused individuals is a common experience. Caring for confused elderly people is probably the most difficult task of all. Carers can experience psychological stress, physical fatigue, and entire families can be disrupted (Marples, 1986). This can in turn lead to anger, bewilderment, feelings of inadequacy and resentment and, in extreme circumstances, to violent physical abuse of the confused individual. Certainly in cases of severe dementia, the most important task that the counsellor can often perform is to support the carers rather than engage in more direct but speculative work with the confused individual.

CHAPTER 20

Bereavement and grief

Bereavement is a term associated with the death of close friends and relatives, although it is often used as a term depicting loss in other ways, many of which have been discussed in earlier chapters. Death, throughout life, is something that happens to other people. We do not generally lead our lives with a lively consciousness of our own mortality. It crosses our mind, impinging at certain times, but we are reluctant to dwell on the subject. There are exceptions; the composer Mahler, whose music was preoccupied with death, springs to mind. But for most it is always some time away; we decide to deal with it later. In general, only those in their later years of life spend time pondering on death, and even then there is a tendency to believe that it is a subject either too remote, or too 'morbid' for serious consideration.

Cultural aspects of death

The reluctance to face death has always been a facet of former cultures, but the way we deal with death has changed considerably in modern western society. Religious belief and traditional customs surrounding death were attempts to help people come to terms with the personal loss in their lives through rituals whose purpose was to focus minds on what had happened. These rituals, and the belief structures which underlie them, are no longer such a powerful social force in western culture (Gower, 1965). Even those elements which are still routinely performed are undertaken without the support of personal conviction, and so with much less meaning to the bereaved. The decline of religious belief is one example of how an element of dominant ideology has been challenged, diminished and largely replaced by other ideas.

The problem with religious approaches to bereavement has always been that they use theological ideas about the after-life in order to take away the pain of death. They tell us that we will meet loved ones again, that they have gone to a 'better' place where there is no suffering. Whilst this emphasis on the next world may actually be helpful to someone who cannot come to terms with the non-existence of a loved one, this is essentially a philosophy of denial. There is a little in such ideas, however deeply the individual believes, to make the present pain and the present social reality any better. They provide little help to people who need to restructure their lives in the real world. The loss of religious rituals is felt so strongly not because they were particularly effective, but because of the failure to replace them with anything else.

The family unit was another important element of our cultural response to bereavement, providing a strong basis of support and a sense of continuity in life. However, as we have seen the family itself is no longer such a strong institution. Its traditional role of caring for the dying was as the ever-present entity which, in the process of its caring, helped develop an acceptance of what was happening to the dying person, and provided a firm basis for the renewal and continuation of life.

The sanitization of bereavement

In more recent years many trends have developed which seek to avoid the feelings of grief that accompany death. The process of dying increasingly takes place outside the home, in hospital or hospices. Even when death occurs within the home, the body is removed within hours, certainly far quicker than was once the case, and taken to a chapel of rest where it is encased in a coffin. Viewing the body of the diseased has become another facet of family life removed from the home. The aim is to ease the pain and discomfort of death for those left behind so that the whole depressing business can be so much more quickly forgotten. Dying has been passed into the hands of the professionals, whose services seek to relieve the bereaved from responsibility, and carry out the necessary business efficiently and unemotionally. In many ways, dying has become a lonely, almost a dehumanized event because we have assumed that what is required after death is professionalism, and not the involvement and support of close friends and relatives.

Even the words associated with 'death' have become taboo, not to be mentioned in 'polite' society. To avoid their use we hide them behind phrases such as 'He's gone', 'passed away', 'at peace', 'at rest', 'sleeping', 'gone to a better place', and even colloquial phrases such as 'snuffing it' or 'kicking the bucket', and so on. To talk openly about death is subtly considered as bad taste, or an indication of morbid interest or curiosity. The less said about the subject the better.

Even common remarks associated with dying are not necessarily reassuring. We comment that sudden death is 'a blessing' because 'at least they did not suffer'. This tends only to give the impression that death is normally accompanied by great pain and suffering, when the fact is that once the emotional anguish has been faced it is more often a calm and peaceful process. Yet at the same time such remarks do little to remedy the loss that is being felt by the person left behind. It succumbs again to the process of denial.

The potential role of counselling

So the processes of death and bereavement have been sanitized. The traditional period of grief and mourning has been largely replaced by an efficient mechanical process controlled by the medical profession, and then by firms of undertakers in misguided attempts to lessen the feelings of loss and bereavement. The old rituals and ceremonies have gradually declined, and with them much of our former knowledge of what to do, what to say, and how to support the bereaved. The old etiquettes and niceties have been replaced by an embarrassed uncertainty. Those who bemoan the passing of the old certainties of faith and ritual probably miss the real point of religious ceremony. It was not so much the belief in life hereafter that was important, but the comfort arising from the opportunities provided for friends and relatives to pay their respects and to give comfort. The abandonment of tradition has left the bereaved in a vacuum, and it is within this vacuum that bereavement counselling can play a part.

The price that we now pay is the failure to recognize the finality of death, its implications for those who have to continue living without a close friend and companion, and how to respond to their troubled emotions. We are conscious of the suffering associated with death, particularly for those closest to the deceased. In our desire to protect them from the pain and turmoil surrounding death, we attempt to shield them from it but in doing so, we are protecting them from a necessary process. Grief represents pain in the short term, but once it has been faced it contains the healing power to help us come to terms with our emotions, enabling us to re-establish our lives in the real world. But whilst the pain of grief eventually heals, the grief first needs to be experienced, and suffered in full.

The common desire of carers to protect the bereaved from grief is therefore a mistake, particularly with older people who more than most are surrounded by loss, grief and bereavement. This desire might arise from understandable concern. When they are already old, troubled, ailing and frail, the tendency to protect them from further pain can be seen as a kindness, and this is why it is a constantly recurring feature of working with older people. In one brief spell in an elderly persons' home, the author came across several cases of older people who had been 'protected' in this manner. A daughter who emigrated without telling her ageing mother. Elderly wives who had not been allowed to attend their husbands' funerals, or view their bodies. Relatives who did not tell their mother of the death of her son. A bereaved wife who was not allowed to remain living in her own home, and was placed in residential care within days of the death.

Consequently, even after the passing of several years, these individuals were still grieving, and in some cases still paying a heavy emotional and psychological price for what had happened. Many became confused, and their confusion dated from the time when death was inappropriately handled by carers. Yet all this was done 'in their own best interests'. To be living happily with a loved one, and then to find oneself living in strange surroundings is social disruption on a monumental scale, designed to create mental infirmity in even the strongest of wills. And it is done to people who are themselves closer to their own death, and all that this implies, than their misguided carers. They would have been aware of the imminence of death; they might even have welcomed the opportunity of discussing it.

No carers, particularly of older people, have the right to deprive the bereaved of their pain. Pain may perhaps seem a strange 'right', but as death is a normal part of life, and as we are all hurt by the death of those close to us, we should not be deprived of the consequent grief by those who mistakenly believe that they know better. Rather than protecting people from their natural grief, the counsellor should assume the responsibility to both prepare them for death, and to help them through the process of grieving. Grief cannot be avoided, but counselling offers the bereaved an opportunity to share it with someone who cares.

Patterns of normal grieving

The work of Parkes (1972) suggested that there were four stages through which normal grieving proceeded. The process begins with the initial shock followed by a period of numbness, which he found was the most common response immediately on death, and which could last anything from a few hours to many days. This numbness is the body's natural tranquillizer, probably very necessary to shield the individual from the intensity of the immediate pain of losing a loved one.

This is followed by a period of yearning and protest, during which the bereaved is totally preoccupied with the deceased person, suffering considerable pain and anguish, constantly going over the events leading up to the death, and the circumstances of the death itself. It is a period of great sadness, tearfulness, self-reproach and guilt. This is often mixed with anger and self-pity.

The third stage sees the bereaved experiencing considerable depression and disorganization, in which aimlessness, apathy, listlessness, hopelessness, restless activity, lack of concentration, inability to sleep, loss of appetite, lethargy and a general lack of purpose dominate. It is a period of social withdrawal and loneliness, of anxiety about future life without the deceased. The final stage is one of re-organization, in which the depression gradually subsides, and interest in normal activities begins to re-emerge.

Yet the experience of bereavement will vary greatly from one individual to another, to such an extent that it is probably unwise to talk of patterns. Bereavement can, of course, also be associated with feelings of relief and emancipation. The degree to which any of these feelings will affect people will vary according to individual personality, and social contacts. Those who have a wide circle of friends and who make new relationships easily will tend to cope better. Recovery time will also vary, from those who are able quickly to repair the damage to their lives to those who spend long periods in mourning, suffering from the normal symptoms of grief.

Older people do tend to take death badly, both because it is largely their generation that is dying, and because death is closer to their own future expectations. This can be particularly vivid when ageing people live in sheltered accommodation or residential care, where deaths occur with relative frequency, and where the modern social tendency to hide from the social realities of death is often too evident.

Worden (1983) looks at the grieving process in a way that may be more helpful to the counsellor. He considers that mourning has four tasks, and that the counsellor should seek to ensure that these tasks are successfully achieved. The first is to accept reality of loss, and to prevent denial. The counselling task here is to help confirm awareness of the reality of the loss. The second task is to experience the pain of grief, where the counselling role is to help individuals go through all their feelings. The third task is to adjust to the environment in which the deceased is missing, and in doing this the counsellor can help the bereaved overcome the various impediments which stand in the way of adjustment. The final task of mourning is to withdraw emotional energy from the deceased and to re-invest it in other relationships. Here the task of the counsellor is to enable the counsellee to feel able to withdraw from past relationships, and to be comfortable in investing in new relationships.

When taking individuals through this process, the counsellor should give assurance that what they are feeling is quite normal, that the grief will eventually pass, and that life will continue. But it is important to do so in a way that does not deny or diminish the pain that they are currently feeling. Indeed, the task of the counsellor is to enable the counsellee to feel, and to feel safe about feeling. Understanding, support and encouragement are the invaluable contributions the counsellor can make, whilst time alone can do the rest.

Patterns of abnormal grieving

Although regular pathways through grief exist, it is also true that grief does not always follow this pattern of recovery. Sometimes, bereaved people feel that they are 'going mad' with grief, perhaps when they believe that they hear the deceased, or set a table and cook a meal with them in mind. Many individuals may continue experiencing grief for several years after the bereavement. Indeed, bereavement can and often does lead to serious psychiatric conditions. Parkes and Weiss (1983) identified three common patterns of grief which they considered abnormal.

1. Sudden and unexpected beareavement

The chief problem with a sudden and unexpected bereavement is shock and disbelief which often delays recovery from the grieving process. Indeed, Parkes and Weiss found that in many cases a 'stubborn persistence' in grieving seriously delayed the time when the bereaved felt able to initiate new relationships. They could not accept the full reality of the loss. They withdrew from social contact and persisted in the belief of the presence of the dead person, with strong feelings of self-reproach and despair and a continuing obligation to the dead. This reaction was found to be quite different from those who had had warning of the bereavement, and although the grief was not necessarily more painful, it was found to be both more disabling and more difficult to recover from.

None of these feelings protected the bereaved person from loneliness, anxiety and depression. The process of recovery and the recommencement of social functioning was seriously delayed, and so was considered to be abnormal.

2. Ambivalent grief

It is widely assumed, with some justification, that the degree of closeness and interdependence that the individual feels determines the degree of grief experienced. The nature and quality of the lost relationship will obviously be an important factor, with close, loving relationships being harder to lose, but this is not necessarily completely so. Within such relationships there is less guilt, and less unresolved business. More tempestuous relationships, whilst we may believe them to be less fulfilling, often fulfil deep personal needs, and separation may supply a 'quieter life' that is neither wanted nor appreciated.

Parkes and Weiss (1983) found that whilst the immediate reaction to a loss of this kind may be one of relief, as time passes feelings of intense despair emerge. This occurs because whilst the conflict within the relationship may have produced real anger and hostility, these feelings co-existed with attachment and affection. The ambivalence was often found to be the result of relationships between individuals who have difficulty in establishing more satisfactory attachments. The response can also be self-reproachful, where the bereaved feels compelled to make restitution for the failures of the relationship, but can find no satisfactory way of doing so. Again, delayed grieving leads to delayed recovery.

Chronic grief

Chronic or intractable grief is excessive in duration, and never reaches an entirely satisfactory resolution. It was associated by Parkes and Weiss (1983) with the end of highly dependent relationships, which they defined as relationships in which the individuals were unable to function adequately in social life without the presence, emotional support or actual help of the partner. Grief is expressed from the beginning, but is associated with high levels of yearning and intense feelings of helplessness, and continues for abnormal lengths of time.

Risk factors determing abnormal grief

The likelihood of the individual experiencing abnormal grief reactions is heightened by the existence of certain factors which have been widely researched. Four general areas of concern have been outlined (Parkes, 1985).

The first area covers the type of death. Problems arise when the bereaved feels that there is some reason for personal blame or when death is sudden, unexpected or untimely, or where it has occurred in circumstances which were painful, horrifying or mismanaged.

The second area concerns the characteristics of the lost relationship. The loss of a very close relationship, and particularly the death of a spouse or a child, can lead to abnormal grieving; but abnormal grief is more likely to occur when the relationship was either dependent or ambivalent.

The personal characteristics of the survivor constitute the third group of factors. Grief has been found to exacerbate personality characteristics so if an individual has a tendency towards insecurity, bereavement will tend to worsen it. Other important pre-determining personality factors are a grief-prone personality, over-anxiety, low self-esteem, previous mental illness, excessive self-reproach, physical disablement or a history of ill-health, previous unresolved losses, and an inability to express feelings.

Social circumstances make up the final group of factors which can give rise to abnormal grieving. Such factors include an absent or unsupportive family, detachment from traditional support systems, unemployment, the existence of dependent children, low socio-economic status, and the prior existence of other losses. Chronic grief can also arise when, for whatever reason, there is a lack of opportunity to grieve.

Where there is any significant combination of these factors, abnormal grief becomes more likely, and the counselling task becomes both more important and potentially more difficult.

Recovery from bereavement – the counselling approach

1. Preparation for bereavement

The timing and circumstances of death have crucial effects on the grieving process. Any support offered to older people prior to a bereavement can beneficially influence subsequent recovery. This is often possible when there has been a long illness, or gradual decline to death. Those who have watched the gradual death of a loved one will often have gone through an exhausting physical and emotional experience. But where this happens, there has at least been more opportunity for individuals to prepare themselves for an imminent and inevitable bereavement. In some cases, people who pass through this experience are able to prepare themselves for death when it eventually comes. But many more fail to do so.

There are several ways in which the counsellor can help to prepare older people for bereavement. The first is to ensure that the counsellee is receiving correct and accurate information, and is not either being misinformed, or failing to accept the inevitability of what is likely to occur. If this is done the counsellee can be enabled to fulfill many tasks which will be helpful at a later stage. The problems and anxieties following death can be anticipated and discussed. Opportunities can be taken for making restitution for any failures or ambivalences in the relationship so that this is done prior to death and does not become a matter of regret later. All the messages of sorrow, apologies, thanks, remorse and love can be expressed. And perhaps most important, the people involved can be encouraged to share memories, both good and bad, and these can be relived for the final time.

The counsellor should give consideration to the entire situation surrounding the death, and wherever possible encourage the bereaved to be involved at all stages of the dying process.

2. *The early stages of grief: support, listening and acceptance*

The early stages of grieving will require important decisions about the availability of care and counselling. Getting the level of support right is vital. There is a tendency either to leave the bereaved individual alone, often because being in the presence of deep grief is too uncomfortable for others; or to insist that the individual is not left alone, either to prevent too much isolated mourning or in fear of what self-harm the individual might inflict. The decision taken over the level of support provided should usually be a sensible balance between these two extreme responses, and based upon the expressed desires of the individual concerned.

Perhaps the first principle of counselling those who have suffered an important bereavement is openness. This requires that counsellors make it known, by word and action, that death is not a taboo subject, and that they are willing to talk about the counsellees' feelings. It is important to ask the bereaved questions about the death, how it happened, the cause, how they found out, details of the funeral, which all indicate that counsellors are willing to move into these areas should the bereaved wish to do so.

Counsellors have to be good listeners, entirely sensitive to the feelings of the individual. They will have to cope with a variety of reactions, varying from tears, anger, hopelessness, a refusal to accept what has occurred, and despair, to feelings of unfairness and injustice, a desire for personal death, and many others. None of these feelings should be denied. It is not the task of counsellors to tell individuals how to react, what they should feel, or what they should do in response to their emotions. Throughout the early stages of grief, the counsellors' task is to listen and understand, with no attempt to understate or belittle the significance of the death to the individual. The only ameliorative that counselling should attempt to bring to the bereaved is the comfort of knowing that someone is there who is prepared to spend time with them.

Sometimes it may be necessary to ensure that the bereaved individual is given sufficient time to grieve. The idea that people should recover quickly from bereavement is common, and attractive because it makes life easier for those close to them who otherwise have to witness their distress. Worden (1983) suggests that particular times can be difficult, mentioning three months and one year after the death as being the most frequent times of personal difficulty. Personal anniversaries, important within the relationship, are also often a problem.

The reverse problem, faced particularly by older people, is that there are insufficient alternatives to grief. Younger people eventually feel the need to return to work, feeling that they are better 'doing' something. This avenue is often unavailable to older people.

3. *Facing up to the reality of bereavement*

Acceptance of the reality of loss should be a primary counselling objective, and this is only possible by full involvement with that reality. This is why it is so dangerous to deny people, older people in particular, the right to see the body, to attend the funeral and to continue to live in the same home. If the counsellor has entered a situation in which these damaging experiences have already occurred, there will probably be a need to take the individual back through the pain of loss and grieving, perhaps by discussions with relatives, visits to graveyards or merely by recounting the circumstances of the death.

The acceptance of reality does not involve forgetting the past or denying the importance of what has occurred. It concerns the recognition that fundamental change has taken place, and that it has deeply affected the counsellee's life. How it has affected it, and what to do about it is what the individual has to decide.

Many bereaved people try to avoid the intense distress connected with grief, either through activity or distracting behaviour, drugs, alcohol or some other form of denial. This should not be surprising given that the intense and apparently unremitting feelings of loss and sorrow can be overwhelming. Indeed, it can seem cruel to insist that they talk about their pain, but the counsellor should seek to ensure that the individual accepts the pain of bereavement, and does not try to avoid it. Only through the acceptance of their grief can individuals begin the process of coming to terms with a new reality over a period of time.

A particular word is required here concerning medication. There is little doubt that modern drugs can tranquillize the pain of bereavement, dulling the immediate awfulness of the new reality. In some situations it may be felt necessary to do so, but as a general rule it should be avoided. Grief eventually has to be faced, and the effect of tranquillizers is transitory. When such a decision is taken, it should be remembered that delayed grieving has been found to diminish the prospects of eventual recovery.

The counsellor should not allow any pretence or fiction to get in the way of eventual acceptance of loss. Many will believe that they will be re-united in another world, and if this is a feature of their religious belief it is important that they are allowed to maintain this, regardless of the counsellor's own feelings. But the counsellor should be careful not to allow unreality, pretence or denial to enter into their discussions about matters in this world, and where necessary should remind the individual of what has occurred. The purpose at all times should be to allow grieving to occur so that individuals can eventually pick up their lives as best they can, and as they see fit.

The task of the counsellor should be to help the bereaved people identify and explore their feelings, and to express them openly. One technique which has been found to be valuable in this respect is to ask them to make a list of their losses in some detail. This assists individuals to explore in depth all those things that the deceased provided, not just the obvious ones such as companionship, but more detailed ones such as driving the car, keeping the garden tidy, doing the shopping, cooking the meals, escorting to social events, accounting for money, and so on.

4. Dealing with social expectations

In counselling grief, the interchange that takes place between the individual and the social expectations surrounding them should be borne in mind at all times. Parkes (1985) states that individual mourning is determined partly by social expectations, but that the response to the mourner will also, to some extent, be determined by the behaviour of the mourner. Some people will believe that they are not grieving sufficiently. They will feel unable to cry, and this will make them guilty. They will not feel a sense of loss as deeply as they think they should. Often, this is a direct result of disbelief and numbness arising from the initial shock of their loss. These people often find it difficult to accept what has happened. They may be pre-occupied with hallucinatory images and visions of the person they have lost. The counsellor has to assure them that what they are going through is a normal process through which they will eventually pass. The advice should be to feel whatever they feel, and to respond in whatever way they wish; not to be concerned with stereotypes about what is right and wrong in such situations.

Alternatively, many people will worry about expressing their feelings. This arises in part because dominant social attitudes tell us that we must not 'wallow' in self-pity, that 'too much' grief indicates that we are not in control, that we are feeling sorry for ourselves, getting hysterical, and that we must pull ourselves together. If we fail to do so, others may disapprove. Again, the counsellor has to assure the counsellee that to cry, to talk about the loss, to express feelings of sorrow and to mourn are not only acceptable, but quite normal.

Anger is a common reaction which is often misunderstood or frowned upon. Negative, hostile attitudes towards the deceased often centre on quite irrational feelings such as being 'abandoned'. However irrational, such feelings are quite normal. Yet to speak or even to feel badly about the dead goes against strong social mores which disqualify such thoughts, however real they may be. As a result, they too lead to strong feelings of guilt.

Are we, in some obscure way, to blame for the death? Did we do everything possible? Perhaps if we had done this, or not done that? If only we had been more sympathetic, if only we could tell them what we felt for them, if only . . . Detectable in much guilt is the idea that other people may blame us for omissions or commissions.

Grief will often alter the way individuals respond to situations and people, and it is important that the counsellor helps them to understand the reasons for these emotional responses. The anger which results can often be displaced. Friends and relatives can be blamed for failing to meet the bereaved persons' expectations and needs. No-one has understood their grief. They become blinded by their feelings, and can refuse to see that they are at least partly to blame for creating their worsening social situation. If these emotional reactions are not understood for what they are, the consequence can be increasing loneliness. Life can become empty, reinforcing their feelings about the lack of meaning that life now has for them.

Often the bereaved question their own sanity because they do not link their lack of concentration, their restlessness and irritability, etc. with their grief. There are many other feelings arising from bereavement which can persuade people that they are going mad. Hallucinations are common, as are actions such as continuing to do the things previously done for the deceased. The counsellor should seek to ensure that the bereaved do not feel that these are unnatural or wrong responses to their situation, and should allow individuals to openly discuss these feelings.

5. Re-emergence from grief

There is no clear end to grief, no time before which or after which grieving becomes acceptable or unacceptable. Individuals make their own pace, and their journey will consist of periods of progress and re-integration, and periods of regression. Anniversaries are often significant times when sadness and grief return. In the normal course of grief, time will diminish the intensity, frequency and the duration of the feelings. Indeed, it is important to remember what many older people tell us; that you never get over the death of a loved one, you just get used to it.

As re-emergence from grief is not a linear process, it has to be remembered that many individuals may wish occasionally to regress into the past, forgetting the pain of the present. At such times they will appear to be making little progress towards recovery, apparently avoiding their sad and painful memories. The counsellor needs to examine such behaviour, and interpret the longer-term meaning. But so long as the bereaved person continues to move toward recovery over a longer period, the overall rate of progress is not important. What would be more significant is if individuals tried to shelter from their feelings behind drugs or alcohol.

Loss through death severely disrupts the regular pattern of life, and this can only be restored through the individuals' own inner resources. The survivors have to be helped to renew some sense of their place in the world, and eventually to come to terms with an experience which originally seemed to threaten their very existence. They have to be able to make sense of something that appeared 'senseless'; they have to find new meaning both in the past and the present. But they have to want to do this themselves.

Yet by the same token, if people do not want to get used to their new reality they can ensure that they do not. They can become trapped by their own thoughts, largely impervious to life around them or the efforts of carers to help and support them. Many bereaved individuals assume a 'sick' role, in which their grief is explained by some medical condition, and treated with anti-depressants and tranquillizers. There is a considerable danger that his medi-calization of grief often prolongs the grieving process, and that many doctors merely play along with it. Counsellors must be aware that grief can be prolonged in this and other ways, and that by merely accepting it they can be colluding in making grief a means of attracting more sympathy, without indi-viduals doing anything to reconstruct their own lives.

The process of recovery begins when individuals begin to withdraw their emotional and social life from the duties and ties they feel they owe to the deceased. The pre-occupation with the old relationship begins to wane, and new opportunities are sought. Reminiscence is one method that the coun-sellor can use to assist this process. Bereavement is a time during which reflection on personal history, particularly with regard to the relationship with the deceased person, can be a helpful, even if painful experience. To go over shared times can help the bereaved appreciate the importance and meaning of the relationship. It can help them re-live aspects of the past, and to grieve over those things which will never be again. The use of old photographs, letters and other memorabilia can assist the process. Grief is a time of intense struggle with the conflicting claims of past and future, conflicts which can be resolved by consolidating what is meaningful and significant from the past, and finding some meaning for the future. What is discussed with the bereaved has again to be a compromise between the needs of the past and the future. To concentrate too much on the past, and what is gone, can tend to diminish the importance and the prospects of the future. To concentrate too much on the future might tend to belittle the past, and lead the individual to feel guilty about any lack of remorse. At all times the guiding principle should be the wishes of the counsellees, and the pace set should be one that they are able to cope with.

The ultimate goal should be to assist the bereaved to live their lives in the absence of the deceased. Where progress towards this seems to be blocked in some way, Worden (1983) suggests that the counsellor should assess which one of the four grief tasks has not been successfully completed (see p. 189). This will indicate the area that has been avoided or neglected, and which should receive further attention.

The process of reconstruction

Death destroys the certainty and stability of former life-styles. There may be a need to establish new relationships and new forms of behaviour, which represents a loosening of the bonds with the deceased, not something which many bereaved people feel capable of doing because it seems to be disloyal. Reconstruction is also difficult because bereavement often brings with it feelings of isolation and alienation. Bereaved people may believe that no-one else can understand how they feel, or what the loss means to them. So they do not want to go out, meet new people or embark upon new activities. Even former associations with people and places can be abandoned in bereavement. Old relationships serve to remind them that they are now alone. Visiting friends emphasizes that whilst they now visit alone, they used to be accompanied. Old activities shared with the deceased can also be abandoned for similar reasons. Many bereaved people also discover the extent to which social organization is geared towards the couple rather than the single person. Older women are particularly reluctant to spend evenings unaccompanied in public places, and also to accept invitations from men. Many also find that there is a loss of social status in being a widow or widower, and there is certainly a considerable loss of pension income. The outcome can be that the life of the bereaved becomes increasingly isolated even from former friends and family.

All this will suggest that the future will be a bleak time, and for many it may well be so. However, the counsellor should seek to present a more optimistic view, and work on the possibilities that each individual has for developing his or her social life. Those who can be encouraged to seek new activities and friends will be part way there; it is defeatism and a depressed view of the future that overcomes most bereaved older people.

So as time passes, the counsellor should encourage the individual to begin to reconstruct his or her life, and in particular to fill the gaps which have been left by the deceased person. The establishment of special bereavement groups can be helpful in dealing with these feelings, and in helping the individual commence the process of social re-integration. By sharing their grief with others who have lost important people, members of the group can support each other through the different aspects of the problems, to see the irrationality of some behaviour, to search for new perspectives in life, and perhaps even to join forces in rebuilding their lives. They see that they are not the only people with such feelings. They can help each other come out of their depression. They can begin to help each other rebuild their lives.

It is often said, correctly, that time is a great healer. Many bereaved people discover in time that the absence of a life-long partner can open up a new stage of life in which they undertake new tasks, either because they have to or because they are no longer prevented from doing so. They find that they can now please themselves, making the post-bereavement period for many a liberating experience. Counselling can help make it so.

CHAPTER 21

Preparation for death

There is never a good time to prepare for one's own death. We are either fit and healthy and it does not appear relevant; or we are too ill to concentrate on it; or it approaches too quickly and we have insufficient time to prepare ourselves. So many older people die without wills, or with important unfinished business. We, and those around us, are unprepared for an unavoidable event that should have been talked about but was always, for one reason or another, avoided.

The counsellor of older people should never knowingly allow this situation to happen, and so must try to overcome the social constraints which prevent death being considered a valid subject for discussion. Older people often throw out comments about the imminence of their own death which we too often either fail, or refuse, to respond to. The reason for this has much to do with cultural attitudes to death which promote a conspiracy to avoid the issue. So we often ignore the possibility that such comments may represent an invitation or need to discuss death. Butler (1974) compares westernized attitudes to death with those of oriental cultures.

> The Western concept of the life cycle is decidedly different from that of the Orient since they derive from two opposing views about what 'self' means and what life is all about. Oriental philosophy places the individual self, his life span and his death within the process of human experience. Life and death are familiar and equally acceptable parts of what self means. In the West, on the other hand, death is considered outside of the self. To be a self or person one must be alive, in control and aware of what is happening. The greater and more self-centred or narcissistic Western emphasis on individuality and control makes death an outrage, a tremendous affront to man, rather than the logical and necessary process of old life making way for new.

If the counsellor sees death as 'the end' then counselling dying people, even counselling older people generally, will receive low priority. If we look upon old age as decline, and death as an outrage, then neglect of ageing people will continue to be the predominant attitude. Instead, the counsellor should try to see death as an integral part of the process of life, and although the final part, no less important to the individual.

All ageing people face death as an imminent prospect, and so it is one which the counsellor should encourage them to consider. Indeed, many older people require little encouragement, and they will tend to supply us with ideal openings for such discussion. Remarks such as 'You don't need to worry about me, I'll be dead soon!' are too often dismissed with a 'Don't be silly, you'll outlive us all!' response. Another common opening for discussion is when older people question the value and purpose of their own lives, and why they should want to continue living. Such questions have many potentially important agendas for the counsellor.

Do such questions indicate that individuals wish to talk about or be reassured of their value and importance to people close to them? Do they indicate a growing despair about their social role, thereby stressing to the carers the importance of giving them the opportunity of discussing their feelings? Are they concerned about their own death, do they feel it is imminent, or do they require reassurance that they are still healthy and well? Or are they concerned about the nature of death generally, whether it will be a peaceful process, or a slow, lingering and painful one?

Dominant attitudes towards death in western society are often quite unhelpful in these respects. We even ponder over the question of whether dying people should be told that they are going to die. The idea that such a fact can or should be kept from a dying individual is strange; most studies and practical experience would indicate that people do know when they are dying, regardless of whether they are formally told or not, either from the way they feel or from the atmospheres and attitudes of people around them. It can lead to farcical situations where both the dying and those around them are aware of the truth, but are not able to face each other with it (Davis, 1979). The failure to be honest reinforces 'death' as a taboo subject, not to be discussed even with the dying themselves, and takes T.S. Elliot's oft-quoted remark 'Mankind cannot bear too much reality' to ridiculous extremes.

The counsellor should always seek to be open. It is a counselling task of some skill to be able to discuss the ill-health of ageing people in such a way that the realization and confirmation of their imminent death is brought to them gently and with care. Ideally, it should only be done by those who have a sound relationship with the individual. The comments and questions about dying and death that older people ask should always receive a considered response, and preferably one which opens rather than closes discussion. Any opportunity should be taken, when appropriate, to ask questions which encourage them to express their feelings about the prospect of death. Dying people are often not as sensitive to the issue as we are. Often they welcome the opportunity to discuss the impending event, but will defer to the 'sensitivity' of friends and relatives who so obviously wish to avoid doing so.

The question of euthanasia

Those who regularly counsel older people will come across the issue of euthanasia. Euthanasia has always been opposed by the two major western religions, Judaism and Christianity, and dominant attitudes in this country continue to reflect and reinforce these traditions. But in other countries, notably Holland and some American states, a more open attitude has developed, and whilst even here the practice is still illegal, it has actually been happening for many years. It is not the intention here to enter into a full philosophical debate on the issue (for this, see for example Downing and Smoker, 1986), but it would be wrong to discuss the counselling of dying people without reference to the issues it raises.

When faced with an ageing individual who expresses a desire to die, what is the counsellor to do? The first reaction should be to discuss the reasons which have led the individual to express such a desire. A statement of this kind can often be an expression of many feelings other than the wish to die. These feelings may be connected with temporary and transitory emotional or psychological stress, or some longer-lasting and deeper depressive state that may respond to medical intervention or counselling support. Alternatively, they might arise from an individual who is demanding attention, and feels that to request their own death is one way of achieving this. Or it might be that the individual wants relief from pain or chronic illness and does not know of any other way of achieving it. If the desire for death arises from any of these then counselling, allied with other forms of caring intervention, may be what is required.

Yet it is also important to accept that many ageing people do actually want to die. There have been many well-publicized cases of people who have genuinely wished to take their own lives. Derek Humphry helped his wife to die, and then wrote a moving account in his book *Jean's Way* in 1978. James Haig, a tetraplegic, made several attempts to end his life, and eventually killed himself in 1983 by setting fire to his home. These more public examples can probably be multiplied many hundred times each year, both by those who successfully end their own lives voluntarily, and by many thousands more who would probably like to do so. Why should this be so? And are there any special factors about modern society which makes euthanasia more attractive to older people than previously?

Advances in medical knowledge are gradually bringing us to understand that death is not a sudden event but a gradual process. Medical science can now prolong life, often well beyond the point where it has any meaning or value to the individual. When this prolongation of life is allied with the historical trend which has denigrated the role and value of older people, the reason for the increasing acceptability of euthanasia becomes clearer. It becomes more understandable that an individual might want to determine the stage at which he or she wishes to hasten what can become an inevitable, undignified and meaningless process. Many people now claim that there should be a 'right to die' (Humphry and Wickett 1986), a right for individuals to decide when to end their own lives. The Voluntary Euthanasia Society, in its 1985 survey, claimed that the majority of people in this country now favour euthanasia which seeks to relieve unbearable suffering and pain. Many other bodies, such as the BMA and the hospice movement, argue against such a position becoming legal. The fear that, once legalized, euthanasia would not remain 'voluntary', but would be used to eliminate groups of people who were considered troublesome, or too expensive to keep alive. The taint of eugenics has handicapped the euthanasia argument since the scourge of Fascism in the 1930s and 1940s and certainly, within a society in which the state and the medical profession are becoming increasingly powerful, it is a strong argument.

The euthanasia issue is far from resolved, and it is unlikely ever to be so entirely. So whilst euthanasia is likely to remain strictly illegal, it is also likely to receive increasing support from many people, and perhaps especially from ageing individuals. Euthanasia will therefore remain a dilemma which is faced by the carers of many older people, and it is one which cannot and should not be ignored.

How is the counsellor to respond to this dilemma? The counselling task is to listen to the expression of feelings, and if these feelings are that life has become meaningless for the individual, that they have no desire to go on living, then the counsellor should listen with all the understanding and empathy that they would give to any other topic. The counsellor can present individuals with all the reasons why they should not feel this way, that other people do care for them, that they are useful and important, that there are things they can do and achieve in their lives. Often this is exactly what is needed. The desire to die can be no more than an expression of depression. The individual might actually want to hear such positive remarks, and be jockeyed out of a mood which might be transitory. In this the counsellors are often in an ideal position; they are able to use all their knowledge and insight of the individual to encourage a more optimistic outlook on life. Clearly, if this is the case, counselling can be an invaluable method of working.

On the other hand, there may be occasions when the counsellor becomes convinced that the individual is not talking from a position of depression, but from a rational and considered point of view. Where this is so, there comes a time when the counsellor cannot continue to argue against what is a genuine expression of feeling. The counsellor will decide, albeit reluctantly, that the individual does wish to end their life. The question will then arise about whether the counsellor should collude, even in listening, to wishes which are against the law. Essentially, it is a dilemma little different to any other in which the counsellor is asked to assist in the solution of a problem. But euthanasia is different both in that it is illegal, and that it concerns the subject of death which raises important, and contentious, ethical and moral questions. The resolution of this has to be a personal one. There is no straightforward or easy answer to a problem which could ultimately set personal commitment to the individual against the law of the land. It is a situation in which the counsellor may benefit personally from counselling, and a friendly priest or doctor who is prepared to discuss the issues involved may well be helpful.

The dilemma increases if the individual implies, or states openly, that he wants help to end his life. There are three courses open to people faced with this. The first, and clearly the legal choice, is to refuse any sort of co-operation. Yet this can be an uncomfortable position for a counsellor to adopt, particularly if empathy with the feelings and circumstances of the individual is strong. Even so, it is possible for the counsellor to explain the position in reasonable and caring terms so that the counsellee is able to understand why what they ask cannot be done.

There are two other responses, one of which constitutes a criminal act under existing law. The 'passive' response would be that medical and nursing staff discontinue any effort to support or prolong life. The 'active' response, which is criminal, would be taking steps which led directly to death. In such a case, the fact that the individual has expressed a voluntary desire for death, even after counselling, someone who takes such action must do so according to his or her conscience, and in full recognition of the legal consequences.

Perhaps to conclude this section, it is important to reiterate here that counselling should be about life, and enjoying life right through to death. The counselling approach with older people advocated throughout this text is one which is essentially optimistic. Perhaps, through counselling, it may be possible to ensure that all old people can be helped to believe that life is worth living, as fully as possible, right to the end. If so, counselling can reduce the desire for death rather than having to deal with the consequences.

Supporting the dying individual

The dying person has many needs. Some are medical, such as relief from pain and the alleviation of unpleasant symptoms. The counsellor should try to ensure that medical assistance is always available, but it is important to realize that dying does not call just for straightforward medical assistance. Clearly, there is a need for correct medical information for the dying. But only in a minority of cases is the best care for the dying necessarily provided by medical staff, in a medical environment. Dying people usually wish to be wherever they feel safe, relaxed and at home. A hospital or medicalized environment is often the worst possible option for many individuals.

Dying people generally prefer to be with the friends and relatives they know and trust, and with whom they have developed sound personal relationships. These are the people who they know will look after their needs without making them feel a burden, so that even in death they can feel that their personal integrity is honoured and respected.

The counsellor can often provide considerable comfort and support for the dying person. The counsellor needs to respond sensitively to the needs of those who are dying, and to their wishes concerning where they wish to be, and by whom they wish to be cared for. Dying people need the opportunity to talk about their anxieties, and to come to terms with their imminent death. They need to talk to someone about their fears, and their feelings of loneliness. It may also be important for the counsellor to ascertain the religious and spiritual needs of the dying person, and to ensure that someone attends to them.

Counsellors can do even more than this if they seek to hand back to the dying individual the responsibility for being in control of his or her own situation. Carers of dying people have a tendency to assume control over their lives. This not only emphasizes and reinforces their dependent situation, but serves to make them more dependent than they often need to be. The counsellor should try to ensure that the dying individual maintains as normal a life as possible, for as long as possible. In all the decisions that have to be taken, the wishes of the dying person should be given precedence.

The process of dying

Kubler-Ross (1970) studied the process through which dying people often pass after they are aware of their impending death, and she found that there were five distinct stages.

1. Denial

The first reaction to imminent death is often one of disbelief and denial, when the dying person is not prepared to accept the fact that he or she has only a limited period to live. Kubler-Ross says this is more typical of someone who is informed prematurely or abruptly, thereby emphasizing the need for a careful counselling approach in this respect. Denial, as with all stages, serves an important purpose for it provides the individual with time to come to terms with an unwanted and unacceptable idea.

It might spur the individual to fight the illness, and this has been known to bring about remission of many conditions, or even a cure. More usually, denial does not last long, particularly with older individuals who will normally be very aware of their physical condition, and sometimes be ready for personal death. Yet whilst denial lasts, counsellors should neither play along with it nor seek to stress too strongly the unacceptable fact of approaching death. Instead they should seek to create an open but sensitive atmosphere in which reality and truth take precedence over avoidance and deception.

2. Anger

Anger replaces denial, and can be a very difficult stage for carers to handle. It can be directed at a variety of people, medical staff, relatives, friends and even God. Everything is wrong – the bed, the food, the room temperature, too many or too few visitors, and so on.

Anger, whilst a natural reaction, can be disconcerting to carers because it is normally directed towards those who are closest to the dying individual. The care they provide may itself provoke anger because it highlights the dying persons' illness, and reinforces their growing dependence upon others. Many good friends can be lost during this stage, but it is important for the counsellor to cope without withdrawing care and approval. Empathy is vital in such situations. Every effort should be made to link with the feelings and thoughts of the dying person, to experience the frustration and fears that have led to the hostile behaviour.

3. Bargaining

The bargaining stage often represents the realization that there is important unfinished business in the dying persons' life. Time is required to complete such business so they seek remission for good behaviour, thoughts, deeds or promises. Often this is allied with a tendency to see their illness as a punishment for past misdemeanours, leading to promises to do everything they consider to be 'good' in return for more time. Implicit in this is often a sense of guilt for the things they have not done, or failed to achieve in their lives.

Counselling should treat this bargaining stage in a similar way to denial; not accepting that bargaining is a possibility, but promoting discussion about the reasons why time has become so important to the dying person, and what needs to be done about the matters which are worrying him or her.

4. Depression

The effort expended in denial, anger and bargaining will eventually subside into depression. In this, individuals experience a sense of grief for all those things which they will never know again – their job, their home, their hobbies, their relatives and friends, indeed, everything that has been important in their lives. This is an important period, as essential to the dying person as it will be later for those who are bereaved by his or her death.

It is also, perhaps, the most important stage in the counselling process, which seeks to give individuals the opportunity of expressing how they feel, what has been left undone, their worries about those they leave behind, and other issues. Again, there should be no attempt to breed a false optimism, for this is quickly seen through. After all, the dying person is losing everything and everybody that is important to him or her, and false optimism can result in a loss of trust and confidence in the counsellor. Instead, and as usual, the ability to listen, understand and respond sympathetically is important. If this is done successfully the individual can pass to the next, and final stage of the dying process.

5. *Acceptance*

The dying person will now have become resigned to his or her ultimate fate, neither angry nor depressed about what is about to occur. The agitation of previous stages will have been resolved. It is therefore a time of relative peace, although this should not necessarily be assumed to be one of happiness. The individual will feel able to say 'goodbye' to loved ones, and perhaps at the same time offer them words of reassurance and comfort. This should be encouraged as it is often extremely important to those who are left behind, and can help in the process of bereavement. Often, it will be a time of increasing weakness and sleep, when the dying person may wish to be left alone in peace, except perhaps for the presence of a few treasured relatives and friends.

The struggle is over. No further counselling will be required.

Directory of useful addresses

General

Age Concern England
Bernard Sunley House
60 Pitcairn Road
Mitcham
Surrey CR4 3LL

British Association of Service to
  Elderly (BASE)
119 Hassell Street
Newcastle-under-Lyme ST5 1AX

British Geriatric Society
1 St Andrew's Place
Regent's Park
London NW1 4LB

British Pensioners and Trades Union
  Action Association
Norman Dodds House
315 Bexley Road
North Heath
Erith
Kent

British Society of Gerontology
Kings College
Department of Geography
Strand
London WC2R 2LS

British Society for Research on
  Ageing
Geigy Unit for Research on Ageing
Department of Geriatric Medicine
University Hospital of Manchester
Manchester M20 8LR

Carers National Association
29 Chilworth Mews
London W2 3RG

Centre for Policy on Ageing
25–31 Ironmonger Row
London EC1V 3QP

Counsel and Care for the Elderly
Tyman House
Bonny Street
London NW1 9LR

Family Welfare Association
501–5 Kingsland Road
London E8 4AU

Help the Aged
St James's Walk
London EC1R 0BE

National Federation of Old Age
Pensioners Associations
'Pensioners Voice'
14 St Peter's Street
Blackburn BB2 2HD

Pensioners Link
17 Balfe Street
London N1 9EB

Social Care Association
23a Victoria Road
Surbiton
Surrey KT6 4JZ

Retirement

Pre-Retirement Association
19 Undine Street
Tooting
London SW17 8PP

Workers Educational Association
9 Upper Berkeley Street
London W1H 8BY

The blind and partially sighted

British Wireless for the Blind Fund
224 Great Portland Street
London W1N 6AA

Partially Sighted Society
Queens Road
Doncaster
South Yorkshire DN1 2NX

Royal National Institute for the
Blind
224 Great Portland Street
London W1N 6AA

Telephones for the Blind Fund
Well House
Mynthurst Leigh
Near Reigate
Surrey CH2 8RJ

Hearing loss

British Association of Hard of
Hearing
7–11 Armstrong Road
London W3 7JL

British Deaf Association
38 Victoria Place
Carlisle
Cumbria CA1 1HU

Hearing Aid Council
1st Floor
Ashton House
471 Silbury Field Boulevard
Milton Keynes
MK9 2LP

National Council for Social Workers
with the Deaf
35 Pleasant Street
Heywood
Lanes OL10 4AJ

Royal National Institute for the Deaf
105 Gower Street
London WC1E 6AH

Communication

Blissymbolics Communication
Resource Centre (UK)
c/o Spastics Society
382–384 Newport Road
Cardiff CF3 7YA

Communication Aids Centre
c/o Charing Cross Hospital
(Fulham)
Fulham Palace Road
London W6 8RF

British Association for Counselling
37a Sheep Street
Rugby
Warwickshire CV21 3BX

Makaton Vocabulary Development
Project
31 Firwood Drive
Camberley
Surrey GU15 3QD

Disabled

Disabled Living Foundation
380–384 Harrow Road
London W9 2HU

Medical

Arthritis Care
6 Grosvenor Crescent
London SW1X 7ER

Chest, Heart and Stroke Association
Tavistock House North
Tavistock Square
London WC1H 9JE

Medical – alternative and complementary

British Acupuncture Association
34 Alderney Street
London SW1V 4EU

British Chiropractors Association
Premier House
10 Greycoat Place
London SW1P 1SB

British Homeopathic Association
27a Devonshire Street
London W1N 1RJ

British Naturopathic and Osteopathic
  Association
6 Netherhall Gardens
London NW3 5RR

General Council and Registrar of
  Osteopaths
21 Suffolk Street
London SW1Y 4HG

Institute for Complementary
  Medicine
21 Portland Place
London W1N 3AF

The Traditional Acupuncture
  Society
11 Grange Park
Stratford-upon-Avon
Warwickshire CV37 6XH

Personal relations

Association to Aid the Sexual and
  Personal Relationships of People
  with a Disability (SPOD)
286 Camden Road
London N7 0BJ

Contact
15 Henrietta Street
London WC2E 8QH

National Marriage Guidance
  Council (now called Relate)
Little Church Street.
Rugby
Warwickshire CV21 3AP

Alcoholism and alcohol abuse

Alcohol Concern
305 Grays Inn Road
London WC1X 8QF

Alcoholics Anonymous
11 Redcliffe Gardens
London SW10 9BQ

Dementia

Alzheimer's Disease Society
158/160 Balham High Road
London SW12 9BN

MIND
National Association for Mental
Health
22 Harley Street
London W1N 2ED

Bereavement and death

CRUSE – BEREAVEMENT CARE
Cruse House
126 Sheen Road
Richmond
Surrey TW9 1UR

Human Rights Society
27 Walpole Street
London SW3 4QS

The Lisa Sainsbury Foundation
8–10 Crown Hill
Croydon
Surrey CR0 1RY

Voluntary Euthanasia Society
13 Prince of Wales Terrace
London W8 5PG

Bibliography

Abrams, M. (1978). *Beyond Three Score Years and Ten*. Age Concern, Mitcham.

Ackerman, N.J. (1966). *Treating the Troubled Family*. Basic Books, New York.

Age Concern. (1977). *Profiles of the Elderly (Vols 1–3)*. Age Concern, Mitcham.

Alcohol Concern. (1987). Alcohol and older people. Unpublished leaflets.

Argyle, M. (1987). *The Psychology of Happiness*. Methuen, London.

Atchley, R.C. (1976). *The Sociology of Retirement*. Wiley, Chichester.

Baltes, P. and Schaie, K.W. (1974). Ageing and IQ – the myth of the twilight years. *Psychology Today*, March, pp 35–40.

Barclay Report. (1982). *Social Workers: Their Role and Tasks*. MacDonald and Evans/NISW, London.

de Beauvoir, S. (1972). *Old Age*. Deutsch/Weidenfeld and Nicolson, London.

Bergmann, K and Jacoby, R. (1983). The limitations and possibilities of community care for the elderly demented. In *Elderly People in the Community – Their Service Needs*, DHSS, pp 141–67. HMSO, London.

Berkun, C.S. (1986). On behalf of women over 40: understanding the importance of the menopause. *Social Work*, September/October, pp 378–84.

Berne, E. (1968). *Games People Play*. Penguin, Harmondsworth.

Birren, J.E. and Schaie, K.W. (Eds) (1977). *Handbook of the Psychology of Aging*. Van Nostrand Reinhold, Wokingham.

Blair, P. (1985). *Know Your Medicines*. Age Concern, Mitcham.

Blumenthal, M.D. (1980). Depressive illness in old age: getting behind the mask. *Geriatrics*, April, pp 34–43.

Bosanquet, N. (1978). *A Future for Old Age. Towards a New Society*. Temple Smith/New Society, Aldershot.

Bowen, M. (1978). *Family Therapy in Clinical Practice*. Jason Aronson, New Jersey.

Bowlby, J. (1980). *Attachment and Loss: Loss, Sadness and Depression*. Hogarth Press, London.

Braithwaite, V.A. and Gibson, D.H. (1987). Adjustment to retirement: what we know and what we need to know. *Ageing and Society*, 7, 1–18.

Brearley, G. and Birchley, P. (1986). *Introducing Counselling Skills and Techniques*. Faber and Faber, London.

British Medical Association. (1986). *All our tomorrows: growing old in Britain*. Report of the BMA's Board of Science and Education. BMA, London.

Brown, G.W. and Harris, T. (1978). *Social Origins of Depression*. Tavistock, London.

Butler, R.N. (1963). The Life Review: an interpretation of reminiscence in the Aged. *Psychiatry*, 26.

Butler, R.N. (1974). Successful ageing and the role of the life review. *Journal of American Geriatrics Society*, 22(12), 529–35.

Cohen, G. and Faulkner, D. (1984). Memory in old age: 'good in parts'. *New Scientist*, October 11th, pp 49–51.

Coleman, P.G. (1986). *Ageing and Reminiscence Processes*. Wiley, Chichester.

Comerford, S. (1986). Reasons to be cheerful . . . *Community Care*, December 4th, pp 18–19.

Cook, J.B. (1984). Reminiscing: how it can help confused nursing home residents. *Social Casework: Journal of Contemporary Social Work*, February, pp 90–93.

Cowgill, D.O. and Holmes, L. (1972). *Aging and Modernisation*. Appleton-Century-Crofts, New York.

Crosby, I. and Traynor, J. (1985). *In Our Care. A Handbook of Workshop Activities for Those Caring for Older People*. Help the Aged Education Department, London.

Cummings, E. and Henry, W.E. (1961). *Growing Old. The Process of Disengagement*. Basic Books, New York.

Dall, J.L.C. and Gardiner, H.S. (1971). Dietary intake of potassium by geriatric patients. *Geront Clin*, 13, 119–124.

Davies, L. (1981). *Three Score Years . . . and Then? A Study of Nutrition and Wellbeing of Elderly People at Home*. Heinemann, London.

Davis, L. (1979). Facing death. *Social Work Today*, 10 (45), 16.

DHSS and WHO. (1978). *A Happier Old Age*. HMSO, London.

DHSS. (1979). *Nutrition and Health in Old Age*. HMSO, London.

DHSS. (1983). *Elderly People in the Community – Their Service Needs*. HMSO, London.

Dixon, J. and Gregory, L. (1987). Ageism. *Action Baseline*, Winter 1986–7, pp 21–3.

Downing, A.B. and Smoker, B. (1986). *Voluntary Euthanasia*. Peter Owen, London.

Doyle, L. (1983). *The Political Economy of Health*. Pluto Press, London.

Enderby, P. (1987). *Assistive Communication Aids for the Speech Impaired*. Churchill Livingstone, Edinburgh.

Erikson, E.H. (1965). *Childhood and Society*. Penguin, Harmondsworth.

Estes, C.L. (1979). *The Ageing Enterprise*. Jossey-Bass, London.
Estes, C.L. (1986). The politics of ageing in America. *Ageing and Society*, 6, pp 121–34.
Exton-Smith, A.N. (1971). Nutrition of the elderly. *British Journal of Hospital Medicine*, May, pp 639–45.
Freud, S. (1905). *On Psychotherapy*. Hogarth Press, London.
Goffman, E. (1968). *Asylums: Essays on the Social Situation of Mental Patients and Other Inmates*. Pelican, Harmondsworth.
Gower, G. (1965). *Death, Grief and Mourning in Contemporary Britain*. Crescent Books, London.
Gray, J.A.M. (1982). *Better Health in Retirement*. Age Concern, Mitcham.
Gray, M. and Wilcock, G. (1981). *Our Elders*. Oxford University Press, Oxford.
Gurland, B.J. (1976). The comparative frequency of depression in various adult age groups. *Journal of Gerontology*, 31 (3), 283–292.
Halmos, P. (1978). *The Faith of the Counsellors*. Constable, London.
Humphry D. and Wickett, A. (1986). *The Right to Die*. Bodley Head, London.
Illich, I. (1977). *Limits to Medicine*. Pelican, Harmondsworth.
Johnson, P. (1985). *The Economics of Old Age in Britain. A Long-run View 1881–1981*. (Discussion Paper 47.) Centre for Economic Policy Research, London.
Judge, T.G. and Cowan, N.R. (1971). Dietary potassium intake and grip strength in older people. *Geront Clin*, 13, 221–226.
Kelly, G. (1955). *Psychology of Personal Constructs*. Norton, London.
Klein, W.H., Le Shan, E.J. and Furman, S.S. (1965). *Promoting Mental Health of Older People through Group Methods*. Manhattan Society for Mental Health/Mental Health Materials Centre, New York.
Kubler-Ross, E. (1970). *On Death and Dying*. Tavistock, London.
Landreth, G.L. and Berg, C. (1980). *Counselling the Elderly*. Charles C. Thomas, Illinois.
McDerment, L. and Greengross, S. (1985). *Social Care for the Elderly*. Social Care Association, Surrey.
Madane, C. and Haley, J. (1977). Dimensions of family therapy. *Journal of Nervous and Mental Diseases*. July, 165.
Marples, M. (1986). Helping family members cope with a senile relative. *Social Casework: Journal of Contemporary Social Work*, October, pp 490–98.
Martin, P. (1987). Psychology and the immune system. *New Scientist*, April 19th, pp 46–50.
Maslow, A.H. (1970). *Motivation and Personality*. Harper and Row, London.
Masters, W.H. and Johnson, V.E. (1966). *Human Sexual Response*. Little, Brown and Company, Boston, Mass.
Meacher, M. (1972). *Taken for a Ride*. Longman, Harlow.
Meade, K. (1986). *Challenging the Myths. A Review of Pensioners Health Course and Talks*. Pensioners Link, London.
Means, R. (1986). The development of social services for elderly people:

historical perspectives. In *Ageing and Social Policy*, Phillipson and Walker (Eds), pp 87–106. Gower, London.

Mayer, J.E. and Timms, N. (1970). *The Client Speaks*. RKP, London.

Monsour, N. and Robb, S. (1982). Wandering behaviour in old age: a psychosocial study. *Social Work*, September, pp 411–15.

Murphy, E. (1982). Social origins of depression in old age. *British Journal of Psychiatry*, 141, 135–142.

Neuberger, J. (1987). *Caring for Dying People of Different Faiths*. Lisa Sainsbury Foundation.

Neugarten, B.L. Havighurst, R.J. and Tobin, S.S. (1961). The measurement of life satisfaction. *Journal of Gerontology*, 16.

Norris, A.D. and Abu El Eileh, M.T. (1982). Reminiscence groups. *Nursing Times*, 78, 1368–9.

Norris, A. (1986). *Reminiscences with Elderly People*. Winslow Press, London.

Parish, P. (1987). *Medicines – A Guide for Everyone*. Penguin, Harmondsworth.

Parkes, C.M. (1972). *Bereavement: Studies of Grief in Adult Life*. Tavistock, London.

Parkes, C.M. and Weiss, R.S. (1983). *Recovery from Bereavement*. Basic Books, New York.

Parkes, C.M. (1985). Bereavement. *British Journal of Psychiatry*, 146, 11–17.

Petty, R. and Sensky, T. (1987). *Depression. Treating the Whole Person*. Unwin Hyman, London.

Phillipson, C. (1982). *Capitalism and the Construction of Old Age*. Macmillan, Basingstoke.

Phillipson, C., Bernard, M. and Strang, P. (1986). *Dependency and Interdependency in Old Age – Theoretical Perspectives and Policy Alternatives*. Croom Helm/British Society of Gerontology, Beckenham.

Phillipson, C. and Walker, A. (1986). *Ageing and Social Policy*. Gower, London.

Philpot, T. (1986). Elderly people in Japan. Respect due? *Community Care*, October 12th, pp 16–18.

Price, J.H. and Andrews, P. (1982). Alcohol abuse in the elderly. *Journal of Gerontological Nursing*, 8 (1), 16–19.

Proctor, H. (1981). Family Construct Psychology: an approach to understanding and treating families. In *Developments in Family Therapy*. S. Walrund-Skinner (Ed.), pp 350–66. Routledge & Kegan Paul, London.

Rogers, C. (1951a). *Client-centred Therapy*. Constable, London.

Rogers, C. (1951b). *On Becoming a Person*. Constable, London.

Rogers, J. (1986). *The Taste of Health*. BBC Publications, London.

Ropper, A.H. (1979). A rational approach to dementia. *CMC Journal*, November 3rd, pp 1175–90.

Rosin, A. and Glatt, M. (1971). Alcohol excess in the elderly. *Quarterly Journal of Studies on Alcohol*, 32, 53–59.

Sargent, S. (1980). *Non-Traditional Therapy and Counselling with the Ageing.* Constable, London.

Scheff, T.J. (1966). *On Being Mentally Ill.* Weidenfeld and Nicolson, London.

Scrutton, S. (1986). 'I don't like to complain, dear.' *Community Care,* December 4th, pp 20–21.

Shakespeare, R. (1975). *The Psychology of Handicap.* Methuen, London.

Sherman, E. (1981). *Counselling the Aging. An Integrated Approach.* Free Press, New York.

Sturkie, K. (1986). Framework for comparing approaches to family therapy. *Social Casework: Journal of Contemporary Social Work,* December.

Sundstrom, G. (1986). Family and State: recent trends in the care of the aged in Sweden. *Ageing and Society,* 6, 169–96.

Szasz, T. (1976). *The Myth of Mental Illness.* Harper and Row, London.

Thienhaus, O.L., Conter, E.A. and Bosmann, H.B. (1986). Sexuality and ageing. *Ageing and Society,* 6, 39–54.

Thompson, P. (1978). *The Voice of the Past: Oral History.* Oxford University Press, Oxford.

Thunhurst, C. (1982). *It Makes You Sick. The Politics of the NHS.* Pluto Press, London.

Townsend, P. (1963). *The Family Life of Old People.* Penguin, Harmondsworth.

Townsend, P. (1979). *Poverty in the UK.* Penguin, Harmondsworth.

Townsend, P. (1981). The structured dependency of the elderly: creation of social policy in the 20th century. *Ageing and Society,* 1 (1), 6–28.

Tudge, C. (1986). *The Food Connection.* BBC Publications, London.

Tunstall, J. (1966). *Old and Alone.* Routledge and Kegan Paul, London.

Turner, P. and Volans, G. (1987). *The Drugs Handbook.* Macmillan, Basingstoke.

Tyler, L.E. (1969). *The Work of the Counsellor.* Appleton-Century-Crofts, New York.

Verwoerdt, A. (1976). *Clinical Geropsychiatry.* Williams and Wilkins, London.

Walker, A. (1981). Towards a political economy of old age. *Ageing and Society,* Vol 1, Pt 1.

Walker, A. (1982). Dependency in old age. *Social Policy and Administration,* Vol 16 (Summer).

Walrund-Skinner, S. (1977). *Family Therapy. The Treatment of Natural Systems.* Routledge and Kegan Paul, London.

Wattis, J. and Church, M. (1986). *Practical Psychiatry of Old Age.* Croom Helm, Beckenham.

Weinberg, J. (1972). Psychologic implications of the nutritional needs of the elderly. *Journal of the American Dietetic Association,* 60, 293–6.

Wilson, R.A. and Wilson, T. (1963). The fate of the non-treated post-menopausal woman. *Journal of American Geriatrics Society,* March, p 347.

Worden, W.J. (1983). *Grief Counselling and Grief Therapy.* Tavistock, London.

About Age Concern

Age Concern England, the co-publishers of this book as well as a wide range of others, provides training, information and research for use by retired people and those who work with them. It is a registered charity dependent on public support for the continuation of its work.

The three other national Age Concern Organisations – Scotland, Wales and Northern Ireland together with Age Concern England – form a network of over 1400 independent local UK groups serving the needs of elderly people, assisted by well over 124 000 volunteers. The wide range of services provided includes advice and information, day care, visiting services, voluntary transport schemes, clubs and specialist services for physically and mentally frail elderly people.

Age Concern England
Bernard Sunley House
60 Pitcairn Road
Mitcham
Surrey CR4 3LL
Tel: 01-640 5431

Age Concern Scotland
33 Castle Street
Edinburgh EH2 3DN
Tel: 031-225 5000

Age Concern Wales
4th Floor
1 Cathedral Road
Cardiff CF1 9SD
Tel: 0222 371821/371566

**Age Concern
Northern Ireland**
6 Lower Crescent
Belfast BT7 1NR
Tel: 0232 245729

Index